E. Margaret Thompson

A history of the Somerset Carthusians

E. Margaret Thompson

A history of the Somerset Carthusians

ISBN/EAN: 9783742856630

Manufactured in Europe, USA, Canada, Australia, Japa

Cover: Foto ©Lupo / pixelio.de

Manufactured and distributed by brebook publishing software (www.brebook.com)

E. Margaret Thompson

A history of the Somerset Carthusians

ST. HUGH OF AVALON, BISHOP OF LINCOLN, THIRD PRIOR OF WITHAM.

A HISTORY OF
THE SOMERSET CARTHUSIANS

BY

E. MARGARET THOMPSON

WITH ILLUSTRATIONS BY
L. BEATRICE THOMPSON

JOHN HODGES
BEDFORD STREET, STRAND, LONDON
1895

Printed by BALLANTYNE, HANSON & CO.
At the Ballantyne Press

PREFACE

THIS little work is not meant as a contribution to the Acts of the Carthusian Saints and Confessors of England, which Dom Victor Doreau and Dom Lawrence Hendriks may be said to have begun in their two books, *Henri VIII. et les Martyrs de la Chartreuse de Londres*, and *The London Charterhouse*. Its aim is to be a faithful narration of the origin, progress, and dissolution of the two communities at Witham and Hinton as a body, rather than a full history of the individual religious of either Priory; indeed, to have written the latter, owing to the extreme paucity of material, would have been an impossibility, except in the case of St. Hugh. But notice has been taken in the following pages of the known monks of both the monasteries, and an account will be found of that portion of their lives which was passed in either of the Somerset Charterhouses, or which affected

PREFACE

in any way either of those communities to which they some time belonged.

There is no need to set down here a list of the authorities to which recourse has been had in compiling this book, since these have been given in the footnotes. It is well to mention, however, that in quoting documents, directly or indirectly, the original spelling has been kept of all names of places, except those of Witham and Hinton, and of well-known towns or cities, in which cases the modern form of the words has been preferred.

The thanks of the writer are due to Miss Mary Baily, of Frome - Selwood, who kindly took the photographs at Witham, Hinton, and Norton St. Philip, from which most of the illustrations have been drawn.

CONTENTS

PART I

WITHAM CHARTERHOUSE

CHAP.		PAGE
I.	ESTABLISHMENT OF THE FIRST ENGLISH CHARTERHOUSE	3
II.	THE CARTHUSIAN RULE	31
III.	AN IDEAL MONK	45
IV.	THE PROSPEROUS YEARS OF THE CHARTERHOUSE	69
V.	DECLINING FORTUNES	119
VI.	THE DESTRUCTION OF THE MONASTERY	156

PART II

HINTON CHARTERHOUSE

I.	THE FOUNDERS	203
II.	A LONG CARTHUSIAN SABBATH	228
III.	BROKEN PEACE	275
IV.	THE SCATTERING OF THE SHEEP OF THE PASTURE	307
V.	A PLEA FOR THE CARTHUSIANS	351
INDEX		367

LIST OF ILLUSTRATIONS

St. Hugh of Avalon, Bishop of Lincoln, Third Prior of Witham	*Frontispiece*	
Witham Friary Church, Exterior	*To face page*	4
Witham Friary Church, Interior	"	19
Supposed Lepers' Window in Witham Church	"	20
A Carthusian—Choir Dress	"	33
A Carthusian Lay-Brother	"	39
Fifteenth Century Font in Witham Friary	"	113
Witham Friary Church, A.D. 1760, with supposed Conventual Buildings	"	199
Hinton-Charterhouse Church, Exterior	"	250
Hinton-Charterhouse Church, Interior	"	253
Norton St. Philip, Exterior	"	254
Norton St. Philip, Interior	"	259
Entrance to the Tower of Hinton Priory Church on the West	"	275
Exterior of the Carthusian Chapter-House, Hinton	"	307
Interior of the Carthusian Chapter-House, Hinton	"	347
Piscina in Hinton Chapter-House	"	350

ERRATA

Page 71, line 1, *for* "prioracy" *read* "priorate."

„ 85, lines 3 and 2 from the bottom, *for* "in the above-mentioned inquisition of A.D. 1273" *read* "at a later inquisition held in A.D. 1273."

„ 88, line 3 from the bottom, *for* "Henry I." *read* "Henry II."

PART I
WITHAM CHARTERHOUSE

A

WITHAM CHARTERHOUSE

OR

THE CHARTERHOUSE IN SELWOOD

CHAPTER I

ESTABLISHMENT OF THE FIRST ENGLISH CHARTERHOUSE

"Through wisdom is an house builded; and by understanding it is established."—Prov. xxiv. 3.

A FEW miles within the eastern border of Somersetshire, and within the bounds of what was once the Forest of Selwood, is the little village of Witham-Friary, or Charterhouse-Witham, a simple quiet grey village, like many another in the West Country, though unlike most in respect to its parish church. Instead of the handsome edifice with the lofty turreted tower so usual in those parts, that building is a somewhat low structure,

in the plan of an oblong without aisles, terminating the east end in an apse, having only a small belfry in the roof. But plain almost to ugliness as it is, that little church has a not uninteresting history, for, with the name of the village, it is all that remains of the first English Charterhouse.

About A.D. 1084, St. Bruno, then a canon in the Cathedral of Reims, became convinced that a religious life could only be led apart from the world, having come to that conclusion whilst regarding the evil life of one of the archbishops there, and, according to the legend, having received a warning to that effect in the speech of a dead friend at whose funeral he was assisting. Persuading six friends to go with him, like another Lot, he fled from his Sodom and turned his face towards the mountains. In the world which he was now quitting he was already well known as a learned and a holy man (indeed, some say he was fleeing from the dignity of the Archbishopric of Reims,* which was likely to be imposed upon him), and he had had several renowned pupils. To one of these, St. Hugh, Bishop of Grenoble, he now applied.

* Montalembert, *Les Moines d'Occident*, vol. vii

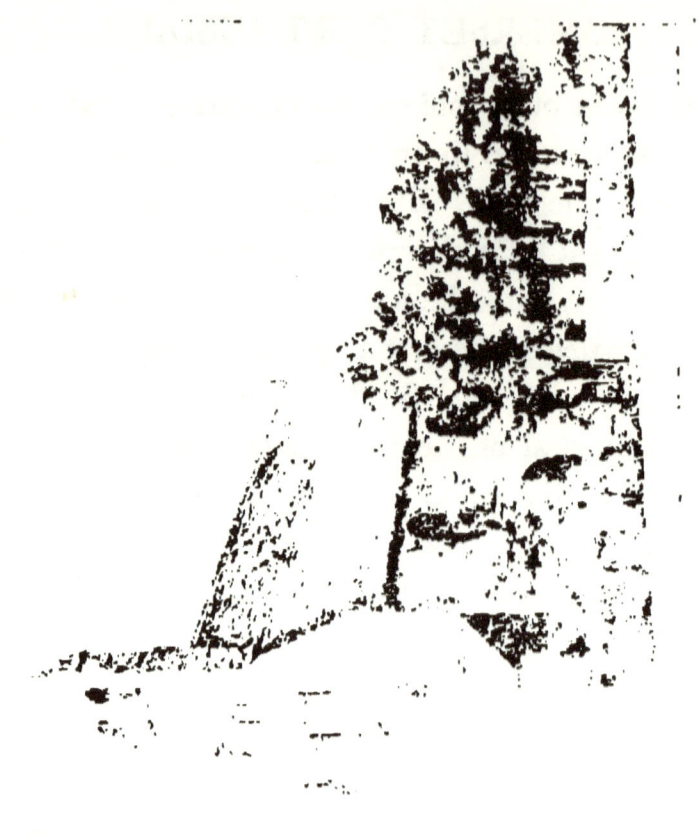

...THUSIANS

...les, tea...
... only a s...
... to ...
... uninter...
... the village, it is ...
... of the English Charterho...
About A.D. 10... St. Bruno, then a c...
the C...l of ..., became c...
a... ly be led ...
that ...
... the ar...
... g...d, havi...
... in the
... ral he w...
... to go ...
Let ... from h's ...
his face ... the mountai...
which he ... quickly be...
known as ... d and a holy ...
... deel... from ...
... Arch... ... of K...s,* w...
to b... in... d upon him), a...
several ... nd p...'s. T... S...
Hugh ...p of ...

WITHAM FRIARY CHURCH, EXTERIOR.

The bishop readily granted the seven companions their desired retreat in the rocky solitude of La Chartreuse. An oratory and some very small cells, built at a short distance from each other, and the cloisters, were erected as speedily as possible. Here, as if impregnated with the very spirit of the stern and wild scenery about him, St. Bruno formulated his harsh rule, taking that of St. Benedict as its groundwork. Here, with long fasts, and in silence for the most part, he and his followers led a hermit life in a desert more terrible than those to which the early Fathers were wont to retire. Their first name, the Poor of Christ, since lost in the later appellation of the Carthusians, was not unsuited to them as regarded their worldly resources, for the sterile soil of the mountains could be little cultivated, so that they had to live on the produce of their flocks, which, in that region of spare herbage, could not have been numerous; indeed, with their scanty fare and general hard way of living, and with their plain style of architecture and churches barren of ornament, they could not have needed much wealth, and it seems were not allowed it; for when Count

William of Nevers,* who later put on their frock, sent them a rich present of silver plate, they returned it. But, in spite of their austerity, the Carthusians excited the admiration of other monks; and laymen, and even women and children, sought to be admitted among them. Their renown for holiness was not less a hundred years later; so that when, in A.D. 1172, Pope Alexander III. commuted the form of Henry's penance for the murder of St. Thomas à Becket from a three years' crusade into the building of three monasteries, it was judged to be for the spiritual welfare of the king and his kingdom that one of them should be a house of Carthusians, whose Order as yet possessed no convent in England.

The site chosen for this new monastery was Witham. In the time of Edward the Confessor it had been a portion of the manor of Brewham, but William the Conqueror had separated it, and granted it partly to Roger de Corcelle and partly to Turstin Fitzrolf.† After the death of both of these, it had reverted to the crown, and

* Montalembert, *Les Moines d'Occident*.
† Domesday Book.

WITHAM CHARTERHOUSE

there continued until now, when Henry II. granted it to the Carthusians. The little band of monks who, at the king's request, had been sent over from La Grande Chartreuse, were henceforth to make their home in a very different tract of country to that whence they had come. A solitude, as was commanded by the rule of their Order, indeed it was, but the solitude of the forest, and not that of a scarcely habitable region; instead of the lofty mountains thickly covered with snow and mist for half the year round, not far off was the gentle undulating range of the Mendip Hills, from which could come no avalanches such as that which in January A.D. 1133 had buried the first cloisters and cells and seven brethren.* But if the newcomers had not to fight against the elements and the physical difficulties of the land, they had to go through many struggles before they were peaceably possessed of it.

Leland the antiquary † says that at first there was at Witham a nunnery. Camden also in his *Britannia* says, "Not far from hence [Nonney

---

* Montalembert, *Les Moines d'Occident*.
† Leland, *Collect.*, vol. . p. 77.

de la Mare] is Witham, where King Henry II. built a nunnery;" but as he goes on to say that after the dissolution of religious houses it came into the family of Hopton, to whom certainly Witham Charterhouse was granted, the word *nunnery* must surely be a mistake for *monastery*. At any rate, the records as to what became of the nuns, who, with the other inhabitants of the village, had to be turned out in order to make a fitting solitary neighbourhood for the Carthusians, have apparently disappeared. But whether the monks had to dispute their rights with a sister-community or not, they certainly had to dispute them with the other settlers on the soil. The first Prior soon wearied of his difficulties; used to the freedom and quiet of the mountains, his delicate mind could not bear the anxiety of planning and constructing, and the constant quarrels with the natives, to whom he and his appeared as monsters, who, not content with their own boundaries, were come to swallow up their acres; moreover, their manners and customs and the strange diet troubled him. Seeing him to be incapable of the management of their affairs, his brethren allowed him to return home. Another monk was sent from La Grande Chartreuse to be their Prior instead, but he too was affected with a like weariness, and soon "by a happy death received the end of his labours and the beginning of life."* The troubles of the remaining brethren continued, and the king himself began to fear lest he should fail in his undertaking of establishing the Order in England. It was probably some time in A.D. 1173, when Henry was negotiating with the Count of Maurienne about a contemplated marriage of the latter's daughter with Prince John, that the Count, hearing of his difficulties concerning Witham, recommended him to entreat the community at La Grande Chartreuse to send to England their present Proctor, who from his office must have gained some experience in monastic affairs. This was Hugh of Avalon, St. Hugh as he was afterwards called. There would be found in this one man, said the Count, not only all the usual virtues, but whatever of long-suffering and sweetness, whatever of magnanimity and gentleness, could be discovered in any mortal being; he would certainly

* *Magna Vita S. Hugonis.*

adorn the whole English Church by the brightness of his "most pure religion and his most religious purity." To none would he seem an undesirable neighbour; none would shun him as a foreigner; every one would regard him as a fellow-citizen, as a brother or an intimate friend; for he himself embraced and cherished all men "in the arms and on the bosom of his unique love."* The king followed the advice given, and sent Reginald Fitz-Jocelin, Bishop of Bath, at the head of an embassy to La Grande Chartreuse.

Being joined on the way by the Bishop of Grenoble, the diocesan of the place, himself formerly one of the community, the royal messengers on their arrival presented their master's letters to the Prior and brethren. The worth of St. Hugh was well known; the Prior at first refused to let him go, and most of the brethren were of the opinion that so valuable a man ought by no means to be sent to so remote a region. But one of them, Bovo, later himself Prior of Witham, said that Heaven might have decreed that by the holiness of this man the sanctity of

* *Magna Vita S. Hugonis.*

the Order might shine forth to the farthest limits of the world. "Think not," he added, "that you will for long be able to hide him, your light, under a bushel. A little while since, Hugh appeared to me by his virtues rather as a bishop than a monk." St. Hugh's own opinion was that he was unfit to rule others, for, surrounded by their sanctity, helped so much by their warnings and examples, he had never, even for one day, had to take care of his own soul independently. But the more reluctant were the monks for the parting, the more urgent were the two bishops and their company in their request. At length, some of the brethren siding with the royal party, St. Hugh appealed to his Prior to let him remain. The Prior, who loved him as his own soul, declared, "As the Lord liveth, never shall that sentence go out of my mouth by which I must order Hugh to desert my old age and widow the Chartreuse of his most sweet and necessary presence!" But finally he consented to follow the advice of the Bishop of Grenoble, and send him across the sea. Then turning to St. Hugh, the bishop said, "And as for thee, Hugh, dearest brother, it is right that thou shouldst imitate in this Him whom thou hast always sweetly followed, the only-begotten Son of the Almighty Father, who, from the deepest secret place of His Deity, deigned to come forth for the salvation of many to the public place of human intercourse." St. Hugh flung himself at the bishop's feet, and begged in vain for a reversal of his decision; then, having given his brethren the farewell kiss of peace and recommending himself to their prayers, he departed with the embassy and came to King Henry, who had him conducted in honour to Witham, where the monks there received him with "ineffable joy," "as the angel of the Lord."

The little community were found in the woods not far from the village of Witham, dwelling in what must have been nothing better than rude huts, for their cells were made out of stakes hedged round with pales and a low wall. In fact, the new Prior had to begin his office by building the convent, for things were in such an imperfect state that it had not even been determined where it would be best to erect the greater and the lesser church, the former with the monks' cells and cloisters, the latter with the dwellings of the lay-brothers and the lodgings of the guests. But the saint would not have the foundations of the holy house laid in injustice; therefore he urged the king to make provision that the inhabitants of the village should take no injury in giving up their ancestral possessions. Henry, admiring his prudence, granted his desires, and offered the people two alternatives: they might, at their choice, either receive dwellings and lands of equal value to those they were leaving at Witham in whatever part of the kingdom they should select, or accept their freedom from serfdom, which would enable them to go to cultivate whatever regions they wished. Some chose their freedom; others chose new land. Thus in the *Testa de Neville* or *Liber Feodorum* (temp. Henry III.) we find:—

In the Hundred of Northairy, Ralf Malet held land worth £8 a year in the same manor in exchange for his land at "Witteham," of the gift of King Henry, father of King John, by the service of the twentieth part of one knight's fee.* That the Charterhouse might be free from future litigation, the king had it proclaimed in all the

* *Testa de Nevilie*, p. 162, b.

towns and villages of Wiltshire, Dorsetshire, and Somersetshire, that any wishing for an exchange of lands must prove their rights to their holdings at Witham within two years.* St. Hugh, mindful that the inhabitants might have laid out much upon their old homes, insisted upon their having compensation, even to the last farthing, for any improvements they might have made. But his sense of duty to his neighbour did not stop here. Referring to the tenements to be evacuated, he said to Henry, "Behold, my lord, I, a stranger and a poor man, have made thee rich." The king answered, as the Prior desired, that he did not know to what use to put such kind of wealth as this. "Therefore," said St. Hugh, "give those buildings to me, that have not where to lay my head." "Wonderful man, dost thou think us unable to build new ones for you? What dost thou want with these?" asked Henry, surprised and puzzled at the demand. "It does not become the royal majesty to inquire into petty details," returned the monk; "this is my first petition to thee, and since it is moderate, why am I to suffer delay in the granting of it?" So

* Assise Roll, 8 Edward I.

WITHAM CHARTERHOUSE 15

the king, still wondering, fulfilled his desire. St. Hugh being possessed of the houses, gave the materials to the ejected natives of Witham, that they might either carry them away to make their new homes of, or sell them. All difficulties of disseising the former occupants of the soil being now surmounted, the monks could turn their whole attention to the work of construction.

As a Carthusian convent is always built on the same system in its main outlines, though the details may vary, in default of any known extant description of the Witham monastery, we will follow that given by Father Doreau * of Charterhouses in general. "The entrance presents to the sight only bare walls, adorned by statues of the saints, and by the predominating Cross. If any openings are made there, they are sashed, and, as if that were not enough, are protected by a strong iron fence against those who might be tempted to a breach of cloister. One's gaze then rests on a gloomy courtyard, flanked by the long buildings which contain, along with the cells of the lay-brethren, their respective obediences, the

* *Henry VIII. et les Martyrs de la Chartreuse de Londres*, chap. iii.

kitchen, pantry, bakehouse, forge, the carpenter's workroom. Adjoining these out-buildings, if it is not included amongst them, is the guest-house for the accommodation of strangers, who come to indulge their curiosity or to fortify themselves with the exercises of the retreat. This court, then, with a few exceptions, however important and ornamented as it may be, offers nothing monastic in its appearance." It is the little cloister which "is the heart of a religious house. In this retired part of the monastery is to be found the chapter-house, where the religious assemble for prayer on certain days, and where they meet whenever the community is invited to consider the reception of a would-be member, or on the temporal affairs of the house. In another place is the refectory, that of the fathers, and sometimes on the same plan that of the lay-brethren, separated from the first by a partition. In either meals are taken but rarely, and then always in silence. A reading in Latin for the former, and in the common tongue for the latter, nourishes the spirit and heart at the same time that a modest pittance repairs the strength of the body." At the end of the little cloister, is the church, with its chapels radiating from it for the use of the religious. The Carthusian church is always without aisles, and, like the refectory, is in two distinct parts. The choir of the brethren is that division where the lay-brethren take part in the service chanted by the monks in the neighbouring choir. Communication to the two choirs is through an open-work gate, which is opened two or three times a year on solemn occasions. Beyond the church is the large cloister, the "enclosed garden" of the monastery, where, surrounded by walls, is generally the burial-ground. "Each cell is a complete dwelling by itself." "Besides the little garden which the recluse cultivates and trims according to his taste, he has a long and spacious corridor where he may walk up and down in the hour for recreation. On the ground-floor a workroom with a stock of tools enables him to make a diversion from his spiritual exercises, which fill up a good part of the day." In the first story is the cell proper, consisting of two rooms, of which one serves as an antechamber to the other, where is all the furniture. The latter consists of "an oratory, a work-table, some shelves filled with books of devotion, a mattress in a recess, two chairs, a 'refectory' in the embrasure of the window."

Looking at it merely as a work of art, there is probably little to regret in the destruction of the Charterhouse at Witham. For, unlike other Orders, the Carthusians eschewed all ornamentation in their architecture; not that, like the Puritans, they thought that the richly carved designs in the mediæval masonry savoured of superstition, and that therefore such decorations rather did dishonour to the house of God, of which the whole monastery might be considered a part; on the contrary, we find that St. Hugh, in whom their ideas were thoroughly instilled, when he came to be bishop, rebuilt the Cathedral of Lincoln in the splendid style of his own days, because it was so much more beautiful than the old.* But in comparison with other things, they probably regarded architectural adornment as a matter of indifference; or perhaps, like St. Bernard, they asked what was the meaning of "that deformed beauty and that beautiful deformity before the eyes of the brethren when reading," fearing that it might be "more pleasant to

* Giraldus Cambrensis.

read in the stone-work than in books, to spend the day in admiring these oddities than in meditating on the law of God."* Nevertheless, what they did build doubtless they built strongly and well, as was the manner of their times. We read how, under St. Hugh's directions, the fabric of the house of God was erected by the hard labour of the workman, with its solid bases and strong supports, so that it should not fall through age; how the roof and walls rose, not of wood, which would rot, but of durable stone.† The present parish church of Witham, whose unusual stone vaulted roof points to its foreign origin, according to the authorities ‡ in these matters, if not wholly built by St. Hugh, must have been the church of the former villagers, which he altered for the use of the *conversi* or lay-brethren; for in the early Charterhouses, not only were the dwellings of the latter separate, but their church was a separate building from that of the fathers or monks proper, that is, those who had taken the vows and entered holy orders. The peculiar splay of the windows suggests the

---

* *Life of St. Bernard,* by J. C. Cotter-Morrison.
† *Metrical Life of St. Hugh.*
‡ *Somerset Archæological Society Proceedings for* 1878.

adaptation of an older edifice to new ideas of architecture; the inside splay measures 2 feet 10 inches, and the outside splay measures 1 foot 8 inches, instead of about five or six inches according to the ordinary width. Now, as St. Hugh wished to roof the church with stone, it stands to reason that the old walls that had supported a roof of wood could not bear up the much heavier material that he proposed to use. Therefore it is to be concluded that he strengthened them by encasing them, as it were, in a stone covering, which added twenty inches to their original thickness. In A.D. 1876 yet further support was given to them by buttresses, which the architect copied from those built by St. Hugh at Lincoln.*

But before they could complete their building

---

* *Somerset Archæological Society Proceedings for* 1893, from the observations of Rev. J. T. Westropp of Witham to the Society. It may be noted here that one of the windows near the east end, known as "The Leper's Window," is supposed to have been opened for passing the Blessed Sacrament to any lepers who wished to communicate; their hospital was at Maiden-Bradley. From the same authority the following fact is also derived. The font, the licence for the erection of which, in A.D. 1458, is mentioned in a later chapter, was found built into the masonry of a modern tower during the restoration of the church in A.D. 1876; the tower was pulled down at the later date and the font restored to the church, where, because of its misplacement, a new one had meanwhile been supplied.

SUPPOSED LEPERS' WINDOW IN WITHAM CHURCH.

the community had to overcome yet another difficulty. Henry, occupied with other affairs, neglected to provide them with funds, so that they had nothing wherewith to pay the workmen, who now naturally fell to reviling and complaining against them. Twice they applied in vain to the king for help, their messengers bringing back each time words instead of gifts. Upon this Brother Girard, a man of somewhat haughty temperament and very proud of the Order, reproached the Prior for dallying there any longer until it pleased that "most hard man," the king, to put a finish to the work; it was an insult to the community, and laid them open to the derision of all, he said. Used to speaking to the great ones of the earth, he was ready to go to Henry and declare his mind to him, and tell him they would return to their own country; let Hugh come with him and hear what he had to say. The rest of the brethren being called, it was agreed that the Prior, with Brothers Girard and Ainard, an aged monk, should go to court. St. Hugh previously warned Girard to moderate his language to Henry. "That prince," said he, "has great sagacity and an almost inscrutable mind, and may be pretending to listen to us in order to try us." The king received them reverently, as if they were angels of heaven, spoke them fair, and promised everything, but again gave them nothing. Then Brother Girard, unmindful of his Prior's advice, burst out into a furious invective: "Whatever you think now to do or to omit to do, my lord king, it does not concern me; I leave you to the quiet possession of your whole kingdom; bidding you farewell, I shall speedily return to our hermitage at the Chartreuse. You think to show us grace in feeding us with your bread when we are not in need of it. Truly we are more content to find shelter on our Alpine rocks than engage in a conflict with such a man, who cares so little for his soul's good. Let him have for himself the riches which he loves so much; neither Christ nor any good Christian is thought worthy to have a share of these." St. Hugh listened to the angry words with amazement and "confusion of heart." Not so the king, who, like a philosopher, waited with unmoved countenance and in silence until the "verbal flagellation" was over. Then turning to the Prior, who was holding down his head in confusion, but whom he had been observing all the while: "What dost thou think of doing, good man?" he asked; "wilt thou too leave us and our kingdom?" The saint returned the gentle answer, "My lord, I do not so greatly despair of you. I pity rather your hindrances and occupations, which impede the beneficial study of your soul; for you are busy, and in the Lord's own time you will follow up these wholesome beginnings." "By the safety of my soul, while I live," cried the king, embracing him, "thou departest not from my kingdom." And forthwith he sent them money and help for the completion of the buildings. The construction now went on without interruption, and, when finished, the monastery was dedicated to the Blessed Virgin Mary, St. John the Baptist, and All Saints.

The charter of the foundation[*] granted by Henry II. prescribes the boundaries of the conventual estates, but it is almost impossible to identify the names, which not only appear in strange guise in the Latinised forms, but pro-

[*] Appendix i. vol. vi. pt. 1 of *Monasticon Anglicanum*.

bably even have been changed with new owners of the lands, for many of them are but the names of fields, paths, crofts, or perhaps of hamlets no longer existing. Then the charter goes on to enumerate the privileges of the monks—" My foresaid house of Witteham, and the brethren of the Carthusian Order serving God in it, are to have and to hold all the foresaid [lands] in free and perpetual alms, well and in peace, freely and quietly, wholly and fully and honourably, with all the liberties, as I [the king] have ever held them ; with all their free customs, as well concerning the election of a prior as other customs which a Carthusian house is wont to have in wood, in plain, in meadows and pastures, in waters and mills, in parks, lakes, fishponds, and marshes, in ways and byways, and in all other places and other things thereto pertaining, free and quit of taxes, danegeld, hidage, scutage, of working at castles, bridges, parks, and moats, and houses." Also the monks were to be untroubled by tolls and other customs due to the king throughout his realm on both sides of the sea, or by attending at the courts of the shire or hundred, or at any lawsuit. And all their lands were to be free from the penalty of murder for ever, and from every other worldly exaction. Foresters and their officers were to leave them undisturbed within their boundaries. If any one shall dare to do anything against this pious donation, either in any way to disturb it or diminish it, the charter goes on, he shall incur "the anger of the omnipotent God and my curse" until he make worthy satisfaction; but for all those who shall cherish it in peace, let there be "peace and reward from the Eternal Father."

It may interest some of our readers to read the charter in its original language:—

"Henricus Dei gratia, Rex Angliæ, dux Normanniæ et Aquitaniæ et Comes Andegaviæ, archiepiscopis, episcopis, etc., salutem. Sciatis me pro anima mea et antecessorum et successorum meorum, construxisse domum in honorem beatæ Mariæ et beati Johannis Baptistæ et omnium sanctorum, in dominio meo de Witteham de ordine Cartusiæ, et sit mea et heredum meorum dominica domus et elemosina: et concessisse eidem domui, et fratribus ibidem Deo servientibus, et dedisse in liberam et perpetuam elemosinam ad sustentationem eorum totam terram infra subscriptos limites, liberam et quietam ab omni servicio. In primis a parte septentrionali a fossato de parco ad Hachstok; ab Hactoch de Posteberry per fossatum de Berwa usque ad pratum regis, de prato regis per medium prati usque ad Hacheweie, de Hacheweye ultra Humburna usque ad Rugalega, de Rugalega usque ad Waletonia, de Waletonia per Hanhesda usque Luthbroka, de Luthbroka per cursum aquæ usque ad Pennemere, de Penemere usque ad maram Willielmi filii Petri, de hac mara usque ad Kincput, de Kincput juxta pontem usque ad Wodecroft-Petri, de Wodecroft-Petri usque ad Fraggemera, de Fraggemera usque ad Cleteweia, de Cleteweia usque ad Fleistoke, de Fleystoka, usque ad Snepsuedesweia, de Snepseudesweia usque ad Ruggesclivaheaved, hinc usque ad Chelsledesweie, de Chelsledeweie percilium montis usque ad Fisborne-Heafole, hinc per cursum aquæ ad parcum; hinc per fossatum parci usque ad Fromweia, de Fromweia usque ad Hachstock. Præterea hæc dedi eis ad pasturas eorum apud terram de Cheddenford Harechina in Hindcome senda usque ad Lecherberg, de Lecherberg usque ad Stemberg, de Stemberg usque ad Hoppewell, de Hoppewelle usque ad Staberga, de Staberga usque ad Sgaldebereg, de Sgaldebereg usque ad Stanamlanam et inde usque ad petram perforatam per medium putei; et de petra perforata usque ad Chinendclive, et inde per vallem usque ad Faldam latronum, et inde usque ad Kingdoneswestende, et de Kyndoneswestende per vallem versus orientem, usque ad viam quæ vadit de Pridia usque ad Chederford, et inde supra pratum Johannis Marescalli, usque ad petram de Pemblestorna, de Pemblestorna per semitam usque ad collem prati Malherbe, et inde usque ad Harestana inter pratum regis et pratum Malherbe, et de Harestona usque ad petram semitæ quæ ducit usque Hindesgravam, et de Hindesgrava usque ad latam viam, et inde usque ad spinam parvam, et de illa spina usque ad Hedewoldesting, et de Hedewoldesting usque ad puteum inter pratum regis et pratum Rugaberga, de puteo illo usque ad Rademera, et inde usque ad petram quæ facit divisam inter pratum regis et pratum de Rugaberga, et de petra illa usque ad aliam petram; et de petra illa usque ad petram de

Cliva, et de petra de Cliva usque ad latam petram, et de lata petra usque ad Merlestresenda, de Merlestresenda usque ad Stanrodam, et inde ad Begesethle, de Begesethle usque ad Esweie, de Esweia ad Sigodesfeld, et inde per vallem de Smelecuma usque ad croftam Rogeri, de crofta Rogeri usque ad Rugelege, de Rugelega ad Clotleg, de Clotleg usque ad crucem de Meleweia, et inde usque Smelecuma, de Smelecuma usque ad Lefiwiesmere et inde ad Snedelesputte, et inde ad Eilstesmede, et inde ad Bikwelle, et inde ad Suthemaste-Rodberg, et inde ad furcas; de furcis per cavum ductum ad platam petram, et de plata petra ad Horswelle, de Horswelle ad Hindeswelle, et inde ad Walborgam, de Walborg ad Herachmam. Quare volo et firmiter præcipio quod supradicta domus mea de Witteham, et fratres ordinis Chartusiæ in ea Deo servientes, omnia prædicta habeant et teneant in libera et perpetua elemosina, ita bene et in pace, libere et quiete, integre et plenarie et honorifice, cum omnibus libertatibus suis, sicut ea unquam liberius tenui, et cum liberis consuetudinibus suis, tam de priore eligendo, quam de aliis consuetudinibus quas habet domus Cartusiæ, in bosco in plano, in pratis et pascius, in aquis et molendinis, in vivariis et stagnis et piscariis et mariscis, in viis et semitis, et in omnibus aliis locis et aliis rebus ad ea pertinentibus, libera et quieta de geldis et danegeldis, et hidagiis, et scutagiis, et operationibus castellorum et pontium et parcorum et fossarum et domorum. De theoloneo vero et passagio, et paagio, et pontagio, et lestagio, et de omni servitio et consuetuedine et omni quæstu pecuniario ad me pertinente sint liberi et quieti per totam terram meam, tam ultra mare quam citra mare, de essartis et regardo forestæ infra terminos suos; et de siris et hundredis et sectis sirarum et hundredorum et placitis et querelis omnibus. Et omnes terræ eorum de quibus solebat dari murdrum in perpetuum sint quietæ de murdro, et de omni exactione et vexatione et inquietatione mundana.

"Prohibeo etiam ne forestarii vel eorum ministri aliquam eis molestiam faciant infra limites suos, nec ingredientibus vel egredientibus per eos. Si quis autem contra hanc piam donationem meam venire vel eam in aliquo perturbare si diminuere præsumpserit, iram omnipotentis Dei, et meam maledictionem incurrat nisi ad condignam satisfactionem venerit. Omnibus vero misericorditer eam amplectantibus, et in pace foventibus, sit pax et remuneratio ab Eterno Patre in sæcula sæculorum. Amen.

"Testibus Hugone Dunholmensi, Gaufrido Eliensi, Johanne Norwicensi, Reginaldo Bathoniensi episcopis, Johanne filio meo; comite Willielmo Sussexiæ, Ranulpho de Glanvilla, Waltero filio Roberti, Reginaldo de Courtnay, Hugone Bardulf, et Hugone de Norwico senescallo, Radulpho filio Stephani camerario, Gilberto filio Reinfredi, Gaufrido filio Petri, Roberto de Whitefeld, et Michaele Bedet, apud Marleburgam."

CHAPTER II

THE CARTHUSIAN RULE

Mundus est Religio est
Turbulenta trepidatio Requies sanctificata
Callis inexplicabilis. Sabbathum Domini.
—THEODORE STUMPWICK, *Schema Monasticæ Religionis Prærogativorum.*

THE stern manner of the Carthusian life won little favour in England, for though within thirty years after St. Hugh's death in A.D. 1200, Hinton Charterhouse, in Somersetshire, was founded in his honour, there were never more than nine houses of the Order here. Capable as Englishmen are of enduring hardship upon occasion for some present end, the generality of them would be far too matter-of-fact to submit themselves year after year to such suffering as the rigid Carthusian rule must have entailed on many of its followers, unless for a more tangible object than the future good of their souls.

St. Bruno's rule was founded on that of St. Benedict; the chief difference between them being that to the vows of poverty and obedience there was added a more thorough system of self-mortification. Poverty among the Carthusians was ensured by their statutes, the appointed number of inmates of a Carthusian institution having reference to it; the monks being thirteen, and the lay-brothers sixteen, "because we think that that number can support themselves on their own resources."* And as the religious were to be limited, so also were their cattle and their hired servants, which last were necessary, as no Carthusian might go beyond his monastery walls, except the Prior and Procurator. They might have 25 paid servants, 1200 sheep and goats, 12 dogs, 32 oxen, 20 bull calves, and 6 pack-horses; if their live stock increased, they were to give the excess to the poor. No wealth was to be spent even on the church; for not only were tapestry and other rich hangings not to be used, but there were to be no ornaments of gold or silver, except in the case of the Eucharistic vessels. All bodily comforts were

* Customs of Guigo I., fifth Prior of the Grande Chartreuse.

A CARTHUSIAN—CHOIR DRESS.

eschewed. The frock was white, with a black plaited cloak for out of doors; two frocks were allowed to each monk, of a better and worse quality, for different occasions. This simple dress, under which they only wore the hair shirt, seems to have been found scarcely warm enough for the English climate, for a general chapter of the Order, held in A.D. 1261, forbids, amongst other things, the wearing of wolf-skins and furs of other wild animals. The bed was a board and a blanket, with a bolster of rags covered with the coarsest skins. Their food consisted of bread, fruit, herbs, and vegetables, varied on feast days by fish and cheese; once a week at least they fasted on bread, water, and salt; flesh they might not eat at any time, not even when ill. Any one wishing to indulge in harsher exercises of mortification in sleep or in diet must first obtain permission from the prior, who, however, had no right to withstand him if he were much in earnest, lest in doing so he should "withstand God also."

But the chief feature in the rule was the complete solitude of the Carthusian's life. The monks of other Orders separated themselves, it is true, from the world; nevertheless, owing to the hospitality which they often maintained on a large scale, they were bound to see not a little of that world. The Carthusians, on the contrary, preferred to close their doors against all comers. In fact, at first they did not have stabling even for those guests who could pay them, nor yet almshouses for poorer wayfarers,* though in their later monasteries they seem to have allowed some accommodation for strangers. One of the customs of Guigo I., their fifth Prior, runs thus:—" To the poor we give alms in bread or anything else that we can, but rarely take them under our roof; for we fled to this hermitage to attend to the welfare of our souls; therefore it is not to be wondered at that we grant more intercourse and comfort to those who come hither for the sake of their souls rather than of their bodies; otherwise we should not have gone to this almost inaccessible place." Women, indeed, they utterly refused to admit on any pretext within their bounds, knowing that, as instanced in Holy Writ, no wise man, prophet, or judge, not Samson, David, nor Solomon, not even the

* *Customs of D. Guigo I.*, cap. lxxxix.

very first man formed by God, could resist the attraction of a wily woman.* But not only did the Carthusians keep themselves more strictly aloof from outsiders than other monks; their system of solitary cells and rule of silence made their lives yet more secluded. They spent their whole time apart from each other with closed doors, meditating, praying, reading, or working, in perfect silence, which was allowed to be broken only in the case of the sudden illness of a brother, or of fire, or of any other unexpected danger, in advertising which few words were to be used. They were to pray in church and repeat the Hours in their cells in as quiet a voice as possible, lest they should interrupt their fellow-worshippers. Even their food was received in silence through a window in their cell. And there are minute rules for preserving the same stillness in their bodily movements during the services in church,—how they are not to look about them, how they must not twist their fingers together, nor swing their legs, nor play with their books while singing, and how they must obtain pardon if they let a book

* *Consuetudines Guigonis I.*, cap. xxi.

fall. They met together only at the services and on chapter-days and festivals, when they also dined together in the refectory and might speak to one another. Even at these privileged times their conversation was to be on serious and non-secular topics appertaining to the observance of religion, and their speeches were not to be prolix, and they were to avoid dissolute or scandalous talk. No one was to whisper or say anything which he was not willing that all should hear. During the common meals in the refectory there would be little opportunity for conversation, as they must listen to some sermon or homily meantime from a reader, who was specially enjoined to read what could be understood by all, and in a voice that could be heard by all. Once a week the monk might walk in the grounds of his monastery, but no one, unless especially sent by the superior—and then he must not receive hospitality of strangers except by permission—was to go beyond the bounds. As a rule, the prior or proctor alone ever went abroad, and then only on the necessary business of the house. The proctor or steward, who had also the charge of the lay-brethren, had to receive any strangers, welcoming them with a kiss, and was to eat with them, if no special fast was going on, sending those who were worthy of the honour to the prior. Although "busy over many things, like Martha," he also was bidden not to shun the silence of his cell, but to have frequent resort thither to read, pray, and think, and compose his mind after attending to temporal matters, and to consider in what he had best instruct the brethren committed to his care.

Even after death the same rule of seclusion was carried out, for no stranger, whether a religious or not, was to be buried in the cemetery of their convent, unless his own people were unable or neglected to give him burial. The graves of the monks themselves, except in the case of the generals of the Order, were and are marked only by wooden crosses without inscriptions, as if to impress all the more on the living the insignificance of all mortal parts of the human person.

The occupation of the monks, besides the performance of the divine offices and their private devotions, consisted principally in transcribing manuscripts, especially the Holy Scriptures and religious books, thus, as they said, preaching the word of God not by word of mouth, but by the work of their hands. The tools and materials for writing on the parchment were part of the furniture of each cell; the proceeds from the sale of the transcripts formed part of the maintenance of the community, the produce of their flocks supplying the rest. Each monk was supplied from the library with two books, of which he was warned to take "all diligent care" lest they should be soiled by smoke, dust, or other dirt. When he was tired of these sedentary occupations he might work at carpentry or in the garden which was always attached to his cell, or might walk in the corridor outside. In addition to this, every monk must take his week of service in the church.

Thus in this routine of services, mortifications of the flesh, penances, and peaceful occupations, the Carthusian's existence ran on in one long fast, as it were, from the day of taking the vows till the day of death.

In one of his *Pensées*, Pascal compares a soldier and a Carthusian:—" Quelle différence entre un soldat et un chartreux? quant à l'obéissance? Car ils sont également obéissants et dé-

A CARTHUSIAN LAY-BROTHER.

…endants, et dans l…
…ais le soldat espère …
… le devient jamais, c…
…ne sont toujou…
…s il l'espère t…
venir ; au lieu …
…are jamais que de…
…t pas dans le s…
…x ont toujours, …
… a toujours et l'autre j…
…han became master of n…
…g must have made him compl…
…self so far as controlling his personal desire
… impulses went, for there could not be a more
…orough system of self-annihilation, leading to a
…ect obedience to rule, personified by the prior
…d chapter of his convent. No military dis-
…line, not even the famous Jesuit system, could
… forth a stricter obedience than was demanded
… shown by the disciples of St. Bruno. An
…isode in the life of Einard, one of the monks
… came to Witham, is an illustration of th…
This Einard was a lay-brother, who … …
… sent forth at different times to hel… …
…r of instituting new houses of the O…

pendants, et dans les exercises également pênibles. Mais le soldat espère toujours devenir maître, et ne le devient jamais, car les capitaines et princes même sont toujours esclaves et dépendants; mais il l'espère toujours, et travaille toujours a y venir; au lieu que le chartreux fait vœu de n'être jamais que dépendant. Ainsi ils ne diffèrent pas dans le servitude perpetuelle que tous deux ont toujours, mais dans l'espérance que l'un a toujours et l'autre jamais." But if the Carthusian became master of nothing else, his training must have made him completely master of himself so far as controlling his personal desires and impulses went, for there could not be a more thorough system of self-annihilation, leading to a perfect obedience to rule, personified by the prior and chapter of his convent. No military discipline, not even the famous Jesuit system, could call forth a stricter obedience than was demanded of and shown by the disciples of St. Bruno. An episode in the life of Einard, one of the monks who came to Witham, is an illustration of this fact. This Einard was a lay-brother, who had been sent forth at different times to help in the labour of instituting new houses of the Order in various parts of Europe; at last, when nearly a hundred years old, he was bidden to go on a mission for the establishment of a charterhouse in Denmark. He had conceived a great dislike to the Danes, and, in fact, feared them as untaught barbarians, and entreated the Prior to release him from this duty. The Prior refused, representing to him that his experience was necessary to the younger brethren of the mission. Einard had entered the monastery in his boyhood, and had as yet shown perfect obedience; but now he boldly declared, that though he should have to make expiation for his disobedience, he would never see Denmark whilst in the flesh. The usual punishment of the refractory was awarded him; old as he was, and in spite of valuable work that he had done in propagating the Order, he was expelled from the doors of the Grande Chartreuse. His superior being inexorable to his entreaties for pardon, he wandered half-clothed and barefoot, suffering meantime bitter cold and hunger, from one charterhouse to another, seeking their intercessions for him. At last, during the bitterest winter weather of that wild region, toiling through snow and ice in the daytime, and resting as best he could without shelter at night, he made his way once more to the Grande Chartreuse, bringing with him intercessory letters from all the priors of his Order. This time his own Prior could scarcely refuse to receive him again; he was readmitted, and soon after sent to Witham, and, notwithstanding all the hardships of his exile, lived another thirty years.

It could not have been the fear of punishment, expulsion, or confinement in the monastery, which was later the fate of the refractory, which caused these ascetics to obey so well, but a true love of the discipline to which they submitted themselves. From their first entrance they knew what this discipline was, for the novices were at once put to the proof and submitted to its harshness and strictness, so that they might form their decision to go or stay gradually and from no sudden or uncontrolled impulse. Youths under twenty, who could scarcely know their own minds, were not admitted to the vows. It was to the grown man, to the man who was capable of understanding the bearing of this harsh mode of life on his own spiritual growth, that the seclusion of the Carthusian cell was granted, and in it, as a rule, he found happiness. We have seen how it grieved St. Hugh to depart from La Grande Chartreuse; it grieved him just as much when, later on, he had to leave Witham, and when at intervals he returned thither, he always went back to the old way of living. His affection for the rule was common to the Order. When he went to La Grande Chartreuse for the first time, he was struck with the expression of calm happiness on the faces of the monks; that happiness is no less expressed in the lines comparing life in the world to life in the monastery written by a Carthusian of much later date, from which the motto of this chapter is taken.

The form of the vow was thus:—" I, Brother N., promise stability and obedience and the alteration of my ways, before God and His clerks and the relics belonging to his solitude, which has been built to the honour of God and the ever-blessed Virgin Mary and the Blessed John the Baptist, in the presence of Dom A., the Prior."*

But the question rises whether in this hard

---

* Cotton. MSS. Nero A. III. fol. 139 *et seq.*, being the customs of the Order as collected by John Batemanson, elected Prior of he London Charterhouse in A.D. 1531.

warfare against the flesh the physical strength was not destroyed. Sometimes it was so doubtless; but generally the contrary seems to have been the case. The Carthusians—and the abovementioned brother Einard is an instance—were as long-lived as other monks, who were remarkable as a class for their longevity. The Carthusian's life was probably not so unhealthy as a life of luxury; if his fare was hard and scanty, at least he could not suffer from pampering his body with unwholesome delicacies or with overfeeding; and if his occupations were quiet, he need not make them too sedentary, as he was always at liberty to do some manual labour, such as carpentering, instead of reading and writing. The vows would be no hardship to him, but more likely added to his content of mind, for, as the Marquis de Montalembert observes, "Le chrétien, le vrai sage, sait bien que jamais les obligations volontairement perpetuelles n'ont rendu l'homme malheureux d'une manière permanente; il sait au contraire qu'elles sont indispensibles au triomphe de l'ordre et de la paix de son âme. Ce qui le torture et ce qui le consume c'est ni la règle ni le devoir; c'est l'instabilité, c'est l'agitation, c'est la fièvre du changement." * The Carthusian, of all monks, must have felt this stability in his hermitage, where he could keep himself "unspotted from the world," whose ways were to him as intricate as an undefined pathway through a forest. To him, his religion, his existence as monk, was a sanctified rest, the Sabbath of the Lord.

St. Hugh of Avalon was a typical Carthusian, therefore it will not be amiss to give some account of his life up to the time when he was called from his duties of Witham] to preside over the See of Lincoln.

* *Les Moines d'Occident*, tome ii.

CHAPTER III

AN IDEAL MONK

"He that loveth pureness of heart, for the grace of his lips the king shall be his friend."—PROV. xxii. 11.

IT was about A.D. 1135, during the era of the Crusades, in an atmosphere of awakened Christianity and revived monasticism, both alike quickened by the eloquence of the great St. Bernard, that St. Hugh was born. Scarcely eight years later, his mother having recently died, his father, William of Avalon, divided his castles and possessions among his other children, and taking him with him, entered the Priory of Villarbenoît, a house of regular canons not far from his own estates and attached to the cathedral church of Grenoble. There was here a school, where, besides moral instruction, sacred and secular letters were taught to noble youths; amongst these St. Hugh was brought up, under such harsh discipline that it is surprising that his loving and lovable nature was not withered by it. For his childish delinquencies he was flogged; and, as intended by his father for the Church, if he was inclined to laugh and play with his young companions, his stern teacher would rebuke him. "The stupid and giddy levity of thy comrades is not permissible to thee, whose lot is different to theirs. Little Hugh, little Hugh! I am bringing thee up for Christ. Joking is not for thee." The boy, "dear to God and man," eagerly drank in the sweetness of the heavenly doctrine,* and soon became proficient in sacred knowledge, for he had an excellent memory, and forgot nothing that he had been taught. His gifts of grace and his natural endowments seemed to be balanced equally in him. Even thus early fervently religious, he did not confine himself to studying the meditations of the saints; he soon put into practice the lessons learnt from them and from a higher Authority, and, fulfilling his duty to God and to his neighbour, he began not only to attend diligently at the divine offices, but also to seek every opportunity of doing services to

* *Magna Vita Sancti Hugonis.*

his brethren. In fact, he showed himself in every way worthy of his father, who was a man of singular modesty, courteous and kind in his manners, full of active friendliness, and most acceptable for his benignity. By the time his son was grown up, William of Avalon had become infirm through age; so now, by the Prior's express orders, St. Hugh, who had served the whole brotherhood with a filial devotion, was intrusted with the entire charge of his father. In after life he used to tell how he led him, carried him, dressed and undressed him, washed him, laid him in bed, and prepared his food, and even fed him, winning in return from him a thousand benedictions, which he greedily drank in as if thirsting. Whether the old man had the gratification of seeing his son ordained deacon on reaching his nineteenth year, and of hearing how already he began to distinguish himself by his earnest preaching, is not related; but it scarcely seems likely that he was living when, a few years later, he was appointed to govern the cell of St. Maximus, not far from Villarbenoît. Here St. Hugh, with an aged canon to advise him, was put in charge of the whole parish, and, through his pure life and ardent way of living, soon made himself valued not only by his immediate parishioners, but also by the people of the country round about.

But scarcely a year was over before there came the turning-point in the young man's career. About A.D. 1160, having left St. Maximus, St. Hugh went on a visit with his Prior to La Grande Chartreuse, and there he realised, whatever other people might say of his wonderful virtues, that he had not even reached the beginning of perfection. He noticed the position of the monastery, almost raised above the clouds and touching heaven, and wholly remote from all the feverishness of earthly things; here there would be excellent opportunity of devoting himself to God alone, as well as numerous books to help his devotions and unbroken quiet for prayer. He saw how the inmates mortified the flesh, but with serenity of mind bore cheerful countenances; he observed their freedom of spirit and their purity of speech, and a great longing was kindled in his heart to become one of them. On disclosing his desire to them, some of the brethren encouraged him, but one of the seniors of the Order, looking at his delicate frame, sternly rebuked him. "How canst thou, O little son," he asked, "presume to think of this thing? The men thou seest inhabiting these rocks are harder than all stone, knowing not how to take pity on themselves, or on those dwelling with them. The mere aspect of the place is terrible, the Order exceedingly harsh; the very hair shirt would eat away thy skin and flesh to the bones." As for the Prior of Villarbenoît, great was his sorrow on learning St. Hugh's intentions, and bitterly did he regret that unlucky visit to the Carthusians; to lose him, he declared, would be to suddenly extinguish the light of his eyes, and to take from him the staff of his old age when he most needed it. Working on him with his tears and lamentations, he finally extracted from him an unwilling oath to remain with him for the remainder of his life, which could not be for long. Nevertheless, further reflection led St. Hugh to the conclusion that an oath thus forced from him and against his soul's benefit was not to be kept; so he stole away and was admitted at La Grande Chartreuse during this same year.

Among his new associates, cleric and lay, he

found many holy and reverend men; the Prior, Basileus, was himself, on account of his eminence and virtues, commonly called saint. As for the rule of the house, rigorous as it was, it was tempered with discretion; the subjugation of the flesh was not allowed to be carried on to the destruction of all physical strength, to which the zeal of both the monks and the lay-brethren might lead; for it was the aim of both alike to maintain strict poverty, to throw aside all superfluity, and even to be sparing in necessaries, and to forget all temporal matters in the contemplation of heavenly prospects. The lay-brethren had received such excellent oral instruction that, though they did not know their letters, if the reader in church made any mistake in the lessons, they would at once perceive it and gently cough their disapprobation. With such teachers and companions, it was natural that St. Hugh should make quick progress in learning and holiness, especially as he spent days and nights over his books and his devotions. But he found that even in the stillness of a Carthusian monastery the path to perfection was none too easy. In after time he would relate how, soon after his entrance there, he was beset by the most violent carnal temptations; how day and night, threatening and buffeting him, the angel of Satan departed not from him. What these temptations were we cannot tell; it might have been that his recent escape from Villarbenoît suggested to him the possibility of shaking off the yoke of the cloister altogether. He was scarcely more than five-and-twenty, and it would not have been unnatural if, high-souled and courageous as he was, and with the eagerness of youth for activity, he had wished to venture forth to try the world, full of dangers as it might be to his soul, and to take a man's part in it. Having gained the victory over himself, such desires might well have seemed to him, to whom monasticism must have been, after all, a second nature, deserving of the extremely contrite language in which he described the internal struggle of those and later days just before he was sent to England, when he was again tempted in the flesh.

Like many another deeply religious man, St. Hugh had unbounded love to all living things. As at Villarbenoît, his care to serve his brethren had led to his being intrusted with the charge of his aged father, so now he was appointed to attend to all the personal wants of an old monk, who in return seems to have looked after his spiritual welfare. But his love did not show itself to his fellow-men only; it condescended also to the smaller beings of creation. The saint could find some solace for his combats with the evil one by taming the little birds and squirrels of that wild neighbourhood to come into his cell, where, during his meals, they would eat at his table, feeding out of his dish or from his hand. The stern Prior, however, forbade him even this one amusement, lest he should take too much pleasure in his dumb friends and allow them to interrupt his devotions. It was not till he got to Witham that he could indulge his affection for animals; there for three years a pet bird lived in his cell, taking its flight at nesting-time and returning later on with its fledgings as if to present them to him; but in the fourth year it came back no more, to his great vexation. Again, when Bishop of Lincoln, an unusually fine swan attached itself to him, showing as much affection for him as a dog.

After some time had elapsed, St. Hugh was

at last advanced to the grade of priest, to which he had long looked forward. In his new office he performed the services of the altar with the most exemplary reverence. He used to handle the sacred elements of the Eucharist as if he were touching indeed the visible Body of the Lord, and by his ardently devotional manner in celebrating the mass, it seemed as if he sang the exultant words of the bride in the Canticles, "My beloved is mine, and I am his." Meantime he imposed on himself the harshest self-discipline, subduing his flesh by vigils, fasts, and flagellations, and, according to the wont of the Order, by the use of the hair shirt. His food was water and dry bread, which hard fare for no sickness or weakness or other cause would he give up until he became a bishop, and by that time such severe abstinence had injured his health. In those days St. Peter, Archbishop of Tarentaise, used frequently to visit the Chartreuse, where he would stay, "like a most prudent bee," for some months in a solitary cell amongst the dwellings of those holy men, as if in some honey-stored hive.*
There he was given a most willing attendant in

---

* *Magna Vita S. Hugonis.*

the person of St. Hugh, whom he found to be also a most congenial companion; for the young monk, besides having at his fingers' ends all passages in Holy Scriptures, the lives of the saints and the writings of the doctors, and besides having the quality of being a good listener, was himself a keen and eloquent talker, and thus could readily converse with the worthy prelate.

At length the days of humble service and of quiet devotion came to an end, and St. Hugh must serve the community on a larger scale as their Proctor, which post was assigned to him about A.D. 1070. This dignity, second only to that of the Prior, gave him the management of the entire establishment, the care of all the secular matters, and the government of the lay-brethren. As was to be expected, in all his duties, both spiritual and temporal, he acquitted himself well. But, as has been related, four years later the Proctor of the Grand Chartreuse became the Prior of the first English Chartreuse (or, according to the corrupted form of the word, Charterhouse) at Witham.

Ever since that expedition to the court which had ended so happily for the new monastery, a firm friendship grew up between the king and the saint: indeed, the latter had so frequent intercourse with Henry, and the royal affection for him was so evident, that it was even thought that he was Henry's natural son, especially as they were somewhat alike in person. Without relapsing into flattery or adulation, never fearing to rebuke him where and when necessary, yet modestly and gently, and alluring him to the right paths, now by subtle argument, now by the splendid examples of great men, he had an immense influence over the king. St. Hugh counselled him on the things concerning Christ, the Church, the tranquillity of the kingdom, the peace of the people, and lastly, his own welfare. By his intervention, Henry's anger was often turned into clemency, and churches and religious houses obtained what they needed. He taught him that earthly cares were nothing in comparison to the heavenly, warning him not to trust to the fugitive winds and prosperity of this world, nor to put his hope in riches, but in the living God, the sole help and eternal happiness of those trusting in Him. He not only vehemently took him to task for keeping bishoprics and abbeys vacant, but often also argued with him on his various excesses. The nobler side of Henry's character led him thoroughly to venerate his Prior, and his reverence for him was said to have been increased after a certain passage of the Channel. The weather was stormy, and the king was in danger of shipwreck; in his terror the words broke from his lips, "Oh! if my Hugh of the Chartreuse were watching now and aiding me with his prayers, God would not forget me for long." Then with deeper groans he prayed, "O God, whom the Prior of Witham serves in truth, through his intervention and merits have mercy on us, now justly overtaken, for our sins, by these dangers." Afterwards Henry not unnaturally ascribed his escape to the mediation of St. Hugh.

As for his rule at Witham, no monk ever realised more than St. Hugh the maxim *laborare est orare*. In his zeal for the welfare of his house, in his industry as its head, in his ceaseless devotions, he showed how labour is one of the truest forms of worship. His own life was one continual act of prayer; even when his body slept, he was heard to repeat the word "Amen" at intervals, as if still awake and praying in mind. His religion was none of that dreamy kind which spends itself in holy thoughts and aspirations, yearning for the Beatific vision, but which never results in holy deeds. Ever loving the Word of God, at his times for receiving carnal food he drank in through his ears and consumed all the more eagerly the spiritual food of the Bible, which condiment was never wanting to his meals, however plain might be the rest of his fare. He told the brethren when in the refectory to have their eyes on the table, their hands at their plates, their ears towards the book, their hearts towards God. At every time and in every place, whatever by reason of that time and place was demanded, he did and bade others do. So long as he was well he never allowed himself much sleep, nor if he was wakeful would he lie in bed; but if for any cause he was roused, if drowsiness did not at once overcome him again, he would rise from his bed to pray. He brought the discipline of the house to such perfection, that persons of various conditions and religious professions flocked thither from all parts of the island, to whose confines the sweet savour of the place had gone forth; men of deep learning and great riches, putting aside the vain wisdom and pomp of the world, sought him out in the humility of his holy and sincere conversation, and put themselves under his rule. But St. Hugh was not too eager to admit new inmates; "prudent and circumspect, neither swiftly nor easily did he open to those knocking at the gate," but received them with "cautious sweetness and gentle asperity." The Prior was sufficiently acquainted with human nature to know that too often it was only a passing fit of enthusiasm that led these candidates for the Carthusian frock to him; but, in spite of his care, overcome by their perseverance in seeking entrance after former refusals, he admitted some who afterwards deserted Witham and went back, not wholly after Satan, but to the tabernacles in which they had formerly dwelt.* There were two who especially troubled him, for, after they had become acquainted with the life at Witham, they bitterly accused him of having seduced them to a place of terrible solitude and hardships; but one of these, some time later, repenting his de-

* *Magna Vita S. Hugonis.*

sertion, sought for readmittance, but was refused. The Prior was always inflexible in these cases, whether to lay-brethren or to monks; there were for such unstable men other religious discipline, which could benefit them better than the stern Carthusian Order, and so on this occasion the supplicant, being turned away, went to Clugni.

Having finished the building of the monastery, St. Hugh turned his attention to the edification of the monks, to which end he greatly desired copies of the Holy Scriptures. These, he said, were to be used as pleasures and riches in time of peace, as arrows and arms in warlike preparation, as food in hunger, as medicine in weariness, especially by religious men leading a solitary life. On one occasion, mentioning his lack of books and of parchment for inscribing them to the king, the latter gave him ten marks to purchase the skins—the Prior having modestly said that one would be sufficient for some time—and promised also to give him a Bible. St. Hugh returned home. Henry, not forgetful of his word, looked about where he might lay his hands on the best Bible. It so happened that the monks of St. Swithun's of Winchester had just made a magnificent copy to read at their meal-times. The Prior, being summoned to give it up whether he would or not, was practically obliged to obey, and accept a promised gift instead of it. St. Hugh, on receiving it, was delighted with the beautiful volume; but later on, when entertaining a monk of Winchester at Witham, he came to learn how the king had beguiled St. Swithun's monastery of it, and though his guest protested that he and his brethren were glad that so holy a man should have it, he insisted on returning it, thinking how grieved they really must have been to part with their costly handiwork, and the monk went back to his own house not more rejoiced at his regained possession than at the courtesy and neighbourly love of his late host.

St. Hugh had been eleven years Prior of Witham when, in May A.D. 1186, Henry held a council at Eynsham, near Oxford. Amongst the matters discussed was the nomination of a bishop of Lincoln, which See had been for many years vacant, the large diocese being in consequence in much disorder. The Prior of Witham was suggested to the canons as a fitting pastor for them; they were very rich and enjoyed much worldly renown, and in fact were somewhat carnally-minded, and at first naturally were rather horrified at the notion. His way of life was so different to theirs that some even made fun of him, but their levity being repressed by the wiser men, they at last were unanimous in electing him. On the election being announced to St. Hugh, he refused to admit it, thinking that the king had coerced the canons. The spirit of the man being revealed to them in this answer, the chapter of Lincoln elected him a second time; but he asked what could wise and polished men like them want from him, an uncultured and inexperienced man? Unless an order to the contrary came to him from La Grande Chartreuse, he would still refuse. But upon application to them, his superiors in France bade him accept the See. The three months that elapsed before his consecration he spent in prayers and preparing himself for the coming change in his existence. He looked forward to his promotion as a sailor, seeing the gathering clouds, waits for an expected storm. The monarchs of those times led their bishops no easy lives, and he feared besides lest he should lose his peace and serenity of mind amidst the manifold duties of a prelate, and amidst the strifes which would probably frequently arise, and lest the outward vanities of the office should sully what inward purity he possessed.

When the time came for his journey to London, where he was to receive consecration, he mounted a horse whose trappings were the skins and coarse blankets that he used as a covering by night or day, while the clerks who accompanied him rode horses whose harness was adorned with gold. Nor could his companions induce him to converse with them by the way either on trivial or serious matters, for as yet he feared to break through his old habits, and their secular mindedness clashed with his humility and spiritual mindedness. When he came to London, he was received most graciously by Henry, who, besides rich gifts in gold and silver, supplied him with various necessaries belonging to his new office. A few days later, on September 29th, he was enthroned at Lincoln.

The first hesitation of the canons of Lincoln to elect the Prior of Witham as their bishop was natural; they probably knew St. Hugh to be a holy man; but holiness, though it would ensure a conscientious performance of his duties to his flock, was not sufficient alone to govern an important diocese. Moreover, brought straight from his monastery, and being the personal friend of the king, it scarcely seemed likely, on the one hand, that he would know how to guard against encroachments on the Church, and on the other, that he would care to lose Henry's favour by opposing his wishes in ecclesiastical matters. But the early years of his episcopate must have allayed all anxieties as to his fitness. St. Hugh, in his abstraction from all worldliness, was an ideal monk; as time went on, he proved himself an ideal bishop. It was largely owing to the Carthusian discipline, ignorant as his way of life might have made him of mundane affairs, that St. Hugh was able to stand where other men would have fallen, either by yielding some point against their conscience, or by the visitation of the king's anger at their resistance; but to this Carthusian worldly rank was vanity and kings' favours nothing; his training had perfected his natural courage until he seemed utterly fearless in all battles for the right, whether against the sovereign or against any other evil-doer of whatsoever station. As to the devout man his religion is his country, and as in his estimation there is neither Jew nor Gentile, St. Hugh looked upon the English not as strangers and foreigners, but as fellow-citizens and members of the same household, and thus, like St. Anselm before him, he fought as warmly for the Church in England as if still in his native land; for although temporal grandeur was nothing to him personally, he would not bate an inch in the possessions and liberties of his See, because these were part of a trust committed to him, and the loss of these, as a true Churchman, he must consider to touch the dignity of the Church as a whole. But it must not be thought that he was a rash and reckless fighter; he was possessed of the wisdom of the serpent combined with the guilelessness of the dove, so much needed by ecclesiastics of high rank under the Angevin rule, so that he could speak and deal with kings and their ministers after a fashion which other men could not have done with impunity, because they would be lacking in his tact and insight into human character. Besides, he knew how to fear God and honour the king at the same time; and though he sharply rebuked, and laid hands on the royal person on one occasion, he always succeeded in retaining the affection and winning the admiration of each successive sovereign, so that even King John was solicitous for his friendship. As for his intercourse with men of lower rank, one anecdote will be sufficient to show his justice and charity to all men. A woman came to him to ask him to remit the heriot ox, for her husband had lately died, pleading that it was the only means of maintenance for herself and her children. His steward warned him that if he did so, he would never be able to keep his land after such a precedent. Being on horseback at the time, Bishop Hugh dismounted, and taking up a handful of mud, said, "I hold the land now, and yet remit the ox to the poor woman;" then dropping it, and looking upwards, he added, "For I do not seek to hold the earth below, but the heaven above. This woman had two bread-winners; death hath carried off the better one, and shall we take the other from her? Such greed be far from us." *

* Giraldus Cambrensis, *Vita S. Hugonis.*

But it does not lie within the scope of the present work to write the life of St. Hugh as bishop, especially as it has been graphically set forth elsewhere.* It must suffice to say here, that he was held in such high estimation of all men, that amidst the vast throng of all ranks at his funeral, not the least loud in their sorrow were the Jews, who as a race at that period were in their turn despised and rejected of men, but to whom this one man, a saint indeed, had dared to show his Christ-like love.

To return to our history of Witham. Once or twice a year, generally in the autumn, the Bishop of Lincoln would return for a holiday of a month or so to the Charterhouse. Whenever he drew near to his beloved solitude, his heart expanded and his face was seen to glow with joy, like that of one returning home after a long absence. Once within the walls, he laid aside his episcopal attire and put on the habit of his Order, his bishop's ring being the only sign of rank that he reserved about his person. He always celebrated mass with the sacrist and his own chaplain every day; but besides this,

* Froude, *Short Studies on Great Subjects*.

as if he were a simple monk again, he took his week of service like the other members of the house; and according to their custom, also, he lived in his solitary cell, which was always kept unoccupied, that it might be free for him on his visits. On Sundays he proceeded with the other members to the refectory door, to receive in silence his weekly loaf, though often, with the prior's permission, he would collect with his own hands the hardest crusts and dry fragments to eat instead. He used to take a great pleasure in washing and scouring the dishes and scuttles of all kinds, rubbing and polishing each as if he were handling "the cup of the Lord." *
Following the rule of the monastery, every Saturday he made his weekly confession, and sometimes more frequently; he would often confess, with the greatest contrition, whatever he had done amiss throughout the year.

One visit to Witham was specially marked in the history of the monastery. It was the evening before the Bishop's departure; he had made his final confession and received absolution, and given his benediction and the kiss of peace to the

* *Magna Vita.*

monks, and had retired to the house of the lay-brethren, where were his own clerks and servants. Thence he went to their church to celebrate the usual nightly praise to God. During the service the west windows were lighted up with a sudden glare. The men standing near the doors rushed out to find the kitchen on fire. It was dangerously near the sacred edifice and the wooden cells of the lay-brethren round about it, and the guest-hall was only six or seven feet apart from it, with a very combustible roof of wooden shingles. St. Hugh discontinued the nocturnal office, and gave himself up to prayer before the altar until the fire ceased. The kitchen was only a kind of wicker construction roofed with thatch, and was quickly consumed by the flames, without damage to the surrounding buildings. Future danger of the like kind was guarded against by the building of a new kitchen of stone, which the Bishop had frequently warned the monks to use for it before. On the morrow St. Hugh bade his Witham brethren farewell for the last time, for his life was nearly at its close. In A.D. 1200 he died, honoured by all men.

CHAPTER IV

THE PROSPEROUS YEARS OF THE CHARTERHOUSE

" Far from the madding crowd's ignoble strife,
. . . . . .
. . . . . .
They kept the noiseless tenour of their way."
—T. GRAY.

IT might almost seem as if Witham Charterhouse had accomplished its purpose in the designs of Providence in having served as the instrument for bringing St. Hugh to England, so little do we know of its history after his promotion to the See of Lincoln. A few charters and patents, an entry here and there on the assize rolls, a rare reference in the chronicles of other religious houses, and two or three letters, are almost the only records left of its existence. Its private documents, its register, its library have been long since hopelessly scattered, if not destroyed, during the complete effacement of the monastery that took place more or less speedily on the dissolution. After the firm establishment of the house by St. Hugh, its necessities were not such as to call forward any of its active members from retirement. The priors who came after him were doubtless good and holy men, but in most cases even their names are not recorded. The monks whom they ruled may have been saints, but what traces they left behind them have disappeared, and of "the eleven learned authors of the English Carthusians," whose books "contain much tending to mortification,"* we do not find that one belonged to Witham. But our ignorance of the Carthusians is, besides the loss of written witnesses, due also to the seclusion of their lives; generally, it would only be in the case of some great emergency that they could appear before the public gaze. When the last sad days for monasteries came, when, if ever, Carthusian fortitude and indifference to suffering and worldly comfort should have been displayed, Witham, the mother of the whole Order in England, as the royal patents style it, was found wanting. But the few known details of its history must now be told.

* Thomas Fuller, *History of Abbeys*, p. 269. The names of the eleven are given in Steven's Supplement to Dugdale's *Monasticon*.

St. Hugh's immediate successor in the prioracy was Bovo, who at the Chartreuse had had a prophetic vision of him as a bishop. In the Cottonian Library there is a small volume* containing miscellaneous manuscripts in various hands and of various dates, among which is a fragment bearing on the history of Witham Charterhouse. From this it may be gathered that Bovo was succeeded by Prior Albert. Under the rule of the latter there were admitted to the monastery four "most excellent men," of whom one was a layman, a certain youth named Theodore, and the three others already priests and monks.

Of the last, the best known is Master Adam the Scot, or the Præmonstrant. "He was of middle height, and for the mediocrity of his stature sufficiently stout, with a merry face and a bald head, and greatly reverenced, as well for his grace of manners as for his circumstances and old age." He had been Abbot of the Præmonstrant Abbey of Dryburgh in Scotland, and was a learned man and a theologian of some note, having written many sermons and several

* Vespasian D. ix.

treatises before coming to bury himself in a charterhouse. The unknown author of the above-mentioned fragment knew of his works as contained in two great volumes entitled, *Sermonarii Magistri Adami*, or *The Discourses of Master Adam*. They were, of course, in Latin. The greater part of them were printed by Migne in his *Patrologiæ Cursus*, vol. 198. Their nature may sufficiently be seen by their titles:—

1. The Book of the Blessed Mary, the Mother of God, and of St. John the Baptist; which is doubtless the same as the work mentioned in the Cottonian fragment as "Concerning the Cousinship of Anne, Mother of the Blessed Mary, and Blessed Elizabeth, Mother of St. John the Baptist."

2. Sermons for Sundays, from the 1st Advent to the 2nd after Epiphany.

3. A Book on the Præmonstrant Order, Habit, and Profession.

4. Concerning the Tripartite Tabernacle: a book in three parts, on the Tabernacle of Moses, in the literal sense of the word; on the Tabernacle of Christ; and on the Tabernacle of the Soul, in spiritual senses of the word.

5. Letters to the Canons of the Præmonstrant Church, on the Threefold Kind of Contemplation.

6. Concerning the Threefold Kind of Contemplation:—Part I. It is to be considered that God is incomprehensible. Part II. It is to be considered how terrible God is to the reprobate. Part III. It is to be considered how loving and sweet God is to the elect.

7. Soliloquy on the Instruction of the Soul; which is a dissertation in two books on the religious life.

According to his namesake, St. Hugh's biographer, Master Adam, "from the first flower of his youth had burnt with a happy desire" for the contemplative life; the first attempts after which he had long been making, when "the wings of the dove being secretly given to him," he flew away to this solitude at Witham, "where for about five lustres he rested in a most happy sleep of contemplation." As our unknown author puts it, having become a monk of the Carthusian Order for twenty-four years, "he lived ever holily and humbly under obedience." But he spent some of that time of rest in writing more treatises, which may be those mentioned in the Cottonian manuscript among his works, which are not included in Migne's collection. These are :—

1. On the Canon of the Mass.
2. On the Fourfold Discipline of the Cell.
3. On the Lord's Prayer, dedicated to Archbishop Hubert.
4. The Mirror of Discipline.
5. A book called The Dialogue of Master Adam.
6. A book called My Own Secret.

When Bishop Hugh took his holidays at Witham, Master Adam was naturally one of those monks with whom he most delighted to talk. To borrow the language of the saint's biographer, "like twin silver trumpets, gleaming with the brightness of heavenly eloquence and with the exercise of regular discipline, they ceased not, by the mutual clangour of sublime exhortation," to stir up in each other a keener zeal for the exercises of spiritual warfare. The recluse would set before the Bishop the examples of the perfect men of Holy Writ and the sayings of worthy prelates, accusing the modern pastors of the Church of laziness, divergence from the footsteps of their predecessors, and of general degeneracy.

He even reproached St. Hugh himself, whom, he said, as a great and good ruler of the Church of God, many men admired, though it was a question where he showed the mere *appearance* of being a worthy shepherd in his acts. The modesty of his life and conversation was all very well, but to what use was he putting the talents committed to him? What interest was he winning for his Master along with those rare tradesmen who, suffering dangers by land and sea, not only had planted the Church, but had supplied and fortified her with their own blood? This "exuberant fountain of celestial doctrine" in return would seek and receive admonitions from the Bishop of Lincoln, with whose character he was little acquainted, judging by his addressing such language to this ever-valiant fighter against oppression of all sorts.

The second postulant to the Carthusian habit never really took the vows. This was Walter, Prior of Bath, whose fleeting passion for St. Bruno's discipline is mentioned somewhat sarcastically in some accounts. He had been sub-prior of Hyde Monastery in Hampshire. He was a "man of much knowledge and religion," and "for the good fame of his sanctity," according to the *Annals of Winchester*, was promoted to Bath, where, "after he had trained the monks to a nicety, thinking to himself how frivolous is the glory of the world and how fleeting honour," he betook himself to the Carthusians, preferring rather to "do himself this much good than to rule over others." At Witham a certain monk of Hyde came to see him. Finding him intent upon pots and herbs, who shortly before had been intent upon souls, he was tickled by the incongruity and addressed him in an untranslatable Latin verse in mockery of his occupation—

> "Domine pater;
> Quod facis est Kere, quod tractas Kirewivere."

Prior Walter, however, was soon found an unfit subject by the superiors of the Charterhouse. Perhaps his former companion's laughter worked upon him, for not many days later he came to himself; and as much by the entreaty as by the injunction of the authorities there, he went back to rule the monks of Bath, understanding at last "that it is holier to save several souls than one alone." On his return, he kept himself strictly to his duties, remaining in office till A.D. 1198, when he died in the Benedictine nunnery at Wherwell, in Hampshire, his body being removed thence for burial to Bath.*

The next monk whom Prior Albert received entered Witham Charterhouse to quit it only at the summons of death, after he had been some years under the vows of the Order. This was Robert FitzHenry, who, having been Prior of the Benedictine House of St. Swithun's, Winchester, for three years, gave up his office there, and, in the somewhat scornful words of Richard of Devizes,† "having laid aside his profession in discontent—or may I say devotion?—cast himself down amongst the Carthusian sect at Witham." Unlike Walter, the Prior of Bath, who, owing to a "similar fervour or madness, had preceded him there, but had not stayed, and having once withdrawn, seemed to think of nothing less than returning," FitzHenry remained permanently in the Charterhouse. Advanced in years at the time of his entrance there, he afforded one of the frequent instances of the vitality of the members of the Order. After spending fifteen

* *Annals of Winchester*, vol. ii. p. 68 of the *Annales Monastici* (Rolls edition).
† *De Rebus Gestis Ricardi Primi.*

years in the silence of his cell, living on scanty fare and enduring the continual discomfort of the hair-shirt, St. Hugh's biographer heard him declare that he enjoyed the best health, and that his youthful vigour had in a measure returned to him since he had been deprived of the plentiful delicacies of his former table. This monk, with another of the Winchester community, Ralph the Sacrist, also used his persuasion on Brother Adam to write what he knew of his master; but at the end of the second book of the Life it is recorded that the old man, with his kindly face, serene mind, snow-white head, eloquent tongue, gentle spirit, and sweet disposition, had "migrated from this light to the brightness of eternal felicity, for which he had waited so long with such yearning expectation in weeping, fasting, and watching." It was for Robert FitzHenry that Richard of Devizes wrote his chronicle of the deeds of Richard I. In spite of his sarcastic remarks, in the mocking dedicatory letter, the author shows that he had after all a lurking sympathy with his former prior. He writes thus:—

"The omen being good, after thou didst go

forth from our church at Winchester to the Charterhouse, I desired much and often to follow thee, perchance to remain with thee, but certainly to see what thou wert doing, after what manner thou wert living, and by how much the Carthusian cell is more excellent and nearer heaven than the cloister at Winchester. At length God fulfilled my wish. I came, and would that I had come alone! I was there, one of three, and those who were with me were the cause of my return. They disapproved of my desire, and made my fervour—I will not say my error—grow cold. I saw among you what I have never seen elsewhere, what I should not have believed, what I could not enough admire. In each of your cells, according to rule, there is a door which you may open at will, but by which you may not pass out, except so much that one foot always remain on the inner side of the threshold of the cell. A brother may go out on which foot he will, whilst the other one stays within the cell. A great and profound oath must be taken by which neither ingress nor egress is allowed. I marvelled also at another thing. Abounding in all temporal goods, having nothing, yet possessing all things, being more merciful and more humane than all men, having the fullest charity towards one another, you halve the result of your charity by giving your guests '*benedicite*' without ministering to them. And a third thing made me wonder. You men living apart from the world in secret and singly, you know all the things that are done as they happen, and even have a foreknowledge of them before they come to pass. Nor wouldst thou believe me to have said this in despite of your more than Pythagorean silence, when I dare to presume that men of as much gravity as of an arduous profession foretell, rather than make up, the idle stories of the world. Howbeit, although the Omniscient God is with you, as is supposed, and in you, and you know all things in Him, not by man nor through man, thou, as thou wert wont to say, hast wished that my occupation should become thy solace; inasmuch as that I should chronicle the new transformations, how the world moves, changing square things into round, especially after our transmigration to the celled heaven, so that having its mobility more fully before thy eyes, the world might grow vile to thee, and that the well-known handwriting of one beloved by thee should recall him to thy memory. O happy I! if that saintly soul, if that angel of the Lord, if that deified man, now made one of the number of the gods, in the presence of the great God deign a little to remember me a man! I have done what thou dost ask; do thou what thou hast promised. . . . ."*

The next Prior of Witham was the former proctor, Robert, who wrote urging St. Hugh to take meat in his last illness, and shortly afterwards attained the highest office in the Charterhouse. Brother Adam prefaces the Life of St. Hugh with an address to his "beloved friends in Christ, Prior R. and those who with him are monks at Witham," by whose commands, he says, he wrote the book. Without doubt this meant the same Prior Robert just mentioned. The Carthusians were not a literary Order (which in part accounts for the scarcity of their records), and this is the last time that we find the Witham community in connection with "the making of books."

The latest sign of favour received by the Carthusians from Henry II. was 2000 silver marks

* Richard of Devizes, *Gesta Regis Ricardi Primi.*

left to their house and whole Order in his will. What portion of the sum fell to Witham is not related.* After his death the latter enjoyed no extraordinary share of royal favour.

The next record to be found concerning the Carthusians of Selwood, as they were sometimes called, is the charter of A.D. 1229, where Henry III. confirms the charter of the foundation granted by his grandfather, which, together with every later liberty and concession to them, the monks took care to get confirmed by each succeeding king.† Down to A.D. 1243 they gained no addition to their grounds, as in the perambulation of them taken by royal order in that year their boundaries were discovered to be the same as those allotted by Henry II.‡ Meanwhile, however, the community itself was increasing, as some time during the next eight years the cell on the Mendip Hills must have been built; for in A.D. 1250 Henry III. exempted the lands of "the prior and brethren of the new Chartreuse on Menedep"

---

* *Gervase of Canterbury* (Rolls edition). Henry's will is given on pp. 298-300.

† Rot. Cart., 14 Henry III., pt. i. m. 9.

‡ *Monasticon*, vol. vi. pt. i. App. II., *Inquisitio Prioratus de Witham*.

from regard of forest, to which, as lying within the bounds of Selwood Forest, they would have been otherwise subject.* This liberty secured in part at least the seclusion of the Carthusians of the lesser house, which otherwise would have been constantly interrupted by the visitations of the royal foresters and bailiffs, and must therefore have been highly prized. The monks at headquarters indeed seem to have taken rather extraordinary measures to maintain the strict privacy of their grounds, if we judge by the account given by the witnesses at an inquisition held on "the Sunday next after the feast of St. Ambrose," in A.D. 1273, concerning the rights and lands alienated from the Crown in the hundred of Bruton.† The wood at Witham belonging to them was enclosed by a ditch, a hedge, and a stone wall; but although it was a part of the forest of Selwood, they would not permit any forester to enter it to take either the deer or wood; and as if they were themselves the masters, they disposed of the beasts there at will. Further, when any one happened to be murdered within their

* Patent., 34 Henry III., m. 1.
† Rotuli Hundredorum, 2 Edward I., No. 23.

enclosure, they buried the body without spectators, "to the prejudice of the king's coroners, his royal dignity and crown;" and if thieves were taken with the stolen goods upon them within their territories, the monks, keeping the goods, made the thieves abjure their grounds, again "to the prejudice of the lord king." As for their resistance to the forest officers, it was probably nothing more than their assertion of their privilege granted to them in the charter of Henry II., that they should not be molested within their own bounds either by the ingress or egress of foresters and their servants. But if the last part of the relation was true, and was not dictated, or at least exaggerated, by the animosity that possibly still survived among their neighbours since their first coming into Somersetshire, it is not surprising to find the Witham monks in frequent collision about that time with both secular and religious persons of the district, though in the latter case litigation may have been prompted by jealousy.

At the beginning of the reign of Henry II., a hospital for poor leprous women had been founded at Maiden-Bradley, and placed under the charge of some secular priests, whom, about A.D. 1190,

WITHAM CHARTERHOUSE 85

Hubert, Bishop of Salisbury, supplanted for a Prior and Canons of the Order of St. Augustine. This priory would scarcely be pleased to see a rival in the patronage of the piety of the country so close to them, and when Henry III. licensed the Charterhouse to enclose the wood, or "la Holt," at Witham, in which, as a part of their manor of Gernefeld (Yarnfield), they had a right of common and a certain amount of firing, called "oldwood underfoot," their feelings must have been very bitter, especially as their claims were not apparently in the least considered until they demanded satisfaction. An inquisition on the matter was held in A.D. 1259 at Frome by Henry de Bracton, the justiciary, and Alan of Walton, the coroner; and the prior and leprous sisters of Bradley asked for £8 rent in Milborne, in Somerset, or for some ecclesiastical benefice, such as Tydolfeshide (Tilshead) in Wiltshire, in exchange for their former rights in the wood.* This or some other equivalent was granted to them, but the Canons were unsatisfied, and in the above-mentioned inquisition of A.D. 1273, reference was again made to the affair, the witnesses

* Inquisition given in the *Monasticon*, vol. vi. pt. i. App. II.

declaring that they had often heard that the king lost 14s. a year, which the Prior of Maiden-Bradley and "his men of Gernefield" used to pay him for the fallen wood, by the monks enclosing the Holt. A few years later they came to open hostilities with the Carthusians. In 1279 the Prior of Maiden-Bradley laid claim to forty acres of land, with appurtenances, in Jernefield (Yarnfield), of which he had been unlawfully disseised by William, the late Prior of Witham, and once more tried to win back the lost common of pasture in the Holt.* As the monks, according to the rule of the Order, might not appear in legal proceedings, the king directed William de Gyselham to answer for them. The assize was held at Somerton. It was there shown that the land claimed lay within the limits of the grounds of Witham Charterhouse as allotted by Henry II., and that, following the tenor of the proclamation made at the time in all towns and villages of Somerset, Wiltshire, and Dorset, warning all claimants of lands within those limits to assert their rights before the end of two and a half years, on pain of losing an exchange for them,

* Assiz. Rot., 8 Edward I., m. 5, 14, 1 ; m. 26.

WITHAM CHARTERHOUSE

the Maiden-Bradley priory, having so made its claim, had been satisfied; and that exchange had also been given for common of pasture in the Holt. All this the Prior of Maiden-Bradley acknowledged, and therefore was amerced for his false claim. This seems to have been a sufficient warning for the Canons to cease from troubling the Carthusians in the future.

Meantime, perhaps for the benefit of their dependent house on the Mendips, the Witham monks had acquired some property at Cheddar, which the inhabitants, justly or not, appear to have resented. In A.D. 1260 certain men broke into an enclosure of theirs at Cedderford, damaged the boundary ditch, burnt the hedge, and having killed one of the prior's servants whom they found there, buried him.* Henry III. had also conceded to them a right to the common pasture at Cedderford, which again proved a source of contention between them and the men of Cheddar, until Edward I. directed his justiciaries in A.D. 1279 to inquire what liberties his father had granted there to the prior and brethren in his charter, and then to settle the dispute. But their

* Rot. Patent., 45 Henry III., m. 7.

interests at Cheddar also clashed with those of another religious body, to wit, the Canons of Wormley or Wormsley, in Herefordshire, who held land in the neighbourhood. In the same year Robert, Prior of Wormley, accused John, the Prior of the Charterhouse, of having unlawfully disseised him of a free tenement and eighteen acres of meadow, with the appurtenances, at Cheddar, but the witnesses declared there had been no illegal disseisin, and as Prior Robert did not appear at the assize, he was amerced for his false claim.*

Perhaps with a view to the ending of all these quarrels, the monks, in November A.D. 1293, obtained from the king, as well as a confirmation of their charter of foundation, a patent confirming the letters patent of Henry III. of 12th March, A.D. 1264. These last had been very explicit in their language. The bailiffs and other royal officers are therein directed to prevent trespass on the Prior's grounds at Witham and Cedderford, Henry I. having satisfied all claims to land lying within their boundaries; the monks are granted permission to enclose what they will

* Assiz. Rot., 8 Edward I., m. 5, 14, 1 ; m. 3 and 5.

WITHAM CHARTERHOUSE 89

within their own boundaries, and to possess the enclosures so made in peace; and all claimants against them are to apply to the king, as he is the defender and guardian of the monks, who, according to the exigencies of their Order, may not plead in trials at law.*

Two other grants to the monks belong to the reign of Edward I. In A.D. 1284, Edmund, Earl of Cornwall, gave "to God and the Blessed Mary, and the religious men of the Carthusian Order serving God at Wytham," an enclosure called Monksham, not far from the Charterhouse, from which they were to receive 100s. yearly rent from the tenant thereof, Lord Robert de Aumare, and from his heirs after him. This was confirmed by King Edward the next year.† Eleven years later, A.D. 1295, the "prior and brethren of Wittenham, of the Carthusian Order," received immunity by charter from all aids, tallages, contributions, and customs whatsoever, levied for whatever cause by "us or our heirs."‡

---

* Patent., 22 Edward I., m. 28; dated 24th November. Carta. 22 Edward I., No. 42; dated 23rd November.

† Carta., 14 Edward I., No. 31.

‡ Carta., 24 Edward I., No. 2; dated Berwick-on-Tweed, 25th August.

In fact, Edward I. appears to have regarded the Carthusians with favour, as he especially wrote to the monks of Witham and Hinton to ask for their prayers during his expedition against William Wallace. "We believe it is not hid from you," runs the letter, "how for the tranquillity and peace of our kingdom, we, with the company of the nobles of the said kingdom, have purposed to repress the frowardness and malice of the Scots, our enemies and rebels, who continue in their obstinacy. And because there is no help in man without God, and therefore we must needs support our weakness with succours from the Divine hand, we affectionately require and ask you, having specially commended ourselves, Margaret, our most dear consort, our children, lieges, and faithful people, and all our adherents, and our expedition in the foresaid parts [of Scotland], or in whatever other place, in solemn masses, prayers, and other kind services, to humbly entreat God and the Lord our Protector for us and for them: that through the help of your prayers, His grace may be increased in us and them, and that with His clemency He may guard us, our said consort, children, lieges, and faithful people and adherents, and our kingdom from all adversities." Concerning the number of masses and prayers, the monks were to send an account to the king. This letter was dated from the manor of St. John of Perth, the 10th of July.*

From Edward II. the monastery gained no new estate, but a patent was issued in A.D. 1309 to relieve the monks both of Witham and Hinton from taxation of their spiritual and temporal goods, and in A.D. 1318 the king granted further, that if any Papal levy should be laid on England, though with his consent, yet both the Somerset Charterhouses should be free therefrom.†

Another document of the year 1318, the grant of an annual livery by Prior Walter to one of the servants of the monastery, has a more domestic interest :—

* "Apud Villam Sancti Johannis de Perth." Rot. Claus., 31 Edward I., m. 7, d. ; given in Rymer's *Fœdera*. The letter to the Witham monks is not there given ; but at the end of that directed to Hinton Charterhouse are the words :—"Eodem modo mandatum est, Priori et Conventui Ordinis Prædicti de Selewode."

† Patent., 3 Edward II., m. 22 ; dated Westminster, 7th February. Patent., 12 Edward II., pt. i. m. 30 ; dated Northampton, 20th July. The temporal goods of the "Prior of the Chartreuse of Selewode at Wyteham" had been assessed at £30 by the taxation of Pope Nicholas IV. [*Taxatio Papæ Nicolai*, p. 203.]

"To all the faithful of Christ to whom the present writing shall come, Brother Walter, Prior of Wytham, of the Carthusian Order, and the convent of the same place, eternal salvation in the Lord. You are to know that, with unanimous assent and will, we for ourselves and our successors have conceded to John called the Fisher and Edith his first wife, one annual livery in our House, to be taken so long as he shall live, to wit, every week seven loaves called Prickelings, and seven flasks of beer, of which one half is to be from the beer for the convent, but the rest from that for the guests: item, a daily dish of the convent pottage and a pittance such as every free servant of ours is wont to receive: item, every year two pairs of new low shoes, and one pair of hose, and one old frock out of those which the monks put off when they receive new ones. We have granted also to the said John for his yearly wages, at the two usual terms of the year, as long as he shall live and be able to work, four shillings of lawful money. But all these things the said John shall receive in our *Firmaria*, from us and our successors on this condition, so long as he, while fit and able to work in the craft of fisher or plumber, or in any other honest work whatsoever appointed by the prior or procurator for the time being, or through any other in their place, shall labour to his utmost as a faithful servant loyally and manfully and without any gainsaying or lying. But if the said John shall become useless through too great age or infirmity, he shall by no means receive the said four shillings wages any more from this place, but nevertheless he shall have in full the said livery of bread and beer, pottage and pittance, together with the tunic, shoes, and hose, from us and our successors all his life without any fraud. If, however, the said Edith, the first wife of John, shall survive him, she shall have weekly the seven loaves and flasks of beer and the forementioned pittance from us nevertheless; but the frock, shoes, hose, and wages she shall not have from here, nor ask nor get anything in their stead. And if it should happen (be it far from him) that John should fail in the foresaid or other duties, or be habitually more remiss than he ought, then he may and allowably can be sufficiently chastised, and also fully corrected, by a deduction from his livery and wages.

In witness of all which our seal is set to this present writing drawn up between us and the said John on either side in the fashion of a fine. Dated at Wytham, the Wednesday next after the feast of the Blessed Barnabas the Apostle, A.D. 1318."*

The Carthusians especially needed servants and labourers, at any rate for their outlying estates, since not only their religious exercises and services took up a large portion of their time, but also their rule did not permit them to go beyond the precincts of the monastery. Thus retired as they were from the world, and perhaps therefore more or less removed from infection, even the Witham religious were somewhat nearly touched by the terrible pestilence of the reign of Edward III., for the Black Death of A.D. 1348 made havoc among the Western folk as among the Eastern. We do not find that any of the monks themselves, as in some of the other houses, were carried off, but their household servants and workmen of all kinds almost all

---

* Translated from Madox, *Formulare Anglicanum;* the original is in the Augmentation Office. The *firmaria*, where the livery was to be given out, was the apartment into which the dues to the monastery were paid.

died. In consequence their grounds for the most part rested untilled and uncultivated in other ways, and when harvest-time came the corn that had been sown "perished miserably" for the want of harvesters, to the no little loss and manifest impoverishment of the prior and brethren. The Statute of Labourers, remedial measure as it was intended to be for the employers, rather hindered than helped the Selwood Carthusians; the clause by which labourers had been forbidden to quit the town and parishes where they dwelt in search of work, though it secured workmen to the inhabitants of the more populous districts, was a great impediment in their case, because their monastery, with all their lands and tenements, lay far distant from towns, and in fact practically deprived them of means of making up the deficiency in their hired servants. At last the monks represented their condition to the king, who in A.D. 1354 issued a patent declaring servants and labourers of those parts, having ended the term of work agreed on with their former masters, to be free to serve the Charterhouse, provided that the prior did not hire more than a necessary number; and in A.D. 1362

Edward directed his bailiffs and other ministers to see that the prior and brethren were not hindered in employing men from the counties of Wilts, Somerset, Dorset, and Devon.*

The other grants of this reign for Witham Charterhouse were as follows :—In A.D. 1343, the confirmation of the charter of foundation, and of the later patents and charters, to which a further clause was added, that if there was any liberty conceded by any of these documents of which the monks had not hitherto availed themselves, they were still to enjoy it in the future without any impediment.† A second confirmation in A.D. 1345, together with a declaration to the effect that the royal and other bailiffs and officers of various towns in the neighbourhood frequently vexed the prior and brethren by exacting customs and dues, notwithstanding their exemption therefrom conceded by former kings, that they, the Carthusians of Witham, "and their successors throughout the whole of our kingdom of England, are quit of murage, tallage, picage, pavage, postage, stallage,

---

* Patent., 28 Edward III., pt. i. m. 20; dated at the Tower of London, 16th January. Patent., 36 Edward III., pt. ii. m. 7; dated at Westminster, 20th October.

† Carta., 17 Edward III., No. 23; dated at Westminster, May 5th.

WITHAM CHARTERHOUSE

and every other custom in force before, perpetually," even should they be imposed under new names by the bailiffs and ministers :* in A.D. 1361 a licence to John of Mershton and John Derby to give in mortmain to the prior and brethren of Witham an enclosure at Radene (Rodden near Frome), consisting of twelve acres of meadow ground, and its appurtenances, called Barbouresmoor, to supply the means of providing daily one waxlight "called a Torche" for the altar of the priory church, to be burnt at high mass during the consecration and elevation of the most holy Body and Blood of our Lord : † in A.D. 1362 a licence to the prior and brethren to acquire twenty pounds' worth *per annum* in land and rents from their own or another's fief, the lands and tenements held *in capite* from the crown being excepted, together with a licence to Robert Cheddar of Bristol, John Hacston, John of Mersshton, William of Coumbe, John of Bekynton, and John of Wotton to assign four messuages and 10s. rent, with the appurtenances, in Bristol, which were held of the king, and a certain messuage besides, to the

---

* Carta., 19 Edward III., No. 3; dated Oxford, 26th October.
† Patent., 35 Edward III., pt. ii. m. 7; dated 26th July.

prior and brethren as a part of the said twenty pounds' worth of lands and rents, these tenements being worth five marks, but according to their true value six marks :* in A.D. 1363 a gift of a hogshead of wine to be received yearly at Bristol from the royal butler at the time being, in return for the prayers of the community for the king's family : † in A.D. 1369 a licence to William Canynges of Bristol to give to the convent five messuages and four shops, with their appurtenances, worth £4 *per annum*, but according to the full value 100s., for the maintenance of a chaplain to perform divine services for the welfare of himself, and of Agnes his wife, and of Geoffrey Beauflour, John Canynges, and Thomas Nottingham while living, and of their souls when dead, the services to be said in the church of the Blessed Virgin at Witham, the tenements being in part satisfaction of the twenty pounds' worth of lands and rents granted to the prior :‡ in A.D. 1376 a permission to Robert and William Cheddre of Bristol to give

* Patent., 36 Edward III., pt. i. m. 8 ; dated Westminster, 2nd May.
† Patent., 37 Edward III., pt. ii. m. 19 ; dated Westminster, 2nd November.
‡ Patent., 43 Edward III. pt. ii. m. 38 ; dated Westminster, 13th July.

to the prior and convent in part satisfaction of thirty pounds' worth of land, tenements, and rent which they had been licensed to receive at various times, fourteen messuages, four shops, and six acres of land, with their appurtenances, in the suburbs of Bristol, the value being according to the escheator and mayor of the town, William Canynges, £12, 8s. 4d., the true value being £15 *per annum*, for the maintenance of a secular chaplain to perform divine services in the church at Cheddar and other charitable works;* and in November of the same year a licence to Robert and William Cheddar, Walter Mullewarde, Henry Wynelescombe, John Woderove, William Combe of Bristol, John Bury, parson of Whateley Church, John Stourton, Geoffrey Waldecote, Thomas Asteley, and Thomas Herdeburgh to assign to the prior and convent, in part satisfaction of forty pounds' worth of land, tenements, and rents which they were licensed to receive, four messuages and seven shops, with their appurtenances, in Bristol and the suburbs, which were held of the mayor and city of Bristol for 13s. 4d. *per annum*, which

* Patent., 50 Edward III., pt. ii. m. 22; dated Westminster, 6th October.

according to the true value estimated by the escheator and mayor of the city, Walter Derby, were worth £10, 3s. 4d.*

Soon after his accession, A.D. 1377, Richard II. confirmed the charters and patents to the monastery granted by his predecessors. From his charter it appears that Edward I. had conceded, in A.D. 1282, whatever lead-mines the monks might find on their estates, which they might work and put to profit as they thought best.† Two years later Richard granted permission to Thomas Erlestoke, parson of Fissherton, and John Bury, parson of Whateley, to give to the prior and convent of Witham, as a portion of the forty pounds' worth of land before mentioned, one messuage, one carucate of land, and eight acres of meadow, with their appurtenances, in Chelternevag and Chelterne Dummer (Chilthorne-Domer in Somerset, near Ilchester), which, according to the estimation of the escheator of Somerset, John de Stourton, are worth 40s. *per annum*, the

---

* Patent, 50 Edward III., pt. ii. m. 11; dated Westminster, 12th November.

† Charter Roll, 1 Richard II.; dated Westminster, 12th January. The patent of Edward I. referring to lead-mines is dated at Chester, 28th of August.

true value being four marks.* In A.D. 1387 the king made the monks a yearly allowance of a hogshead of wine, which they were to receive from Bristol, for the use of the lead-miners working in their grounds on the Mendips.†

After Richard's deposition, the Witham Carthusians, for five marks, received from the new king, in A.D. 1400, a confirmation of the previous concessions to them, together with a fresh grant to the effect that neither the monks nor the lay-brethren of their house, nor their servants, should be sued at law or troubled in any way on account of their buying or selling, for the profit of the convent, skins of their own or other people's beasts, tanned or to be tanned in their own tannery, the price being settled between themselves and the skin-merchants.‡ Eight years later their estates were increased by three messuages, sixty acres of land, and eighteen acres of meadow ground, with the appurtenances, in Woky and

---

* Patent., 2 Richard II., m. 39; dated 12th July.
† Patent., 11 Richard II., pt. i. m. 39; quoted in Collinson's *History of Somerset*.
‡ Patent., 2 Henry IV., pt. i. m. 30; dated at Westminster, 1st October.

Yerdele, the gift of John Wykyng and Isabella, formerly the wife of Thomas Tanner of Wells, and by two messuages, with their appurtenances in Maiden-Bradley, the gift of Robert Neel, clerk, and Thomas Bathe. The prior had to pay twelve marks for his licence to receive these tenements.*

A far more important addition was made to the territories of the Charterhouse during the reign of Henry V. The Benedictine Abbey of St. Peter and St. Paul at Préaux, in Normandy, in the time of the first Henry had received certain possessions in England. These were the manor of Toftes in Norfolk, and its church of St. Margaret, and the manor and church of Spectesbury, in Dorsetshire, both given to them by Robert de Bellomont, Earl of Mellent and Leicester, and the manor and church of Warmington, in Warwickshire, presented by Henry Newburgh, Earl of Warwick. At each of these places the monks of Préaux had built priories, those at Spectesbury and Warmington being generally considered as cells to that at Toftes, or Monk's Toft, Toft Monachorum, as it came to be

---

* Patent., 10 Henry IV., pt. i. m. 9 ; dated Westminster, 1st February.

called.* During the continuous war with the French under the three Edwards, the alien priories were seized,† in case they should prove convenient nests to the enemy for hatching conspiracy. Some were afterwards restored, but Richard II. retained many of them in his own hands. Thus at the end of the fourteenth century the above-mentioned manors were in the charge of Ludovic de Clifford,‡ but somewhat later, in A.D. 1404, Henry IV. conferred them, and Aston in Berkshire, also formerly belonging to the same Norman Abbey, on Sir Thomas Erpingham and John Heyles, a priest, with the right to the tenths, oblations, fees, rents, and services, advowsons, liberties, franchises, escheats, and all other privileges and emoluments proceeding thence that the Priory of Toftes had enjoyed. Erpingham and the priest, however, did not enjoy the property for long. A few years after they conveyed their interests in it by indenture to the prior and convent of Witham of the Carthusian Order in Selwood, for the term

* *Monastic. Anglic.*, vol. vi. pt. ii.
† *Henry VIII. and the English Monasteries*, by Dr. Gasquet, vol. i. ch. ii.
‡ L. T. R. Mem. Rolls, Mich. 9 Henry V., Rot. 9.

of the life of Sir Thomas. In A.D. 1413, Henry V. ratified the conveyance by letters patent; and granted further, that after the knight's death the Charterhouse might retain the manors* of Warmington, Spectesbury, and Aston for ever, with the revenues, advowsons of vicarages, chapels, and chantries, all rights in woods, waters, and mills, and every kind of liberty appertaining, such as the Abbots of Préaux and the two secular owners after them had enjoyed, the whole being worth per annum £64, 7s. 9¼d. The same patent licensed the monks of Préaux to cede their rights for ever to the Carthusians,† though this must have been a mere form, for, partly owing to the attacks in Parliament on Church property during his father's reign, Henry V. suppressed the alien priories altogether the very next year (A.D. 1405). In return for this patent, the prior of Witham was to have paid fifty marks, and for the confirmation of the other charters and patents of his house, 100 shillings; but while Sir Thomas Erpingham lived he exacted such a heavy charge

* The revenues of Monk's Toft were granted by Edward IV. to King's College, Cambridge (vide *Monasticon Anglic.*).
† Patent., 1 Henry V., pt. iii. m. 20; pt. v. m. 36; dated Westminster, 15th July.

from the monks that they found themselves impoverished by their bargain with him. Henry VI., however, had pity on them, and remitted the fifty marks and other arrearages owing to him, out of his special grace towards "the first house and mother of the whole Order in England;" in A.D. 1441 he himself confirmed their possession of these manors.* A less important benefit fell to the lot of the Charterhouse during the time of the three Lancastrian kings, in the form of six quarters of salt, which the prior received annually from the manor of Caneford in Dorsetshire.† But among all the various grants and gifts that the kings or private individuals bestowed on the community since the foundation, to us in these days the most curious token of esteem was shown to them in a legacy. Foreign spices, judging by the frequency with which certain quantities of some of them were given and taken instead of money payments, were more appreciated by our ancestors than by us, in pro-

---

* Patent., 7 Henry VI., pt. i. m. 12; dated Westminster, 4th December. Patent., 19 Henry VI., pt. i. m. 14; dated at the Palace of Westminster, 28th November.

† Escæt., 14 Henry VI., post-mortem, John, Duke of Bedford; vide Collinson's *History of Somerset*.

portion to the greater difficulty of obtaining such luxuries. The Carthusians were, doubtless, as glad to season their very plain fare as their contemporaries, and would find quite acceptable the bequest of Richard Ryborg of Salisbury in A.D. 1360, consisting of five marks to the prior and convent of Witham Charterhouse, and to each monk there, a pound of ginger, and to each brother (that is, lay-brother) half a pound of ginger.*

Meanwhile the whole Carthusian Order had been affected as well as their fellow-Christians by the Great Schism; even among them there were two rival Papal parties, each recognising a separate prior as visitor-general of their Order. But in A.D. 1409 the unity of the Church was restored by the Council of Pisa, Gregory XII. and Benedict XIII. being both deposed, and Alexander V. being elected. Following the example of the Fathers of the Council, the Carthusians, meeting together in A.D. 1411 to acknowledge the new Pope, put out of office both the vicars-general, and unanimously chose the Prior of the Chartreuse

---

* Hoare, *History of Modern Wiltshire*, vol. vi. (*Old and New Sarum*), p. 96.

of Paris instead.* After this the chapter turned their attention to the government of the Houses, for not unnaturally, during the late unsettled times, discipline had often grown lax, and the original strict simplicity of the rule had been infringed. To this end some of the old constitutions with fresh details were re-enacted, and new regulations made, as well as new arrangements in the religious services and ritual. It would be out of place here to quote the whole code, to which each year brought a fresh addition as time went on, but those constitutions formulated between A.D. 1411–24, though they apply to the Carthusian monasteries generally, refer in some particulars to the English houses especially, these having now increased to eight, including Witham, and are interesting as showing the life of the Order; therefore an account is subjoined of some of these.†

Sometimes, it appears, weary of their confined monastic life, the inmates would break away and

* *Histoire des Ordres Monastiques*, vol. vii. chap. lii.
† Cotton. MS. Calig. A. II. Constitutiones generalium capitulorum Ordinis Cartusiæ ab anno 1411, in quo facta est Unitas Ecclesiæ et Ordinis, h. e., quando Alexander Papa V. in verum et summum Pontificem erat susceptus, ad annum 1504.

wander out into the world, to "the peril of their own souls" and "to the scandal of very many," and few of their superiors were sufficiently zealous to see to their capture. But now all the priors and procurators of the Order were enjoined to seize any such fugitive whom they should come across, and send him back under safe custody to the house from which he had gone forth, and at the expense of the latter, or to some other house where he might be imprisoned until the next general chapter, provided it were not above three days' journey distant from the house of his former profession, in which case the chapter would decide who should pay the expenses. In England, it was observed that certain persons of the Order did not fear to disturb the silence and solitude of their cells by entertaining others there; hence the old rule was repeated, that no one was to eat or drink with another in his cell, whether that other were an inmate or a stranger, the case of the prior and proctor being excepted. Offenders against this statute were to observe an abstinence for a certain time, during which they were to eat but once, and then on the floor of the refectory, without their wine and customary pittance, so often as they should transgress; the prior failing to enforce the rule was also to fast and to be put out of office for a week. The English manner of singing also did not please the mother-house at La Grande Chartreuse, who enjoined on her children here to follow her ways, especially in the art of making pauses in the middle of a verse, and to use her tunes, so that they should not make too much noise. In A.D. 1415 a concession was made to the English houses; henceforth their visitor, or other prior deputed by them for the purpose, need only attend the general chapter every leap year; in other years they were to send letters from their province to the nearest priors on the other side of the sea, namely, to those at Bruges or Antwerp, who should despatch their business for them, they paying a fair share of the expenses. The growing civilisation of Europe and the gradual development of the various branches of art which was leading the way to the Renaissance at the end of the century, was not without effect upon the followers of St. Bruno, for the fathers of the Order had occasion to observe that in many of the Charterhouses about the altars there were strange pictures, and other kinds of painting also were "multiplied, against the holy simplicity and humility" of the Order, in the glass windows and other places, representing shields and arms of secular persons and figures of women, "at which notable men were not a little shocked;" hence they ordained that all such pictures and quaint paintings should be removed where they could cause no grave scandal, and that new ones should not be set up, admonishing at the same time the visitors of the different provinces to look to the matter, and the priors not to fail in punishing the disobedient.

To enforce these regulations, and to insure uniformity with the other houses of the Order in the performance of divine services, the General Chapter in A.D. 1424 ordered a special visitation of the English Province, where there was, moreover, to be counteracted something graver than differences in ritual—a tendency towards relaxation of Carthusian discipline.* A sign of the latter was the custom, then in vogue in the Charterhouses in England, for the servants to wear party-coloured clothing, and in that attire to accompany the priors when they went out. This must have

* *The London Charterhouse:* Dom Lawrence Hendriks.

been particularly distasteful to the good fathers, considering how much it was against the spirit of the Order, whose members, Giraldus Cambrensis in the *Speculum Ecclesiæ* relates, used to refuse to change their customary dress for travelling even in times of danger, unlike other monks, who would put on the habits of laymen. The Prior of Antwerp, who was Visitor of the Province of Further Picardy, and his assistant, the Prior of Chapelle in the diocese of Cambray, were charged to conduct this visitation in England. The Provincial and his assistant generally made their inspection every two years; their duty was to inquire into the spiritual and temporal state of the monasteries in their care; to see whether the priors performed their office conscientiously, and did their best to promote the welfare of the communities under them; and to look to the conduct and morals of the monks, assigning due punishments where needed. The fathers and brothers of the convent were to answer truthfully all questions put to them, and in conscience were bound to report whatever was wrong in the discipline or administration of the affairs of their houses, or in the life of any member. The visitors, after the examination of the inmates, wrote their report, in which the statutes of the Order bade them avoid exaggerated praise or blame, and keep to the naked truth, which was to be expressed in the simplest words. The report written, they repaired to the chapter-house, and read it before all the monks, except the novices, making such additional remarks as they saw fit; after which they took their departure.

Whether the Witham monks were the worst transgressors or the most faithful upholders of the ancient Carthusian traditions is not discoverable; but it is not unlikely that they spent some of their increasing wealth in the introduction of over-much adornment of their holy places; for we hear of a beautiful old rood-screen in the church cruelly torn down by a modern priest of the parish. That the community were growing rich is scarcely to be doubted, as they were evidently maintaining a more extensive scale of hospitality than formerly, since Bishop Beckington, a few years later than this visitation, caused them to build a dormitory, which, not being needed by the religious themselves, must have been used for their guests.*

* *Itinerarium Will. Worcester.*

FIFTEENTH CENTURY FONT IN WITHAM FRIARY.

WITHAM CHARTER.

During the time of the same Bishop of Bath and Wells we have another glimpse of the lay-house in connection with the world by the Carthusians. In former days the laity, prompted by a greater fervour and devotion towards the Priory of Witham, took the habit and profession of lay-brothers, and dedicated themselves to the labour of tending the lands of the Charterhouse and other necessary and helpful work on its behalf. But in the later ages such persons no longer thus associated themselves with the interests of the monks, and therefore, for a long past, the convent had been obliged to employ hired people of both sexes, who, for convent needs, had to dwell even within those bounds that would have separated them from the world. It was for those so employed on the grounds that the prior in February A.D. 1458 procured Beckington to allow wish to erect a baptistery, not in the chapel of the Friary dedicated to the Blessed Virgin (that is, the church of the lay-brothers, "Friary" in the case of Witham, meaning merely "company" or "brotherhood"), and to form a cemetery in a certain part of the glebe. After making

During the time of the same Bishop of Bath and Wells we have another glimpse of the Charterhouse in connection with the world beyond their precincts. In former days the laity, prompted by a greater fervour and a warmer devotion towards the Priory of Witham, putting on the habit and profession of religion, were wont to dedicate themselves to God by ploughing and tending the lands of the Charterhouse, and doing other necessary and helpful rural labours in its behalf. But in the later degenerate times secular persons no longer thus associated themselves with the interests of the monks; therefore, for long past, the convent had been obliged to employ instead people of both sexes, who, for convenience-sake, had to dwell even within the bounds that should have separated them from the world. It was for those so employed on the grounds that the prior in February A.D. 1458 petitioned Beckington to allow him to erect a baptismal font in the chapel of the Friary dedicated to the Blessed Virgin (that is, the church of the lay-brothers, "Friary," in the case of Witham, meaning merely "frèrie" or "brotherhood"), and to form a cemetery out of a certain part of the glebe. After making preliminary inquiries as to the truth of the representations made to him, the Bishop granted the requisite licence for the font on May the 20th next year, and commissioned William, Bishop of Sidon, the prior of Mottisfont in Hampshire, in his stead "to dedicate, consecrate, and bless the ground to be used for the burial of the devout bodies of the secular persons." *

In collecting these scattered details of the history of Witham Charterhouse, we have now reached the epoch of the Wars of the Roses; but that long struggle did not touch the fortunes of the Priory. Henry VI. exempted it in the Act of Resumption passed in A.D. 1455, which was not to be in any wise "prejudiciall to any Graunt or Graunts, Confirmation or Confirmations, made by us by our letters Patentes to the Priour and Covent of Wytham in Selwode, in the Counte of Somersete, of the order of Charterhouse, ne to theire successours of the Manours of Warmyngton in the Counte of Warrewyk, Spectebury in the Counte of Dorset, and Aston in the Counte of Berk, with their appurtenances;

---

* Thomas Beckington's *Register*, in Harl. MSS., No. 6966, f. 90.

nor to any Graunte or Grauntes, Confirmation or Confirmations, made by us by our Letters Patentez to the Priour and Covent of the house of the place of God of Henton, in the said Counte Somers, of the said Order." Having in A.D. 1461 paid 20s. on one occasion, and one mark on another, to Edward IV. for his confirmation of the patents and charters of his predecessor, because these were considered insufficient, Henry VI. being king *de facto sed non de jure*,* the Charterhouse neither gained nor lost anything by him. After the accession of the Yorkist House until the breach with Rome under Henry VIII., the want of materials necessitates a blank in the history of the monastery.

But before proceeding further, it may be well to subjoin here a list of the priors of Witham, collected from various sources. The dates prefixed are rarely those of their election, but denote the years when they certainly held the office.

* Rot. Patent., 1 Edward IV., pt. iv. m. 6 ; dated Westminster, 20th July. Rot. Patent, 1 Edward IV., pt. vi. m. 32 ; dated Westminster, 3rd December.

THE PRIORS OF WITHAM.

A.D.
- 1173? The first Prior.
- 1174? The second Prior.
- 1175–76. St. Hugh arrived at Witham.
- 1186. Bovo succeeded St. Hugh.
- 1191. Dom Albert.
- 1200. Dom Robert.
- 1279. Dom William, Prior some time previous to that date; succeeded by Dom John.
- 1318. Dom Walter.
- 1387. Dom John de Evercriche.
- 1402. Dom Nicholas de la Felde.*
- 1458. Dom John Pester (or Porter).†
- 1500–1. Dom Richard Peers elected, and held office thirty years.
- 1532. Dom John Huse.
- 1534. Dom Henry Man.
- 1536. Dom John Mychell, the last Prior, who surrendered the House in A.D. 1539.

The following list of prominent monks of Witham is taken from two volumes of manuscript notes on the history of the Order in the British Museum.

* The last two named priors are given in Collinson's *History of Somerset*.

† According to Collinson, "Pester;" Dugdale gives the name "Peslir," as in Cole MS., vol. xxvii. f. 87^b. The name is printed "Porter" in the *Somerset Archæological Society's Proceedings* for 1878.

MONKS OF WITHAM.

A.D.

1180. B. Eynard, made his profession at the Grande Chartreuse, afterwards monk at Witham under St. Hugh, and died in the said year, being the 126th of his age and the 105th of his profession.

1185. Dom Radulphus, who had been Sacrist at Winchester, became a monk of Witham under St. Hugh.

1186. B. Bovo, a professed monk of La Grande Chartreuse, distinguished by the gift of prophecy, became 4th Prior of Witham, and died about A.D. 1200.

1200. St. Hugh, Bishop of Lincoln, and 3rd Prior, died.

1340. 17th November, Dom Adam, S.T.D., a professed monk of Witham.

1468. Dom Daniel Long and Dom Robert Mayle, both priests and professed monks of Witham, died.

1474. Dom Hugh Bostalben [or Bostauen], a priest who had also made his profession at Witham, died.

1475. Dom William Browne, Prior of Beauvale Charterhouse, died. Having been formerly Prior of St. Anne's Charterhouse, near Coventry, he had made his profession first at Beauvale, and secondly at Witham.

1482. Dom Stephen de Dodesan, a monk professed first at Witham, then of the Charterhouse of Jesus of Bethlehem, near Sheen, died.

„ Dom Thomas of London, died.

„ Dom John Welde, died.

1484. Dom Nicholas Buke, a professed monk of the Charterhouse of the Blessed Virgin Mary of Witham, died.*

---

* Additional MSS., No. 17,092, ff. 23, 368, and Additional MSS., No. 17,085, f. 124. Brother Adam, the author of St. Hugh's biography, and Girard, Count of Nivernais, have been omitted from

In explanation of the above, it may be well to remark here, that when a monk was allowed to change his monastery for any reason, the second Charterhouse might require him to make a second profession (that is, might require him to take the vows of the Order a second time); but this was not always the case. Here, too, we will remind our readers that the English word *Charterhouse* is merely a corruption of the French word *Chartreuse*. Every house of the Order was called a Chartreuse, after the parent convent near Grenoble. The Order, however, took its name from the Latin form for Chartreuse, *Cartusia*, sometimes spelt Chartusia in the English royal patents.

the list, though these MSS. include them, because it is doubtful whether they belonged to Witham (*vide* Mr. Dimock's Preface to the *Magna Vita*).

CHAPTER V

DECLINING FORTUNES

"Men's hearts failing them for fear, and for looking after those things which are coming on the earth."—S. LUKE xxi. 26.

IN A.D. 1531 the first actual step was taken towards the separation from Rome, for it was then that the clergy ceded to Henry VIII. the ambiguous title of Supreme Head of the Church so far as the law of Christ allowed. When it is considered that this concession was wrung from them as part of the price of their pardon for a breach of the Statute of Præmunire, with which the king most unjustly accused them on account of their submission to Wolsey's legatine authority—an authority never called in question by himself until it no longer suited him to acknowledge it—and when it is remembered that the doings of Luther and the German Reformers were well known in England, and that their opinions were gaining ground here amongst all classes, it is not surprising if the dismay and alarm that Catholics must generally have felt caused a spirit of restlessness and a sense of coming change even among the English Carthusians. At any rate, two or three Charterhouses were at that time much troubled by unruly monks; moreover, the one year's novitiate allowed in those days would often be too short a period for the postulant to rid himself of the influences that had affected him while still in the world, or for him to know whether he had thoroughly discarded all the thoughts and feelings of a secular man; and thus it was scarcely avoidable that the irrevocable vows should have been now and then rashly taken. This is the explanation that suggests itself of a few letters written at this date to the prior of the London Charterhouse, one by the Prior of Witham, and the others concerning Dom Alnett Hales, a future monk of Witham. These letters are in volume viii. of the *Calendar of State Papers*, amongst the correspondence of A.D. 1535, but are marked as of doubtful date; but as Henry Man, the English General of the Order of that date, was not likely to trouble himself about the discipline of monks or "the slander of the

Religion" (*i.e.*, of the Carthusian Order), and as Prior Richard Peers of Witham did not hold office later than A.D. 1532, and for other reasons needless to discuss here, they must belong to earlier years, probably A.D. 1531, when Dom John Jonbourne, Prior of Sheen, was the Provincial Visitor.* The letter from Witham, given farther on in full, concerns Dom (or, as that title was formerly written, *Dan*) William Bakster, a professed monk of the Charterhouse, Smithfield, who for some unrecorded transgression had been sent to his brethren in Somersetshire, but who had to obtain the permission before he could return home, not only of his own prior in London, but also of the head of the English province, Prior Jonbourne.

"*The Prior of Witham to the Prior of the Charterhouse, London.*

"Ryght reverend fader in our Lord, I recummende me unto you with vere glad desire to here of your good helth; owre geste Danne William Bakster desyreth you to have an answer of his letter late sent unto you; he is vere busy in

* Dom Laurence Hendriks: *The London Charterhouse.*

desyring to cum home to you agayne. God knawyth if he wold stabyll him selff he myghte lyve with us in grete reste and quietnes, and I am sure non of our cloyster gyveth hym contrary cause; he hath wrytyn a nother letter to the Fader of Shene to have his wylle fulfylled. I pray God it be not *ad ruinam ejus*, but to hys profyt of wurship of our relygion. He wold have no spekyng of his transgressions, but it is not in my power to stop menys mouthes. Our Saviour Jhesu stabyll him in goodnes and preserve you and youres from all adversyteis. Amen.

"Writyn at Witham in hast the xxth day of July. Fader, we have sent you brevys* for our brother Dan William Burton, Jhesu have his sowle. We beseche you they may be convayed shortly.

"*Per fiilium vestrum Ricardum priorem ibidem Christi inutilem.*"

[Addressed]:—*Venerabili in Christo patri domino priori domus Cartusiensis prope Londoñ dentur.*†

---

* The Office of the Dead, recited alone in the cell on the reception of the *Obiit* of a member of the Order. [Hendriks, as above.]
† *State Papers of Henry VIII.*, vol. viii. No. 611 (8).

Alnett Hales or Halys was a Carthusian of London, who, being sick in mind and body, had been sent to the Charterhouse of Mountgrace in Yorkshire; his prior wished to exchange for him Thomas Barker, a professed monk of the latter monastery, who had committed the great offence of breaking his vows and wandering out of bounds without permission; but for some reason or other he wished that Barker should be dispensed from punishment, and wrote to the Visitor-General about the matter. The correspondence on the two monks affords an excellent illustration of the way in which the Carthusians maintained discipline, and at the same time a picture of Carthusian life. As for sending Barker to London, Prior Jonbourne replied, "in this holy feste called Alhalowentyde," that he could not promise it, as he did not know to what expense Mountgrace Charterhouse had been put in maintaining Hales. But as for dispensing Barker's punishment, "God forbid, father," he wrote, "that I should discharge an apostate. The monk has been out of the house of his profession four weeks at the least, hurting therein in special his soul, to the displeasure of God and to the slander of the Religion, how much

I know not well. He was taken at Oxford for a spy or a man out of due order, and presented to a commissary there and examined; a batchelor of divinity, a brother of one of the Mountgrace community, being present at the examination, recognised him, and he was committed to a strong prison until I sent for him. I wrote to you to take him to discharge your expenses for your brother at Mountgrace. Let me know whether you will punish him after the form of the Order. If he order himself religiously with you, in process of time he may be more favourably dealt with. If you will not receive him, I propose to set him in our prison until his father prior send for him." *

Somewhat later, Jonbourne made a visitation of Witham and some of the other Charterhouses, amongst others to that of the Isle of Axholme, where he found "Dane Alnot Halys" arrived from Mountgrace three or four days before him. Although the sick monk had been sent without his commands, he permitted him to remain, and wrote to the prior in London to provide him with

* Abbreviated from *State Papers of Henry VIII.*, vol. viii. No. 611 (7).

necessaries, for he remarked, "Your said brother will not be content without his necessaries; I understand his pilch was destroyed in carrying from Mountgrace to Axholme; what else he wants I know not."*

Robert, the prior of Axholme Charterhouse, also wrote himself:—"Dan Hales has been with us since the Assumption of our Lady. The Prior of Mountgrace, without authority or licence, sent him hither for your pleasure. I was content to receive him, for we have a brother at Mountgrace by order of the General Chapter, but we had no commands for an exchange. Our brother is a strong man, and readeth and singeth right well, and at his departing had all necessaries for his body and bed. Your brother is a weak man, not able to bear the burden of our religion, neither in fasting, reading, or singing. He wanteth many things necessary, as in raiment and bedding. His pilch [cloak] is worth no money. I have delivered unto him a pair of blankets, and all other things unto him, as I do to our brother: he continually crieth of me to send him home to you,

* Abbreviated from *State Papers of Henry VIII.*, vol. viii. No. 611 (6).

and greatly we be unquieted by him, for he thinketh he is laughed at. We are few in number, and some of us are weak, and to sing at all we need a strong man to help us. Good father, we pray you take your brother home, or provide another place for him. We shall be content to receive Dan Thomas Barker, who is with you, if we must have any one."* But this proposal concerning Barker was not accepted, for having been sent to London, he stayed there until A.D. 1534; and Hales for a time remained at Axholme, until at last he was so "marvellously mended" that his brethren there would have been content to keep him with them "but for his mind and desire," which were for another change. Upon his "fatherhead" being petitioned on the subject, Dom Jonbourne consented to his being sent to the Charterhouse of St. Anne's, near Coventry, "for the salvation of his soul and the solace of his body," and wrote to the prior in London to agree to the plan, "Father, for the love of God, take ye good heed to this matter, for as it seemeth there is jeopardy therein."†

---

* Abbreviated from *State Papers of Henry VIII.*, vol. viii. No. 611 (1). † *Ibid.*, No. 611 (5).

Hales did eventually go to Coventry, and still later to Witham; upon the dissolution of the latter Priory he received the grant of a pension as a monk of the house, which seems to imply that he was no longer reckoned to belong to the London community.

It must have been soon after the disposal of these two monks that Prior Richard Peers ceased to govern Witham Charterhouse; he had held office for thirty years, and as in those days young men were not set at the head of the Carthusian monasteries, he must have been of advanced age. He lived in his own Priory a little longer, and evidently was one of those from whom the oath to the Act of Succession was demanded, for a few months after that incident, in A.D. 1534, he wrote the following letter in defence of the liberties of Beauvale Charterhouse in Nottinghamshire :—

Letter from Prior Richard Peers of Witham.

"To alle cristen peple to whome this present writing shall come, I, Dan Richard Perys, monke of the Charterhouse of Wyttham, and late prior of the same by the space of xxx yeres and con-visitor sumtyme of th'Order of the Charterhouse within this Realme, sende greting, and I lete you witte that by all my tyme, and as ferre as I knowe or ever herde synes the furste tyme of the graunte made unto our house by our founder, king Henry the secunde and his noble successor king Henry the thredde: By vertue of the said graunte we have use and thies liberties following: Furste we have used to have within all our boundes sanctuary to almaner of persons for murder and felonie and to tarie at their pleasur, and in caas at any tyme the said felons have ben taken out of our boundes by violence, they have ben afterwarde restored unto us again, and the parties that soo violently have taken them hath made satisfaction for their soo doing. Also we have view of frankplege, wayf, and stray, bloodwyte, all the kynge der that come within our boundes we have hunted and kylled, and lycensed gentlemen our neybours being our frends and lovers to hunte and kylle at our libertie. Also noo sherif, noo baillif or cunstable, but oonly our owne baillif doo at any intermedle or execute any maner of thing within our said boundes. Nor yet fforesters, lieutenants, verders, nor any of their officers doth at any tyme fetche outt the kinge dere or hunte within any of our boundes, but onely by our licence. Thies with many moo expressed in our said graunte we have used hitherto by vertue of the saide graunte. This I do wryte because I am credibly informed that the Charterhouse of Bevall, who hath like liberties as we have, be nowe interrupted and letted to use their said liberties. And because the shriefe officers ther be not afferde to take strayes and execute other their offices within their said boundes. Wherfor I beseche you all to whom thes presents shall come to thynke that I do not thus wryte for any maner of affection for our house or any other house, but only for the declaring of the trouth. Beseching you therfore to take credence to premisses, and from hensforth to suffre the said house of Bevall, forsomuch they have like liberties in all thinge as we have, peasably without interuption to use their liberties as we do ours, and to take credence unto the premisses; for they be true, as ferre as I knowe, as wol answer afor God at the dredefull day of jugement, and for more credence to be given herunto, I the said Dan Richard Perys have subscribed the writing with myn own hand the xxvii[th] day of October, in the xxvi[th] yere of the reigne of our soverain Lord king Henry VIIIth.

> "*Per manum dom. Ricardi Peers nuper prioris ibidem per annos xxx.*"*

Prior Richard could scarcely have seen more than the beginning of the misfortunes of the English monks of all Orders. Death must have spared him from realising the truth—

> "That a sorrow's crown of sorrow is remembering happier things,"

for his name is not amongst the members of the Charterhouse at the Dissolution, and there is no further record of him at all after the above date. But the letter of his successor, Prior John Huse, written in A.D. 1532 to Secretary Cromwell, shows no sign of coming troubles.

Prior John Huse to Cromwell.

"Ryght worshypful Syr, acordyng to my dewty, I humbly recomend me vn to your good master-

* *State Papers of Henry VIII.*, No. 1269, vol. vii.

shyppe, beseechyng Almighty God to reward
you everlastyngly in hevyn for the grett charyte
you have shewed and doyth to me your pouer
bedman, et my pouer brethern yor continuall
bedmen, in solicityng my mater vn to the Kynges
Grace, whom I understand by my proctor ys
thorough your favorable information ryght good
and gracious vn to me and my pouer House in
recevying us his pouer bedmen vn to his gracious
protection, in lyke maner as hys noble progenitors
hath don befor hys tyme, grantynge allso vn to us
that he will defend the ryght of our foundacyon
agenst all men, so that we shall not sew nor be
sewed of no person or persons, but to gyve us
to continuall prayar for the prosperous estat of
hys grace and all hys noble progeny. Wherfor I besech your mastershype that you will
optayn the Kyng's commyssyon of defence for
our tuycion under hys grett seale. Ande that yt
wyll plese you to accept Mr. Hyde, the berer
herof, to gyve attendance on you for that whyche
shall pay all the costs and charges therof. Ande
in the meane whyle I beseche you that I may
have the Kyngs letters patent for my lord of
Glastonbury that he doo not enquiet us any mor

herafter, but to repare vn to the Kyngs Grace, our gracious protector and founder. Thus I recommend you to our Lord Jhesu, Who have you in His keeping. From Wytham, the viith day of Aprell, by your pouer bedman, John Huse, prior there.

[Addressed]:—*To his speciall and singler good master, Mr. Cromwell, be these delyvered.**

John Huse was not to preside over the declining fortunes of his house; his prioracy did not continue much longer. A monk of the same name signed the Oath of Supremacy when it was last tendered to the inmates of the Charterhouse in Smithfield on 18th May 1837. Judging by the somewhat obsequious language of the above letter, it seems possible that he was the former Prior of Witham whom William Trafford, the unworthy successor of the martyred John Houghton, may have persuaded to follow him to the London monastery in order to help swell the number of "the perjured," as those yielding to

* *State Papers of Henry VIII.*, vol. v. No. 920. Richard Whiting, thereafter murdered rather than martyred during the Suppression, was the Abbot of Glastonbury.

the king must inevitably be regarded by the upholders of the Papal supremacy.

It is to be supposed that the letter written by Huse had the desired result, as nothing further is to be found on the matter. Whether the paper concerning "the prior and friars of Wytham," mentioned in a catalogue of documents belonging to Cromwell or in his custody, is on this or another subject does not appear. In the same year, A.D. 1533, among Cromwell's "remembrances" there is a reference to the warrant for the restitution of temporalities to be signed for "the Friars" of Witham.*

Somewhere about January, A.D. 1533, the desire of Anne Boleyn's heart was partly fulfilled in her secret marriage with the king; for a portion, at least, of the following Lent, although no sentence of divorce had as yet been pronounced against her rival, she openly assumed the title of queen, and on Easter Eve, April 12th, she went to mass in royal state. Pious people, in the world or out of it, were not unnaturally much troubled in mind by their

---

* *Calendar of State Papers*, vol. vi. No. 299, ix. G., and No. 299, II.

sovereign's barefaced desertion of his lawful wife and scandalous intercourse with the Lady Anne, and among them the Carthusians—who, according to Cardinal Pole,* bore, with the Brigittines and Observants, the greatest name for holiness at that period—were unlikely to be the least distressed by the passing events.

Indeed, Father Hord, the Prior of Hinton Charterhouse, carried on the debate even in his sleep as to whether he could consistently acknowledge Henry's new queen; being sorely perplexed, he not unnaturally dreamed about the matter, after which he was so discomforted that he went to Witham to unburden his mind to his brother prior. It is a sign of the times in which he lived that one of the Witham monks should have ventured out of the monastery to detail his story to Lord Stourton, and that the latter thought it worth while to repeat it to Cromwell, though, fortunately perhaps for both the priors, that period in Henry's life had not yet quite come when the slightest hesitation of the humblest subject to approve of all his proceedings could be construed into an act of high

* Quoted by Lingard in his *History of England*, vol. v.

treason, so that no consequences attended the following letter:—

Edward Lord Stourton to Cromwell.

"Ryght honorable and veray singuler good master, In my most hartie maner I recommaunde me unto your goode mastershipe with lowly thanks for your manyfolde goodnes to me and my frendes shewide. And wher ther was delyvered unto me by a frende of myne the vii day of this present monyth of M[ay?] one of the monkes of the Charterhous of Wytham in the countye of Somersete, named Dan Peter Watt, who hath deposed before me and others credible persons that the prior of the Charterhous Henton within the countie aforsaide came in tyme past to the Prior of Wytham aforesayd in the Lent tyme and said that he had the nyght before a marvelous vision, and declared the same in the maner and forme following. That he saw a stage ryall [where] upon stowde (as he thought) all the nobles of the realme; they by one consent drew up into the sayd stage the queenes grace that now is (as he thought) by a lyne. Wheronto he put his honde with ayde to the same, and so sodaynlie cam ayen unto his remembraunce and sore repented his foly that he had so moch doen in prejudice to the law of God and holy Chirch. And forder saide (stryeking himself upon the breste with his fyste), "God defend that ever I shold ever consent to so unjuste and unlawfull a dede." Farther the sayd Dan Peter saith that he hath mor other secrets toching the welth and preservation of our soverayne the lorde the kyng and queenys noble grace. Which thynge he wyll not (as yete) shew unto me, but reserveth hyt untill such tyme as he may cum by your meanes to the speche of the kyng or queenys noble grace. The Witham monke I do now send up to you with thes my servante the berer of this letter accordyng to the reasonable request of his appellation and as I am bounde to doe as knoweth Jhesu Who preserve you in honour with long lyffe. Writen at Bonam the xix daye of the monyth above writen. By your owne assured with hart and mynd accordinglie. Also I pray yow wyll continue your favourable goodnes unto my frende your bedman the prior of Shirburne and all thinge concernyng the same shalbe at your commaundement.

[*Signed*] EDWARD STOURTON."

[Addressed]:—*To the ryghte honorable and veray goode master Cromwell of the Kynges honorable councell this be delivered.**

A few days after the writing of the above letter, the sentence of divorce having been passed at the Archiepiscopal Court at Dunstable, Anne was crowned, and the unhappy Katherine was left to break her heart alone, in spite of the Pope's decision somewhat later in her favour. In the following November, the Act of Annates, the completion of the Act of A.D. 1532, transferring those payments from the Pope to the English crown, brought about the final breach with Rome. Meantime Anne had given birth to the Princess Elizabeth, whose position as heir to the throne was secured by the passing of the Act of Succession in March A.D. 1534. During the following summer the ecclesiastics and religious had to take the oath in approval of that Act, which was made especially obnoxious to many of them, because in their case the addi-

* *State Papers of Henry VIII.*, vol. vi. No. 510.

tional acknowledgment was required that the Bishop of Rome had by right no more authority in England than any other foreign bishop. Lord Stourton administered the oath to the inmates of Witham Charterhouse, but did not find all of them compliant "to the kyngs high commaundement." "The prior himself," he relates on June 13th in a letter to Cromwell, "is gone in pylegremage and this xiiime days hath byn from home, and vii of his monk[s] wull not take no othe untyll they se the sayde prioure swear fyrste; and when the sayde prioure comythe home I wull go to them ageyne acordinglie; but if he and they or ony of them make refusall that to do, I pray you to send me your mynde howe I shall order my selff with them and how they shall be ordered."* As there appears to have been no further correspondence on the matter, probably Stourton's second visit to the monastery was more successful.

Scarcely more than a year after their subscription to the Oath of Succession, the seclusion of the monks of Witham was again interrupted by visitors on a royal errand. The Act of Annates,

* *State Papers of Henry VIII.*, vol. vii. No. 834.

granting to the king the first-fruits of all benefices, and the tenth part of each year's income from the spiritual and temporal possessions of ecclesiastics, as has been related above, was passed in the autumn of A.D. 1534. To make sure that his new revenues should amount to the correct sum, Henry appointed commissioners to survey all church property in England and Wales. After swearing to perform their work faithfully, the commissioners received minute instructions as to how they were to proceed. In the case of the religious houses they were to find out the names of the chief governors, and of every "spiritual person" that had any distinct dignity, office, cure, or chantry, and the names of all offices of any kind belonging to the houses, and of all sorts of "spiritual promotions" in their gift, together with the clear yearly values of each of the latter; and where alms and fees for masses had been wont to be paid, they were even to discover not only "the names of the persons and places whereunto and to whom such annual and perpetual rents and pensions had been yearly paid," but also the names of the persons for whose souls such alms had been given.* It was to these searching inquiries that the Selwood Carthusians had to submit some time early in A.D. 1535. The total yearly value of all their possessions was found to be £215, 15s., about £2589 according to the present rate of currency. The details are given in the following pages.†

ARCHDEACONRY OF WELLS
DEANERY OF FROME

THE PRIORY, OR CHARTREUSE HOUSE, OF WITHAM.

Declaration of the extent and yearly value as well of all possessions, Temporal as Spiritual, belonging to the said Priory, and assessed in the presence of the Commissioners of the Lord King in the time of Henry Man, the Prior there.

BERK'
ASTON

	£	s.	d.
Value of rents after the deduction of xiijs. ivd. annual fee to Thomas Sadler the bailiff there	ix	xvij	x

WARWIK
WARMYNGTON

	£	s.	d.
Value of rents besides xxvjs. viijd. yearly fee to Thomas Draper the bailiff, and ivs. annual rent to be paid to the King for his manor of Kyngton	xxv	x	ij

---

* Introduction to the *Valor Ecclesiasticus*, by Rev. Jos. Hunter.
† *Valor Ecclesiasticus*, vol. i. pp. 157-158.

DORS'
SPETISBURY

	£	s.	d.
Value in rents after xxvjs. viiid. deducted for the yearly fee of William Fry the bailiff there	xxxv	—	x

WILTES'
FONTEL GYFFORD

Value in all rents there after the 2s. annual rent to the King and 2s. annual rent to the Prior of Maidon Bradeley	—	lvj	—

SOMERS'
MERSTON

Value of all the rents per annum	iiij	xv	iiij

CLYNCK

Value of the rents of all the tenements there per annum	—	xxvj	viij

BRADDELEY

Value of the rents of all the tenements there per annum	—	xj	iiij

BRISTOL

Value of the rents of all tenants and tenements *per annum* after deducting xvs. yearly rent to the Abbot of St. Augustine's there for one tenement in the high neighbourhood, lxjs. rent to the chamberlain there for divers tenements on the bridge, ijs. yearly to the custodian of Retclyffe church, xvd. rent yearly to the Prior of St. John's, London, for a tenement in Temple Street there, besides £x yearly to the custodian of the church of Cheddar for a certain chantry called Cheddar's Chantry, vjs. viii. to the prior of the Kalendars there, vijs. viijd. to the chaplain of the chapel of the B.V. Mary and lxs. fee to David Harrys, bailiff there .

£ xj   s. xj   d. vij

BERK'
NUEBURYE

Value in rents besides ivs. viijd. yearly rent to the Abbot of Redynge, and iijs. iiijd. fee to Henry Burges, bailiff there. — xliiij vij

SOMERS'
WOKES AND YEARDESLEY

Value of the rents of all tenements yearly . — xlij vj

CHILTERNEFAGG

Value of the rents of all the tenements yearly . — xxxvj viij

MORELOND

Value of the rents of all the tenements there yearly besides iijs. iiijd. fee to Thomas Sutton, the bailiff there . . . . — xlviij vj

WITTAM AND HIDON

Rents of the demesne land there remaining in the hands of the prior and indicated by four lawful men . .

£ lx   s. —   d. —

Payments from the land there with cxvs. ijd. from the sale of wood . . . . vj — xxij

} lxvj — xxij

Billerica

	£	s.	d.
Farm rents of the demesne land *per annum*	xiij	vj	viij

Westbarne

Farm rents of the demesne land *per annum*	xv	vj	viij

Quarre

Value in farm rents *per annum* of the demesne land	x	xiij	iiij

Moncksham

Value in farm rents *per annum* of the demesne land	iiij	xiij	iiij

The Priory also received from certain enclosures the following rents :—

	s.	d.			
Este Poundehayes	viij	—			
West Poundehay	x	—			
Hollemeade	x	—	vij	viij	—
Newhichyns	liij	iiij			
Hickesparke	xxvj	viij			
Drowfe	xl	—			

The Spiritual Profits follow—

Wittam Frarye

	£	s.	d.
Value of the greater and lesser tenths of the rectory with the oblations	—	lxiij	ij

Aston

	£	s.	d.
Value of certain other annual pensions received from the church there	—	liij	liij

Warmynton

	£	s.	d.
Value of certain other yearly pensions received from the church there	—	xiij	iiij

Spetisbury

	£	s.	d.
Value of certain other yearly pensions received from the church there	—	xxx	—

Nueburye

	£	s.	d.
Value of certain other pensions received yearly from the church there	—	xxiij	iiij

Wilbye

	£	s.	d.
Value of certain other pensions yearly received from the church there	—	vj	viij

Total for the five above: £ ix s. ix d. x

Total value of the spiritual and temporal possessions above mentioned . . ccxxvij — xx

But from the above sum there were certain payments to be deducted, as follow :—

	£	s.	d.
In yearly payment to Nicholas FitzJames, steward of all the above-mentioned possessions	iiij	—	—

WITHAM CHARTERHOUSE

	£	s.	d.		£	s.	d.
In yearly payment to Robert Bugett, bailiff of Witham and Marston . . .	—	xl	—	} xj	vj	viij
In money paid to Helie Byrche, chaplain of Witham Frary, every year . .	—	cvj	viij			
Sum of the allowances . .	—	—	—			
And thus there now remains clear after all deductions made . . .	ccxv	xv	—			
The tenth thereof .	xxj	xj	vj			

The process of valuation could hardly have been agreeable to the inhabitants of any of the religious houses, for besides receiving directions to examine the registers, books of accompt, and Easter books of each monastery, the commissioners were bidden to search any other writings which might be thought necessary by them, and to use their discretion in finding out other ways and means of coming at the truth. Judging by the set of officials a few months later, the discretion of royal agents led them to very dubious ways for finding out truth, and to show very little consideration for those whose peace they had come to disturb. To the Carthusians of Selwood, who from their earliest days had hitherto been exempt from inspection by ministerial persons of whatsoever authority, except the Generals of their

K

own Order, it must have been exceedingly annoying to have their private documents ransacked and to be questioned upon oath concerning the details of their property. But if the Witham monks were inclined to murmur, the commissioners probably found a willing coadjutor in their Prior, Henry Man, who was soon to prove "the assuryd beydesman and servant" of Cromwell, as he signs himself, in more than the merely formal meaning of those words.

Witham Charterhouse had but two priors who became bishops; between the one, Hugh of Avalon, who during his priorate, the third from the beginning, helped to establish the foundation of the monastery on a firm basis, and Henry Man, who after his priorate, the third before the suppression, as Visitor-General of the English houses, helped to make easy the fall of the Order; between St. Hugh, who, rightly sometimes called the patriarch of the English Carthusians, died Bishop of the important See of Lincoln, and Henry Man, who, a traitor to his Order in the eyes of a faithful few, died Bishop of the insignificant See of Man, there is a great contrast. Both were young men when they adopted the

Carthusian habit; the stern discipline and silent prayerful life strengthened the one in holiness and stability of character, but had no effect on the other, unless it made him, being probably a man of excitable temperament, more restless by confinement, and inclined to spend the hours of devotion in his cell in vain speculations and faithless seekings after signs of heavenly wrath or favour. Hugh, even amidst his high estate, remained a true monk, careless of worldly considerations, and, to the last, fearless of worldly disgrace or punishment or death, resisted all manner of oppression, and never truckled to kings or their ministers; Man, truly converted to Henry's views or not, received advantage from the proceedings of that tyrant, and after beguiling his brethren to follow his submissive conduct, and, subsequently to the suppression, accepted promotions under the new *régime*, in the first years of which the noblest of his Order and of the faith in which he had been brought up had been martyred or judicially murdered.

Henry Man, a native of Lancashire, having, after a course of education at Oxford, become a

Carthusian at the time when the king's desire was first drawn to the goods of the monasteries, was the Proctor* of the Charterhouse at Sheen. Judging by his letters, he was at this period of his life devout enough, but, like many other men whose fervour is largely emotional, he was too prone to believe in visions and dreams as divine warnings; hence it was only natural, when wiser and better men than he were half inclined to consider her hysterical fits and hallucinations, with the attendant denunciations of coming woe on Henry VIII., of importance, that he should give credence to the "Holy Maid of Kent," especially as he probably then disapproved of the divorce and of the king's supreme headship of the Church, which was shortly to be acknowledged. Indeed, he was so carried away by his admiration of Elizabeth Barton as to write of her to her confessor, Father Bocking, in somewhat extravagant language. "Let us," he said, "magnify the name of the Lord, who has raised up this holy virgin, a mother indeed to me and a daughter to thee, for our salvation. She has raised a fire in

* *Proctor* is the contracted English form of the word *procurator*, the Latin name of the steward of a charterhouse.

some hearts like the working of the Holy Spirit in the primitive Church." "God has been pleased," he wrote later, "to give me some knowledge of His secret and wonderful works which He does daily in His specially elect virgin named Elizabeth Barton, your spiritual daughter. This knowledge doth more fervently 'accend' my heart in the love of God than anything that I ever heard spoken, or anything that ever I have read in Holy Scripture." "Put my good mother Elizabeth," he asked, "in whom is my trust above all mortal creatures, in remembrance to offer me up in sacrifice to the most glorious Trinity, and to beg the grace for me to mortify myself, so that I may live only for Christ." He had personal interviews with her, and talked enthusiastically * of her virtues with Sir Thomas More. The latter, after the Nun's confession at Paul's Cross, sent to warn the Proctor of Sheen that she had proved herself a hypocrite, but "the good man" had so high an opinion of her that he would scarcely believe it. The execution of Elizabeth and her deceived supporters † must

* *Cal. State Papers, Henry VIII.*, vol. vi. Nos. 835, 1149 ii.
† *Ibid.*, vol. vii. No. 287.

have been a rude shock to Man; but it also must have alarmed him as to whether he might not have to endure some punishment for having listened to her. Henceforth he was the humble servant of Henry and Cromwell. The administering of the Oath of Succession to the Carthusians of Sheen in May A.D. 1534 was attended with no difficulties, for the Prior and Proctor showed themselves "faithful subjects, honest men, and obedient to the laws," not only giving their own subordinates a good example, but also exhorting the Friars Observant at Richmond to subscribe also.* Shortly afterwards Henry Man was rewarded, no doubt at Cromwell's instigation, with the higher post of Prior of Witham Charterhouse. There, as has been related, he received the commissioners for the ecclesiastical survey. A few months later, however, he was back at Sheen as Prior there, and about the same time was commissioned by the royal Vicar-General to be Visitor of the English Carthusians, instead of John Houghton, the head of the London Charterhouse, one of the earliest martyrs for the Papal supremacy. Mention will be made

* *Cal. State Papers, Henry VIII.*, vol. vii. No. 622.

WITHAM CHARTERHOUSE

of Prior Man again, but his later fortunes as regards the history of Witham are of no further interest.

Meanwhile the king had come to recognise that English monasticism, on the whole, could not bring its conscience to bow to his supremacy in the Church, and therefore, although it might refrain from rebellious acts, it would be well to do away with it, especially as its property would afford new funds for his constantly decreasing treasury. Hence he and Cromwell planned that show of righteousness, the Visitation of the religious houses, which, in the light of recent historical researches, was too apparently only a framework on which to fabricate the grossest scandals that could be invented against reputed religious men. The appointed Visitor for the south-western counties was Dr. Layton, who, as one of the clerks of the Council, had examined Sir Thomas More and Bishop Fisher in the Tower. In August A.D. 1535 he was inspecting the monasteries on the borders of Somersetshire and Wiltshire, and towards the end of the month was at Witham. On the 24th he wrote to Cromwell, "Witham the Charterhouse has professid and done all thyngs accordyng as I shall declare you at large to-morrowe." *

That short report, with its absence of charges true or false, against the monks, may mean that their lives and characters were so wholly unimpeachable that Layton's "swift reed," as he calls his evil pen, could find nothing to relate about them. On the other hand, it shows a timid submission in them to the king's proceedings, natural enough considering what had been the fate of their brethren in London. Henceforth the Prior and brethren, according to the royal injunctions always imposed by the Visitors, were to observe and teach the king's supremacy, and to do their best "to fulfil the statutes of this realm, made or to be made, for the extirpation and taking away of the usurped and pretended jurisdiction of the Bishop of Rome within this realm;" they were to instruct "all committed to their care that the king's power is, by the laws of God, most excellent of all other under God in earth, and that we ought to obey him afore all other powers by God's prescript." All statutes binding them to obey the Bishop of Rome or any other foreign

* *State Papers of Henry VIII.*, vol. ix. Nos. 42 and 168.

potentate must thereafter be abolished from their books or muniments. No one, either Prior, Proctor, or brother of the monastery, was in future to leave the precincts, a rule which it was found impossible to keep if the house was to continue to exist at all, for, as Ap Rice, one of the Visitors, pointed out to Cromwell, recluses as the Carthusians were, they recognised the necessity of having a system by which the Prior, intrusting the supervision of the monks to a Vicar, could himself go out on the business of the convent. To ensure less communication with outsiders, entrance must be through "the great fore-gate alone," and this was to be kept by a specially appointed porter, and to be opened only at certain hours. Also, every day all members of the convent, under the pain of punishment, must attend a lesson of Holy Scripture for an hour—an injunction advisable enough, but very objectionable to many, as Cromwell appointed supporters of the New Learning to give these lessons. Other directions concerned the management of the monastic property and a stricter observance of the rule of the house, which was to be kept so far as it agreed with Holy Scripture and the

Word of God. The Prior must expound to his brethren that "true religion is not contained in apparel, manner of going, shaven heads, and such other marks, nor in silence, fasting, uprising in the night, singing, and such other kind of ceremonies, but in cleanness of mind, pureness of living, Christ's faith not feigned, and brotherly charity, and true honouring of God in spirit and verity;" and "that they assure not themselves of any reward or commodity any ways by reason of such ceremonies and observances, except they refer all such to Christ, and for His sake observe them." They must not show relics and "feigned miracles" for lucre to pilgrims, who were to be exhorted to give their offerings to the poor instead. Further, every brother who was in orders must daily pray in his mass for the king and "his most noble and lawful wife Queen Anne."* Besides these injunctions, some of which were excellent enough if only the whole scheme of the Visitation had not been a cloak for an unjust robbery, it was left to the discretion of the Visitors to add more—that

---

* The injunctions are printed in the *Collection of Records* appended to Burnet's *History*, pt. i. bk. ii. No. 2.

is, they were allowed a free tether to tyrannise, according to their dispositions, over the unhappy religious, who, to escape from their exactions, not infrequently paid heavy bribes to them and Cromwell. The community of Witham later on wrote letters complaining of extra expenditure, which probably was in part incurred in this way. Fear of what may be is as hard to endure to some natures as actual suffering; this must be the excuse for the monks for what some would call weakness on their part in thus staving off evil which might end they knew not where.

CHAPTER VI

THE DESTRUCTION OF THE MONASTERY

> "Then might ye see
> Cowls, hoods, and habits with their wearers tost
> And fluttered into rags."—*Paradise Lost*, Book III.

WITHAM Priory, having an income of over £200 a year, was still allowed to drag on an unhappy existence for another three years after the Visitation. During that time it witnessed the dissolution of the lesser monasteries on the ground alleged by Henry (in spite of the fact that the correspondence of his agents produced no graver accusations of immorality against them than against the greater houses), that they were dens of vice, whereas in the others "religion was right well kept;" and the disastrous attempt of the Pilgrimage of Grace to restore the old order of things, resulting in the dissolution by attainder of those houses that had shown however slight sympathy in word or deed with the rebels.

But the Charterhouse was not left to itself any more. In March A.D. 1536, Dr. Petre, afterwards Sir William, one of the commissioners for monastic affairs, must have been transacting some business concerning it, for amongst Cromwell's fees for that month there is noted—"Dr. Peter for the fees of Witham and Seen (Sheen), 10 March, 20*l.*"*

Care was taken also that the Carthusians should understand "the Word of God" after the royal ideas of right interpretation. Although not a preaching Order, the commission to Henry Man for the Visitation of their religion, commanded the brethren to preach it within their monasteries. Man himself did not think this sufficient for the dissemination of the opinions which he had embraced, and suggested that "Prioures of our Order (to whome it is lawfull and sometyme necessarie to goo and Ryde abrode) shall preache not onlye within the howses whear they dwell, but allso in other churches whear they come wheare as they thynke convenient."† Doubtless Cromwell gladly conceded this, even

---

* *Cal. State Papers of Henry VIII.*, vol. xi. Appendix No. 16.
† *State Papers of Henry VIII.*, vol. xi. No. 244.

though it would, contrary to the injunctions quoted in the last chapter, afford frequent opportunity for absence from home on the part of the heads of the various houses.

In this year, A.D. 1536, the last Prior of Witham, John Mychell, began his short-lived rule, receiving also a commission to act as Visitor to the Order with Man. Either because he thought it best to temporise, or because he was of the opinion that the Pope's supremacy was not one of the vital points of the Christian faith, he must have been a sufficient upholder of the royal head of the Church to be chosen by Cromwell for this post; but considering that he held a place of trust among the little band of Carthusians reunited for a short time under Queen Mary, it must be concluded that he held with the Romanists on the question in his heart of hearts. But whatever were his real convictions, in August A.D. 1537 he with Man had the delicate task of reconciling to the royal supremacy the uneasy consciences of Maurice Chauncy and John Fox, two of the London Carthusians. The success of the Visitors was not great, for they reported the two brethren to Copinger, the confessor of

Sion, as not obstinate, but still "scrupolose." In fact, Chauncy and Fox were sent on to Copinger, in the hopes that he might remove their doubts; for as they went by the authority of a book that they each had, and were prepared to argue the points in it, they were likely to take up too much of the time of Man and Michell, who had "myche busynes with certen other" also.*

These matters were occupying the Prior of Witham while Cromwell was making applications to his brethren at home for one of their farms called Westbarne. The poverty of their house was growing, and in spite of the submissive tone of their letters to Layton on the subject, they were unwilling to let him have it, as they must not expect to receive rent from him. The correspondence shows that in the end they were obliged to grant it to him so far as they could without the consent of Michell, who without doubt did not withhold it, his office having been given to him probably to make things work smoothly between Cromwell and the Charterhouse.

* Cotton. MS. Cleopatra, E. iv. f. 247.

Letter from Witham Charterhouse to Dr. Layton.

"Well-belovyd Mr. Doctor with dew recommendatyons and thanks for all kyndnes shewyde un to us youre pore beydemen (undeseruyd on our parte) we recommend us un to yow certyfyeing yow that we have receyvyd yowre letters and as myche as we maye do not offendyng god and our rule, we have done. In our father's absens also, for the forther accomplessyng of the same, we have sent the letters of my lorde privye seyle and yowre letters also un to owre father prior for to have hys advysse and assent therto; and as shorteley as we kan here Redy Worde from owre father prior, we do trust sone after yow shall have a answer from us to my lorde privy sele, that shall content hys lorshype and yow also. Now good Mr. doctor yff we dyrst be soo bolde with yow as to opyn owre necessyte and poverte off owre pore place un to yow and fynde yow frendely un to us in that cause (as we truste that you wylbe) and as conscyens wyll (we do thynke) bynde yow, we pray yow to sumwhatt ponder owre grete payments that we have payede and must paye for the Whyche we have solde plate off owre Churche, stoke off catell a grete parte, sale off wodde to the most that kan, and also borowyd and browghte owr howse in dette for the same, and off very trewthe we kan nott tell by whatt menys we shalbe abyll to pay the nexte grett payment att Chryssemas un to owr nobyll prince, excepte favowre of Relaxacyon therof or sum helpe be by lettying of this ferme fallen in owre hands wherefore we lamentabely beseche yow with the gretest Instance that we kan, that with the ye off pete and compassyon yow wyll so ponder owre poverte (that owre pore place be nott forsett for defowte off the nexte payment) and that for god's love and charyte un to us, yow wyll be a frendely solycytor to my lorde pryve seyle in thys cause for us. As we may dayly pray for yow un to the blessed Trynyte who ever preserve yow.

"Wrytten the xxiiij daye off September from the Charterhowse off Wyttham.

"YOWRE PORE BEYDEMEN
THE CONVENT THERE."

[Add.]:—*To the Ryght Worshypefull Mr. Doctor Layton thys letter be delyverd with spede.*

[Endorsed]:—*From Witham to doctor Leighton.**

---

* *State Papers of Henry VIII.*, vol. xii. pt. ii. No. 744.

Letter from Witham Charterhouse to Cromwell.

JHESUS.

"Ryghght honorable and owre syngler good lorde, after lowly commendacions wyth humble subication according to owre dutye, your lordeshyppe shall understand that we be rygght sory to here by Mr. Doctor Leatons letters that your lordshippe shulde esteme us not to be fully wyllyng that yo shulde have a leese of owre ferme called the West barne, accordyng to your desyre in your loving letters. And therfore now to expelle all suche inquientys owt of your lordshyppys mynde, we the covent with all owre harts grawnte you owr good wyllis; besekyng your lordshyppe to ponder owre greate charges off payment to the kynges grace now att cristmas, and that in case owre father prior can not make provision for the same, so sone as he is bownden, your lordshyppe wylle graunte hym ferther days, and accepte owr good wyllis at thys tyme, for we can not religiously send owt owre covent seale before hys comyng home, nor without hys consent, as knowyth the blessyd Trinite who ever have your good lordshyppe in hys mercyfull tuicion. Amen.

From the Charterhowse Wytham the xith day off October.

"BY YOUR DAYLY BEDEMENE
THE CONVENTE THERE."

[Add.]:—*To the Ryght honorable and our syngler good lorde my lorde prive seale be thys delyvered with spede.*

[Endorsed]:—*Oct. xj°. The Couent of Wytham.**

From the same to Dr. Layton.

"Ryght worshypfull mr. doctor, we lowly recommend us unto you, wyth owre dayly preyer, thankyng you for your charytable counsell. We have made my lord privey seale an answer accordyng to the same trustyng your mastershyppe wylbe a solyciter to hym for us, and speciall for forther respyte to pay the kyng as we desyred you in your former letters, and in so doyng ye shall bynd us to do you that plesure we can and to be your dayly bedesmen to our mercyfull Lorde Jhesu long to preserve you to Hys plesure.

"From Wytham the xith day off October.

"BY YOUR DAYLY BEDEMEN
THE COVENT THERE." †

[Add.]:—*To the Ryght worshypfull Mr. doctor Laton dd.*
[Endorsed]:—*The Couent of Witham to mr. Docter Leyton.*

---

* *State Papers of Henry VIII.*, vol. xii. pt. ii. No. 882.
† *Ibid*, No. 883.

Letter from Richard Layton to Cromwell.

"Hit may please your lordshipe to be advertissede that forasmuche as at my laste beyng with yowe then deliveryng your lordeshipe letters from the covent of Wittham for a ferme of thers, wiche ther letters (as I myght conjecture by my letters they also sent from them unto me) purportede not so full a graunte unto your lordshipe as I wolde they shulde. I therfore immediately after my departure from them unto Harrowe sent my servant unto them with newe letters persuasious, willynge them to make unto youre lordshipe a full and a fast promes forasmuche as in them was, wiche thyng I suppos they have done as I may conjecture by ther letters, wiche here inclosede I sende unto you, and in casse a brabullyng felowe one basyng make any sute unto your Lordshipe for any former graunte the folyshe prior shulde at any tyme make hym, with that you have nothyng to do; the hole covent now hathe made yowe a graunte; the priors graunte without the covent is nothyng, yours his sure. Shake ye off therfore lightly such besye gentilmen medelyng in [?] mañes matters, what your matters, what your lordshipe shall commande me further in this or any other your affairs, I am and ever shalbe redy at your commandement. Thus I pray Jhesu preserve your lordshipe long in honoure with incresse from Harow xvij° octobris by your lordshippes most assured to commaunde

"RICHARDE LAYTON, *preste.*"

[Add.]:—*To the right honourable and my veray good Lorde my Lorde Cromwell Lorde privy seale.*

[Endorsed]:—*Oct. xvij°. Doctor Layton.*[*]

A few months earlier than the date of these letters the London Charterhouse, in yielding itself to the king, had afforded the first example of the nominally voluntary surrenders of the monasteries. In fact, the work of the general dissolution had already begun; for although, in the following March, Cromwell declared that Henry "does not devise for the suppression of any religious house that standeth except they shall desire it themselves with one consent, or else misuse themselves contrary to their allegiance, in

[*] *State Papers of Henry VIII.*, vol. xii. pt. ii. No. 934.

which case they will deserve the loss of their lives as well as of their possessions," the process of gathering all monastic property into the king's hands, either by confiscation or by overawing the religious to surrender it, continued without an interval until A.D. 1539. Those words of Cromwell, indeed, were but a ruse sanctioned by royal authority to prevent the alienation of any of it, which would incur loss to Henry. It was foreseen, either by the Vicar-General or his master, that the monasteries would anticipate their fate; for in few cases could the statements made on the part of the king deceive. The least danger was that the abbots and priors, caring less for property which would soon pass away from the communities which they governed, would cease to be such "good husbandmen," and so lessen its value. Sometimes, too, the monks, hoping to save for themselves some portion from the universal ruin, conveyed their lands cheaply to some "lover" of their Order, with the understanding that in the event of no dissolution or of reunion with Rome they should have their estates again; here and there perhaps they sold (and at any rate were accused of having done so) some of their chattels, for money could be hidden away from the piercing scrutiny of the royal agents; or they secreted some of the church plate, either for selling afterwards or for use again on the restoration of the old course of things. Thus it was that commands were issued to the religious forbidding them to dispose of their possessions in any way upon rumours of a suppression—a command in itself little likely to allay their fears, since in the natural order they were permitted without such interference to dispose of their property as they concluded best for their house. In the case of Witham Priory, Walter Lord Hungerford was appointed steward, doubtless to look after the management of the estates to the king's advantage, for his nomination to that post by Cromwell just then could hardly have been to any other end. The Proctor of the Charterhouse, Tristram Hyckemans (to adopt one out of the several ways of spelling his name) was also the Vicar-General's nominee; but he did not supervise the affairs of the monastery to Prior Mychell's approval, though what his proceedings were is not recorded; the two chiefs quarrelled, and called in the new steward to settle their dispute. On the 10th of

September A.D. 1538, Lord Hungerford wrote to Cromwell upon this amongst other matters thus:—

"Whereas you were pleased to prefer me to the stewardship of the Charterhouse, Wytham, Soms., I have of late been desired thither upon a dispute between the prior there and his proctor, and perceive by examination that the proctor is no good husband for the said house. Seeing your letters in the proctor's behalf, I advised the prior to let him continue till your Lordship should know further from me of his demeanour. The house is undone if he remain in the office, as you will further learn from the bearer, Harry Pany, whom please credit."*

How the dispute terminated, or whether it lasted during the remaining months of the Priory's existence, does not appear.

Henry, who was always anxious to have, if he could have nothing more, the show of legality at least on his side, preferred the monks to go through the form of a free surrender, and his commissioners were directed to always endeavour

---

* From the abstract in the *Cal. of State Papers*, vol. xiii. pt. ii. Appendix No. 39.

to bring about these so-called voluntary submissions. In Somersetshire, John Tregonwell and William Petre had the task of persuading or terrifying the religious into confessing their unworthiness and the worthiness of the new Supreme Head to possess what was lawfully their own. In January A.D. 1539 they visited Hinton; on the 25th they wrote to Cromwell that the Prior's "conscience would not suffer him willingly to give over" his house, and that in the whole convent three only were "conformable."* " In the mean tyme," they continued, " because wee thought thatt thother Charter howse, takyng example by this, wyll nott conform themself, we have determyned (your lordeshippes pleasure savyd) to differ the same unto our return." The commissioners came back to the neighbourhood in March; and whether affected by the obstinacy of their brethren at Hinton or not, the monks of Witham signed the deed of surrender of their house in the presence of Petre a few days before them, that is, on the 15th of March. The document was as follows :—

---

* Quoted by Mr. Archbold in his *Somerset Religious Houses and their Suppression*, from R. O. Crom. Corresp. xliii. 74.

"To all the faithful of Christ to whom the present writing shall come: Dom John Mychell, prior of the House or Priory of the Blessed Virgin Mary of Wytham in the County of Somersett, of the Carthusian Order in Selwodde, and the Convent of the same place, eternal salutation in the Lord.

"Know ye that we, the foresaid Prior and convent, with unanimous consent and assent, with deliberate minds from our certain knowledge and pure motive, for certain just and reasonable causes moving our souls and consciences especially, voluntarily and willingly have given, conceded, and by the presents give, concede, confirm, return, and confirm to the Illustrious Prince and our lord, Henry the eighth, by the grace of God King of France and England, Defender of the Faith, Lord of Ireland, and in earth Supreme Head of the English Church, All our said House or Priory of Wytham aforesaid, and also all the manors, domains, messuages and gardens, courtyards, tofts,* lands, and tenements, fields, meadows, pastures, woods, underwoods, rents, reversions, ser-

* *Toft*, a place where a house has formerly stood.

WITHAM CHARTERHOUSE

vices for grinding, tolls, knights' fees, wardships, rights of bestowing in marriage, neifs,* villeins, with their appurtenances, rights of common, liberties, official jurisdictions, court-leets, hundred courts, views of frankpledge, fairs, markets, parks, warrens, fish-ponds, waters, fisheries, ways and roads, waste soil, advowsons, nominations and presentations of churches, vicarages, chapelries and chantries, hospitals and other ecclesiastical benefices, and whatsoever pensions, portions, annuities, tenths and oblations of the rectories, vicarages and chantries, and all and every the emoluments, profits, possessions, hereditaments, and rights of ours whatsoever, as well within the County of Somerset as in the Counties of Wiltes, Dorsett, Gloucester, and elsewhere within the kingdoms of England and Wales, and marches of the same, pertaining, belonging to, appending from, or resting with the same House or Priory of Wytham aforesaid; Also whatsoever charters, evidences, writings, muniments of ours regarding or concerning in any manner the same House or Priory, manors, lands, tenements, and other premises, with their appurtenances or any

* A *neif* was an unfree dependant.

parcel of them: To Have, Hold, and Enjoy the said House or Priory, site of foundation, circuit, and precinct of Wytham aforesaid, and all and every the domains, manor, messuages, lands, tenements, rectories, vicarages, pensions, and the other premisses, with all and each of their appurtenances to the foresaid invincible prince and our lord King, his heirs and assigns forever: To Whom in this matter we subject and submit ourselves with the full consequences of the law, and the said House and Priory of Witham, and all our rights of any kind, as is right, and by these give and cede to the same royal Majesty, his heirs and assigns, all and every kind of full and free faculty, authority, and power ourselves and the said House or Priory of Wytham aforesaid, together with all and singular the manors, lands, tenements, rents, reversions, services, and each of the premises, with all rights and appurtenances, to dispose of at the liberty of his royal will to whatsoever uses please his Majesty, to alienate, give, convert, and transfer, the disposal, alienation, donation, conversion, and transfer to be made in anyway by his said Majesty, are hereby ratified, and ratified and agreeable and sure we promise to hold them forever by the presents. And that the presents may have all their due effect, elections moreover of ourselves and our successors, and all quarrels, provocations, appeals, actions, litigations, entreaties, and our other remedies and benefits to ourselves for example, and to our successors in that affair by reason of the disposal, alienation, transfer, and conversion aforesaid, and of the rest of the premises of whatsoever suitors, and from all suitors to be, all errors of fear, ignorance, or of other cause or dispositions, exceptions, objections, and allegations being entirely put away and rejected openly, publicly, and expressly, out of our sure knowledge, and with spontaneous minds we have renounced and ceded, as by writings we renounce and cede and withdraw from them. And we the forementioned Prior and Convent, and our successors the said House or Priory, precinct, site, mansion, and church of Wytham aforesaid, and all and singular the manors, domains, messuages, gardens, courtyards, tofts, fields, meadows, pastures, woods, underwoods, lands, tenements, and all and singular the other premises, with the whole of their appurtenances, we warrant against all people forever by the presents. In witness whereof we the foresaid Prior and Convent have caused our common seal to be set to the presents. Given in our chapter-house of Witham aforesaid the xvth day of March, in the thirtieth year of the reign of King Henry above-mentioned." *

The seal of red wax is still in good condition; it represents our Lord on the cross between two figures, presumably of the Virgin and St. John, and in the lower portion an ecclesiastic with a crosier in his hand. The legend runs thus— S . COMMUNIE . BE . MARIE . DE WITHAM . ORDINIS . CARTHUS. The names of the monks are signed in the margin of the document in the following order :—

John Mychel p'or.	John Lawson.
John Wele.	John Myllott.
Thomas Secheforde.	Richarde Wodnet.
John Dove vicar	C. De nycss (?).
John Mychhyllson.	Nicholas Lychefold.
John Clyffe.	Thrustanus Hyckmās.
John Smyth.	

Thus Wytham Charterhouse chose, as it were, to deal her own deathblow rather than receive it

* *R. O., Augmentation Office, Deeds of Surrender of Monasteries*, No. 270.

from the merciless king's hand. Her last years had not been glorious; not only had she not produced a single martyr, but from the beginning to the end of the monastic troubles she had manifested so little of the martyr's spirit as to have shown scant signs of resistance to what was a series of extremely unjust actions, be they looked at in whatever light they may. The Hinton Carthusians, indeed, surrendered also; but their surrender was preceded by strong opposition to the royal commissioners, and conscientious hesitation as to whether it were right to yield "upe that thynge" which was not theirs "to give, but dedicate to Allemighte Gode for service to be done to hys honoure contynuallye, with other many good dedds off charite."* But among the records of the elder Charterhouse there is nothing like the sad letter of Prior Horde to his brother in London (from which these words are taken), where, though looking upon the Priory and the purpose of its foundation as a trust committed to him and his brethren, and not to be lightly or hastily yielded, he confesses the fear

* Ellis's *Original Letters*, 2nd series, vol. ii. p. 130 (MS. Cleop. E. iii. f. 270).

"off the Kyngs hye displeasure and my Lorde Prevy Sealis;" for which cause he ultimately persuaded the monks under him to surrender.

But although the end of Witham Charterhouse appears not worthy of the beginning, much allowance must be made for the community. The later Priors were certainly not of heroic natures; had it been ruled by a St. Hugh or a John Houghton, whose brave endurance of King Henry's cruelty has won him in recent years the well-merited beatification from the Roman See, there might have been another tale to tell. As for the compliance of the monks during the earlier stages of the scheme of dissolution, resistance usually entailed death, and if they thought the Papal supremacy—again tacitly rejected in their deed of surrender where the king is styled Supreme Head of the English Church—was no cause for which to die, they were not the only men of their class who did so think. Temporising too often suggests cowardice, but after all discretion is the better part of valour, and the Selwood Carthusians may have thought it wiser to bow to the royal will for a time than to endure the agony of soul and body that the inmates of the London Charterhouse were made to undergo, and, like them and the "Blessed" John Fisher and Sir Thomas More, suffer a perhaps useless martyrdom; for even if Henry himself, once so zealous for the Roman Catholic faith, never retraced his steps, to all devout sons of the Pope England's perpetual separation must have seemed an impossibility. Even to these rather remote monks of the West, the knowledge of the debased and debasing lives of the recent successors of St. Peter must have penetrated, and probably helped, the question once being put, to make them doubt whether the Papal supremacy were really divinely instituted. In the matter of surrendering their monastery and property, nobler as it always is to oppose illegal actions, from a worldly point of view it was their wisest course; resistance at that date was utterly useless, and refusal to surrender generally meant, if nothing worse, deprivation of the poor pittance that the king's greed allowed to the religious out of their own property which he robbed from them.

As it was, all the monks of Witham received pensions, appointed by the king's commission near the time of their surrender, "every of them to have one quarter's pencion at thannunciation of our Lady next cumyng and att the feast of Saynt Mychell tharchaungell next after that one half yeres pencion, and soo from half yere to half yere duryng their lyves and the lyfe of every of them," or until they were presented to any ecclesiastical benefice or were otherwise promoted, was added in the patents issued on the 24th April next year. The accompanying list of the recipients* and their pensions was made out and signed by Cromwell, John Tregonwell, William Petre, and John Smythe. Rather strangely, considering it could not be much later than the date of the foregoing deed, there is no mention of the monk who signs himself "C. De nycss," and the name of Alnett Hales occurs instead, as it does in the patents. The last two names on the list must be those of lay brothers.

Ffurst to John Mychell, prior	xxxiii^{li}	vi^s	viij^d
To John Wele	vj^{li}	xiij^s	iiij^d
To John Dore	vj^{li}	xiij^s	iiij^d
To John Smythe	vj^{li}	xiij^s	iiij^d
To Thomas Segeforde	vj^{li}	xiij^s	iiij^d

* Dugdale, *Monasticon*, vol. vi. pt. ii. App. iv. From a Pension Book in the Augmentation Office, from which the list of pensions is also taken.

To John Clyffe	vj^{li}	xiij^s	iiij^d
To John Lawson	vj^{li}	xiij^s	iiij^d
To Nycholas Lychefylde, impotent	viij^{li}	—	—
To John Mychelson . . .	vj^{li}	xiij^s	iiij^d
To Richard Woodnett . . .	viij^{li}	—	—
To John Mylett	vj^{li}	xiij^s	iiij^d
To Alnett Hales	vj^{li}	xiij^s	iiij^d
To Thruston Hyckemans, late proctor	viij^{li}	—	—
To Hugh Bytt	—	xl^s	—
To John Swansea . . .	—	xl^s	—
Summa of the yearly pencions	cxxj^{li}	vj^s	viij^d

Besides the above annuities the patents granted to Prior Mychell the gift of £8. 6s. 8d., and to each monk 33s. 4d., except to Nicholas Lychefylde, Thrustan Hyckemans, and Richard Woodnett, who had 40s. each.*

The Carthusians once turned out of house and home, almost nothing is known of them. Except in the case of the Prior, whose large salary would argue that he could not have lost favour with the king or Cromwell, their pensions could scarcely be sufficient for their maintenance. Moreover, they were appointed to receive the allotted sums from the Treasurer of the Augmentations or from the Receiver of the revenues of their late monastery. This meant a journey to wherever that

---

* R. O. *Augmentation Office*, *Misc. Bks.*, vol. 233, ff. 247–250.

official might be, or in the case of their being incapacitated from travelling, the payment of some person to draw the pension for them; in addition to these expenses there was a fee of 4d. to those concerned in the disbursements of the money; so that the pensions were yet smaller than they appear.* Whether they found friends to help them, whether they went back to their relations, or how they passed their lives, is not to be discovered. To one or two of them a living may have been given later on, but this is extremely doubtful. More certainly some of them, like others of their Order,† went abroad, not from fear, but to lead the old secluded life in foreign Charterhouses. The following extract from the Acts of the Privy Council (A.D. 1547, June 9th) is an illustration of this fact:—

"This daye forasmuche as the Lord Protectour's Grace and Counsaile were enfourmed of certain Inglishemen, late monkes of thorder of the Charterhowse, who reteigning still in their hartes their old supersticion and popish monkery, had fownde the meanes to convey themselfes

* Dr. Gasquet, *Henry VIII. and the English Monasteries.*
† Mr. Archbold, *Somerset Religious Houses and their Suppression.*

secretely over the sees into Flandres, where they have againe received their monkes habite and profession, and nevertheles procured with their frendes here to have the payment of their pencions to them alloted by the Kinges Majeste contynued unto them as if they remaigned still in somme partes of Ingland, lyke as also certaine other Inglishemen late religious persons of their confederacye were of late detected that they intended shortly to have folowed the former for the semblable purpose, in case they had nat in the meane tyme been apprehended; therefore considering how the Kinges Majeste, by the meanes of conveyaunce over the sees of sundry suche popishe persones late religious, hath been and may be gretely defrauded in allowing them still of their pencions as if they contynued here his Highnes true subjectes, and that it may be that his Majeste hath lykwise been deceived in the contynuance of payment of suche pencions to dyvers late religious persones uses and behaulfes, who before the tyme lymited therefore were deceased, and for the avoidance of the like errour and losse that his Highnes shuld susteigne by theis deceiptes hereafter, it was this day with thadvise and consent of the said Lord Protectour's Grace and Counsaill decreed that from hencefourth the pencioners of any late Religious Howse dissolved, having pencions yerely during time of lief of his Highnes graunt, shuld no more be paide the same at thandes of the Particuler Receivour of the Courte of thaugmentacions, &c., but shuld hooly be referred to the Tresorer of that Courte, so as either at their next tyme of payment at Mighelmas next comming they shuld personally present themselves before the said Tresorer, or his deputes, to be viewed, whither they were the same persones to whom such pencions were assigned. Or in case they did nat so personally present themselfes they shuld at lest sende uppe to the saide Treasorer, by him whome they deputed to receave their pencion for them, a certificat in writing under thandes of two Justices of the Peace in the shyre where they abide, or at leest under thandes of oone Justice of the Peace and oone other jentilman of reputacion of that shire, declaring that the persone whome they beare witnes of is there remaigning in lief, and in lawfull state to receive the saide pencion. And that this said Order, either for the personall presentacion of the saide pencionaries or the sending of their testimonies, shalbe contynued in fourme before expressed from tyme to tyme as their paymentes shall arise due to thintent that the Kinges Majeste be nat otherwise charged then of right shall appertaine."*

This order was natural enough, considering that at that date, as again for so long after Queen Mary's reign, the question of the Papacy was quite as much a matter of politics as of religion in the eyes of the rulers of the country, but it was extremely hard on the Carthusians. To act against conscience at a great crisis, however mistaken conscience may be, is one thing; to live perpetually a double life is quite another; and to those who had bowed to King Henry through fear, the continually necessary concealment of their real opinions, and the unreal profession of the views enforced by tyranny, must have been galling beyond measure, especially as the monks, through long habit prone to self-examination, would be often looking back to those days of weakness with a sense of shame for which they must have longed to atone, if in

* *Acts of the Privy Council*, vol. A.D. 1547-50, pp. 97-98.

no other way, by at least leading the old existence more earnestly than ever. But to live as a monk in England, even to appear in the cowl, was utterly forbidden. To go abroad was their only resource, and now that their pensions were stopped, the refugees were thrown entirely on the charity of the foreign religious of their Order, who, brethren of theirs as they were, too much regarded them as strangers, and did not always welcome the prospect of having them as constant inmates of their Charterhouses.

At last Mary, the hope of all adherents of the Pope, ascended the throne, and once more the parent-house of the Carthusians gave its care to the maintenance of English piety. In A.D. 1555, Dom Maurice Chauncy, who, with Brother Taylor, also of the London Charterhouse, had taken refuge with their Flemish brethren at Bruges on the suppression, received orders from La Grande Chartreuse to return home and attempt the re-establishment of the Order in the island. In May the two religious, with Dom John Fox, who had followed them into Flanders, reached London. They were received, as was fitting, by Sir Robert Rochester, who had lost his brother in the cause of the Pope. Being comptroller of the royal household, Rochester was able to give them apartments in the Savoy, and took the earliest opportunity to introduce them to Cardinal Pole, and then to the Queen, who, from that time until their removal, supported them in the Palace at her own expense. In the summer of A.D. 1556 Father Fox died of a fever, and was buried by Sir Robert in the Savoy Chapel. Chauncy wrote thereupon to headquarters to procure another monk, and Dom Richards of St. Anne's, near Coventry, was sent to him from a Dutch charterhouse, where, having escaped from England, he had made a second profession. But the latter after five weeks also died, and was buried beside his predecessor. Utterly disheartened, Dom Maurice thought of returning abroad. By this time, however, the existence of the small community was well known, and several monks, who meanwhile had been living in the world, became anxious to join them. The Savoy Palace was scarcely a fit Carthusian monastery, so that other quarters had first to be found. The consequence was that before the year's end, through the assistance of Cardinal Pole, once more there was a Charterhouse at Sheen. On December 31st Pole appointed Chauncy Prior. In the spring of A.D. 1557 the General Chapter of the Order confirmed the nomination; for though resenting the Cardinal's interference, doubtless under the circumstances they felt it hardly politic, as well as ungrateful, to offend him by rejecting it. Nevertheless, they added that in so doing they intended to derogate in nothing from the privileges of their Order.*

Queen Mary having already issued the charter for its re-establishment, the monastery was now settled. The community at first consisted of nine monks and three lay-brothers, but soon seven more monks returned from the Continent. Several of the nineteen had shown weakness more or less during King Henry's persecution, but none, in all probability, regretted their past failures in heroism as much as their Prior, who, with the terrible warning of the torments and martyrdom of his leader, John Houghton, and his comrades before him, after great suffering of body and mind most bravely endured, had at last given way to

* *Charta Cap. Gen.* A.D. 1557. Quoted by Dom Lawrence Hendriks in *The London Charterhouse.*

WITHAM CHARTERHOUSE 187

the royal supremacy. Father John Mychell, the last Prior of Witham, now Chauncy's vicar at Sheen, could certainly not be reckoned among the strong adherents of the Pope. Seemingly after the dissolution of the Selwood community he had, like Dom John Cliffe and Brother John Swansco or Swymestowe, remained in England, these three alone out of the number of their house still drawing pensions at the beginning of Mary's reign.* It does not appear whether Swansco and Cliffe also went to Sheen. The former Proctor of Witham, Thrustan Hyckemans (or Tristan Holimans, according to one authority), on the other hand, must have been abroad, and returned with the last addition of seven monks.

The renovated Priory of Sheen soon came to an end. The stern exclusive Catholicism of Mary was succeeded by the more liberal, if less ardent, Churchmanship of Elizabeth, soon to develop into the utterly hostile Anglicanism. Prior Chauncy saw that England was no more a place for monks. Having already buried at different dates the aged Father John Wilson, once Prior of Mountgrace, who had died soon after

* *Cardinal Pole's Pension Book.*

his return to England, Father Fletcher of the same house or of Hinton, Fathers Robert Abel and Robert Marshall of Mountgrace, and Father Robert Thurlby of the original Priory at Sheen, he judged it best to go back to the Continent at once. Of those that followed him across the sea, there was but one Witham monk, Dom Hyckemans. It may not be amiss here to give a list of these last spiritual descendants of St. Hugh and then to sketch the outline of the later history:—

> Prior Maurice Chauncy of London died July 12th, A.D. 1581.
> Roger Thomson, a novice of Mountgrace, died Oct. 12th, A.D. 1582.
> Tristan Holimans or Hyckmans (of Witham), died Dec. 6th, A.D. 1575.
> Leonard Hall *alias* Stofs of Mountgrace, died Oct. 10th, A.D. 1575.
> Nicholas Dugmere of Beauvale, died Sept. 10th, A.D. 1575.
> Nicholas Bolsand of Hinton, died Dec. 5th, A.D. 1578.
> William Holmes of Hinton.*

The Charterhouse at Bruges was again the place of refuge. In A.D. 1561 the General Chap-

---

* Dr. Gasquet, *Henry VIII. and the English Monasteries*, vol. ii. p. 487. Nicholas Bolsand must be Nicholas Balland of Hinton. William Holmes does not appear in the list of monks who surrendered Hinton Charterhouse.

ter of the Order appointed Chauncy to the Priorate there, in spite of his being a foreigner. Unfortunately, the English monks were not popular with their brethren, for besides causing the overcrowding of the house, they wished to have a separate novitiate of their own, in the prospect of a future restoration to England. Frequent disputes arising, Prior Maurice was ordered the next year to be particular to choose, if not Flemish officers, at least those able to speak the language, and six years later he was authorised to look out for a suitable dwelling for the English Carthusians to live in apart. In A.D. 1569 therefore, having been assisted by the charity of other voluntary exiles from England and of various foreign friends, they settled in St. Clare's Street, Bruges, naming their house Sheen Anglorum. Here they abode until, barely nine years later, the Protestants turned them out. Once more the community were scattered, but some settled together again at Louvain under the protection of Don John of Austria. Unhappily that prince died shortly afterwards, and for some time they led a struggling existence, the support coming from others being too small to meet their needs. It was on a journey to the King of Spain for the purpose of seeking his help that Prior Chauncy died at Paris in A.D. 1581.

As was meet for these sufferers in the Papal cause, aid at last came from the Pope. Sixtus V., hearing of their difficulties, issued a bull addressed to Cajetan, Cardinal Protector of England and the English Carthusians, and to Cardinal Allen, requiring all the visitors and priors of the Order to provide a proper house and maintenance for them, and to send to that house all those dispersed among the Continental charterhouses. The bull could not have benefited them much, for few of the foreign Carthusian monasteries had any funds to spare; the King of Spain, however, pensioned them. Before A.D. 1596 they were able to take possession of a sufficiently large house in Bleek Street, Mechlin, and from that date prospered so well that in A.D. 1626 they removed, with the consent of Philip III., to Nieuport, where they had purchased two houses with a garden. This was the last Sheen Anglorum that the wanderers set up, and here an English community existed until their Charterhouse was suppressed with

WITHAM CHARTERHOUSE

other monasteries in his dominions by the Emperor Joseph II. in A.D. 1783, when, by a strange turn of the wheel of fortune, some of these Carthusians took refuge in England. One of them, Prior Williams, did his best to maintain here the rule of his Order, though living among his relations at Little Malvern Court, Worcestershire, where he, the last monk of his house, also died.

At this day, not the least zealous in praying for the reunion of all England with Rome—a subject dear to the hearts of all true Christians in spite of the many differences between them, and not only to the sons of the present saintly-minded Ruler of St. Peter's See—are doubtless the Carthusians of St. Hugh's Priory at Parkminster in Surrey, one of whom is our authority for the last paragraph.*

Having followed the monks through their troubles so far as is possible, there remains to be told the destruction of their original home in Selwood Forest.

In prospect of the sale or other distribution of the monastic lands, in each case a rental

---

* Dom Lawrence Hendriks, *The London Charterhouse.*

was made out. That for Witham Priory is as follows :—

	£	s.	d.
In the County of Somerset.			
Witham—Rents and farms	69	9	10
Witham—Farms of site with orchards	18	13	4
[*In the County of Dorset.*]			
Aston—Rents farmed out	5	7	2
Aston—Pension from the rectory	2	13	4
[*In the County of Warwick.*]			
Warmyngton—Rents of free tenants	1	1	8
Warmyngton—Rents farmed out	18	2	5
In the County of Leicester.			
Ulstrope—Rents of free tenants	0	13	8
Wilscote—Rents farmed out	6	15	5
Warmington—Pension from the rectory	1	0	0
In the County of Dorset.			
Spetisbury—Rents of free and customary tenants	16	2	4
Spetisbury—Pension from the church	1	10	0
Spetisbury—Farm of the manor	18	10	0
[*In the County of Wilts.*]			
Fontell—Rents and farm	3	0	0
[*In the County of Somerset.*]			
Monkisham—Firm of the manor	4	13	4
Merston—Rents farmed out	4	2	0
Feltham and Clink—Rents, &c.	2	0	0
Mayden Bradley—Rents of tenants	0	12	0
Moreland—Rents of tenants	2	11	4
Newbery—Rents farmed out	1	9	4
Newbery—Pension and portion of the rector	1	6	8

	£	s.	d.
Wokey—Rents, &c.	1	15	0
Yerdeley—Rents of tenants	0	8	0
Chiltern Vage and Chiltern-Dommer—Farms	1	16	8
Bristoll—Assessed rents of customary tenants	18	15	8
Bristoll—Assessed rents of conventual tenants	25	15	4
Hydon—Farm of the grange	40	0	0
Witham—Farm of the rectory	6	1	8*

As everywhere else, there were various would-be purchasers and grantees of the above scattered estates during the immediately ensuing years. But the division of the spoils, except the very grounds of the Priory, need not be recorded here, as no longer concerning the history of the Charterhouse. In A.D. 1544, Ralf Hopton, Esq., received a grant of the site of "the late monastery or Priory of Witham, otherwise called Charterhouse Witham," with all houses, buildings, lands, stables, dovecotes, orchards, gardens, and soil within and around the site; the whole of the pasture called Hedstoke, the enclosure and wood called Home Park and Pound Close, a corn-mill,

* *Computatio Ministrorum Domini Regis.* Abstract from Roll, 31 Henry VIII., in the Augmentation Office, given in Dugdale's *Monasticon*, vol. vi. pt. i. App. v.

the meadows Aldershaies, Studleigh Fostok, Holte, Little More Park, Great More Park Chelfurd, Newlands Southfield, Tylemeade, Gurneham, Tanner's Close, Elm Hies [Hayes?], Le Grove, Cowelease, Little Wood, Longham, Pykemead, Parkefeld flat and Parkfelde with their appurtenances, a flour-mill and enclosure called Newpit, and an enclosed pasture, Pitlespound Close, and two other enclosures called Estbitroy and Westbytroy. The foregoing were estimated as 446 acres. There was granted besides to Hopton a whole grange called the Frary Grange, with its "dayhouse or dayrehouse" and the other buildings there, and three enclosures at Witham, Westpoundhays, and Middepoundhays of 4 acres, lately held by John Giffard, and Estpoundhays of 3 acres, lately held by William Morvell; two dwellings in Witham, the "Heyhouse," with a plat of ground thereto annexed, and "Fat Oxenstall," lately held by Roger Rasing, with a dovecote, a carpenter's shed, and a little barton near by; the enclosures Oldeorchard and Windelease of 24 acres, Corier's croft of 10 acres, Moreleas of 10 acres, Wolfehill of 20 acres, Hollowedmeade of 4 acres,

Rowestable of 2½ acres, Newmeade of 10 acres, Oxenlease of 7 acres, Skinner's croft of 1 acre, with all the commodities and appurtenances thereof; also the rectory of Witham, with all the rights belonging to it; also Hidon Grange, with all the land and pastures and the water-mill, as well as all the profits issuing from Witham, Westbarne, Billerica, Quare, and Lez Frary. The wood called Le Holt in Witham was, however, granted to the Earl of Oxford, otherwise Hopton received all that the late Prior had held, except that the great trees were reserved to the Crown. He was to pay for the property £79. 16s. 8d. yearly for twenty-one years to Henry and his heirs; the reversion of the house and site he bought for £572. 16s. 8d.*

Next year also the King granted to Hopton and his wife Dorothy "the grange called Le Quarre or Lee Quarre grange, or whatever else it may be named," with all the land appertaining to it lying in Selwood, as well as a pasturage on the Mendips that could maintain a hundred sheep, which had formerly belonged to Witham

---

* *Rot. Orig.*, 36 *Henry VIII.*, 2 pars. 54; *Ibid.*, 37 *Henry VIII.*, 7 pars. 24.

Charterhouse. This Ralph Hopton was the grandfather of the Cavalier Sir Ralph, later Lord Hopton, one of the generals of the royal army in the West during the earlier part of the Civil War. The latter dying without issue, the Witham estates passed through the marriage of his sister to the family of Wyndham. About a century afterwards, Mr. William Beckford, Lord Mayor of London, bought them of a later Wyndham, the Earl of Egremont; he in his turn sold the property, which was finally purchased of the new owners by the Duke of Somerset.

But besides the estates, there were the movable goods out of which the king could make a profit, if indeed the more valuable of these were not somehow purloined before the authorised officials could lay their hands on them. Unfortunately, in the case of Witham Priory there is no inventory to be found; but considering that the Carthusian rule did not permit the possession of precious things for use or ornament except for the service of the altar, it is not likely that the monastery had much valuable plate or many costly vestments. Its library would soon be dispersed or destroyed,

WITHAM CHARTERHOUSE

the illuminated books and manuscripts being too often regarded as rubbish. As for original works, it can scarcely be said that the English branch of the Order did much for literature, which leads to the supposition that not many were lost at Witham. On the other hand, as the royal goldsmith, John Freeman, had pointed out, there were "merchants within his realm ... a great sort," who would give the King "a goodly payment" for the lead from the roofs of monastic buildings. The suggestion, if indeed it had been needed, was adopted. In fact, that useful metal, so long the protection of the wonderful mediæval architecture, was in the end the cause of its ruin; for even where the stone-work was not carted away as material for new buildings, rain and frost and other atmospheric influences must in time fret away the masonry, when once the roof had been torn off to abstract the lead. This happened at Witham.

In the Minister's Accounts of the Augmentation Office* there is recorded 108s. wages to the plumber Richard Walker for melting down

---

* *Minister's Accounts* in the R. O. (Exchequer and Augmentations), 30–31 Henry VIII., No. 224, quoted by Mr. Archbold in *Somerset Religious Houses*.

fourscore and two pigs of lead procured from the church, cloister, bell-tower, and the other buildings of the Charterhouse, weighing about 43 fodders 9 cwt. 8 lbs. From the same source we learn that the three bells of the monastery, weighing about 200 cwt., were sold for £14 to Richard Morian, and that the "superfluous buildings lately belonging to it were purchased for £20 by Ralph Hopton." As regards the bells, their price, £168 in the present currency, does not seem high compared to their great weight; this was doubtless owing to the fact that the buyer would probably have to melt them down before he could use them, and was not likely on that account to give a large sum for them; moreover, upon the destruction of the religious houses, bell-metal must have become plentiful and cheap.

The ruins of the Charterhouse were allowed to exist for more than two centuries after the dissolution. In A.D. 1760 one of the churches was still standing, with some of the original conventual buildings almost contiguous to its west front, and with some others more or less altered near its east end, of which that supposed to have

WIDOW CRUSE OF ELIJAH. 1 KINGS 17: 8-24. (See page 288.)

been the guest-house is now used as the parish library or reading-room. These very buildings, which later occupants so easily adapted for a farmhouse and out-houses, seem to mark it as the lesser church of the lay-brethren, near to which would be their own dwellings, the guest-house, and all the more secular buildings of a Carthusian establishment. In A.D. 1458 the Prior of Witham petitioned Bishop Beckington, as we have seen, to be allowed to put the "chapel of the Friary" to the uses of a parish church for the secular persons living within the bounds of the Priory. Upon the suppression, this chapel, like others elsewhere, was probably spared because it had really become by that time the parish church for the people of the district.* This little

* It is scarcely to be doubted that the church in question is that chapel, and not the larger church of the monks, which, with "the solid bases and firm columns" mentioned in the *Metrical Life of St. Hugh*, has long since disappeared. About sixty years ago the little church underwent a strange transformation; some of the adjacent buildings, if they had not been pulled down before, were removed, and an incongruous square tower was erected at the west end in an entirely different style of architecture. At the same date, an old and beautifully carved rood-screen of oak was ruthlessly destroyed; the entrance to the loft above it, with the steps formed in the thickness of the masonry, may still be seen in the north wall of the interior. In the same wall, a few feet farther to the west, there is a blocked entrance to a passage which Collin-

WITHAM FRIARY CHURCH, A.D. 1760, WITH SUPPOSED CONVENTUAL BUILDINGS.

Church of St. Mary of Charterhouse-Witham—its severe style of architecture harmonising with the ascetic life of its builders, redeemed from ugliness within by the beautiful concentration of the arches of the stone roof—is the sole relic still in some measure devoted to its original holy uses, not only of the first English Carthusians, but also of the whole branch of the Order in England. Not the least significant note of the vast difference between their age and the present is that this church—built, if ever church was, that it might be the house of prayer—stands with locked doors during the long intervals between the hours of service, when it may indeed be entered, but by the sight-seer, and not by the would-be worshipper.

son, the author of *The History of Somerset*, described in A.D. 1791 as winding round to the east end of the church and leading to the monastery, and the traces of which were probably also removed during these alterations. In A.D. 1876, Mr. Burney, the then parish priest of Witham, with a wiser spirit of restoration, took down the tower, and enlarged the church westwards in a style in keeping with its original architecture, at the same time raising the outer roof and covering it with red tiles.

PART II

HINTON CHARTERHOUSE

HINTON CHARTERHOUSE

OR

THE HOUSE OF THE PLACE OF GOD

CHAPTER I

THE FOUNDERS

"Lord, I have loved the habitation of Thy house, and the place where Thine honour dwelleth."—Ps. xxvi. 8.

ON the occasion of a visitation of the religious houses in his diocese, St. Hugh went to Godstow. In the church there, in the middle of the choir, right before the altar, he saw a tomb decked with silken hangings and surrounded by lamps and wax-lights. Naturally he wondered who was lying thus in such state near so holy a spot—in a place, in fact, that was usually reserved for the most worthy. Upon learning that it was no other than Fair Rosamund, although his informants represented to him that King Henry for love of her had been a generous benefactor to that church, he replied with his accustomed disregard of the rank of the transgressor and regard for the plain truth, which would not allow him, after the fashion of later sentimentality, to look on this king's mistress almost in the light of an injured saint: "Bear the body hence, for she was an harlot, and bury her with the rest outside the church." He feared otherwise that the Christian religion would become less esteemed, and that other women, hearing of her honourable burial, would hesitate the less to follow in her steps. "And thus was it done," curtly adds Roger of Hoveden, who relates the incident in his Chronicle.

Henry and Hugh were both dead in A.D. 1222, the date of the foundation of the second English Charterhouse. That the king's bastard son, William Longespée—especially if, as later traditions say, his mother was Rosamund Clifford herself—should have founded this priory, seems like a possible act of atonement for the parents' breaches of marriage chastity, the keeping of which whole, as the wise and pure-minded Carthusian taught, could merit heavenly bliss as well as virginity, and for their sins against the dignity of womanhood, which the saintly bishop held so high, because, "whereas to man it was not granted to be, or to be called, the father of God, yet to a woman it was given that she should be the parent of God." * But it is not known whether the Earl had any motive beyond religious ardour in establishing the monastery; the greater part of his life was passed in warfare, during which he must have become inured to hardship, and there may have been something in the discipline of the Order that met with his sympathy as well as its known sanctity. The monks of Hinton, however, owed their origin scarcely less to Ela d'Evreux, his Countess; indeed, the new Charterhouse had no eminent man of the Order to watch over it, but only these two secular persons, one of whom was much engrossed in the affairs of a very turbulent world. The history of the founders is not without some savouring of romance, but it is also illustrative of the times in which they lived, both from a religious and a social point of view, and a short relation of it may not be inaptly inserted here.

* *Magna Vita S. Hugonis.*

Both the name of his mother and the date of the birth of William Longespée are unrecorded by the earlier choniclers. The first known incidents in his life are the grant to him by his father, Henry II., of Appleby in Lincolnshire in A.D. 1188, and ten years later his marriage with Ela, the Countess of Salisbury. Among the followers of William the Norman had been Walter d'Evreux, Count of Rosmar, who for his services received the domains of Salisbury and Amesbury; his great-grandson was Patrick, the first Earl of Salisbury, and the father of William, the second Earl, who married Eleanor de Vitré. From this last marriage Ela d'Evreux was born at Amesbury in A.D. 1188. Eight years later death had removed both her parents, and the child had become the ward of the king, according to the feudal law. Her relations and friends, however, did not care to have her under the royal guardianship, but privately carried her off to Normandy, with the intention of bringing her up in the strictest secrecy; this purloining of so valuable a commodity, so to speak, from the hands of King Richard, though he was not likely to have borne it with equanimity, does not seem to have entailed any punishment on the family. The royal guardian indeed took measures to recover his ward, but they were of a very gentle nature. At that time there was in England a knight named William Talbot; this man, presumably with Richard's orders, dressed himself as a pilgrim and crossed into Normandy, where he stayed two years searching for the hidden abode of the little Countess. At last, having discovered it, putting off the pilgrim's weeds, he donned those of a harper and entered the house. Being a man of merry temperament, and well versed in the tales of ancient deeds, he was readily received as a friend. By what means he obtained possession of her does not appear, but when a convenient season was come, Talbot repaired to England, taking Ela with him, and brought her to Richard. And very "joyfully," according to the Register of Lacock Abbey, the King received her, as no doubt he did, for he now had the bestowal of the hand of the heiress. He must have almost immediately given her to his brother William Longespée as they were married that same year. The Earl of Salisbury, as he now was in her right, had then for wife a girl of ten years old. This was only one instance of a not infrequent mediæval practice, namely, child-marriage, against which but a rare voice even among the clergy was to be heard now and then.* In this case the union, however, does not appear to have been unhappy.

Salisbury was in the favour of his brother John no less than of Richard; for throughout his reign he held various high offices, being at divers times Lieutenant of Gascony, Warden of the Cinque Ports and Constable of Dover, and Warden of the Welsh Marches, besides being employed occasionally in an ambassadorial capacity. As a prominent partisan of John, Roger of Wendover reckons him during the time of excommunication among those "most wicked counsellors," "who, desiring to please the king in all things, gave their advice not with regard to reason, but with regard to his will."† His most notable feat occurred a few years later in A.D. 1213, when he was sent against Philip of France, who, preparatory to an invasion of England, had begun to attack the lands of Ferrand of Flanders, the ally of

* During his episcopate St. Hugh enjoined on his clergy the refusal to celebrate such marriages. *Magna Vita*, p. 174.
† *Flores Historiarum*, vol. iii. p. 237, Hist. Soc. edit.

John. Outside Damme he found a large French fleet; he and his party attacked it and won the victory, which caused the French king to desist from his purpose of invading England.

In the following year he was marshal of the king's army in Flanders, and having joined forces with Count Ferrand and the Emperor Otto, fought Philip Augustus on the 27th July at the battle of Bouvines, where John lost his last chance of re-establishing his influence at home by the glory of a decisive victory on the Continent. The Earl was taken prisoner by the French and delivered to a kinsman, Robert, Count of Dreux; the latter afterwards exchanged him for his own son, who had previously been captured by King John. On his return to England, he found his brother in a desperate position, but for the present he clung to the fortunes of his house and did not join the insurgent barons, although he saw the expediency of acquiescing in their proceedings, and counselled the granting their demands at Runnymede. When December came, he was still their open enemy, and as one of the leaders of John's army in the south, he concerted measures with Fulkes de Breauté for watching London and cutting off the supplies of the barons; with his party he overran the neighbouring counties, and early in A.D. 1216 committed the worst act of his life, which was to join Fulkes in the devastation of the Isle of Ely. Indeed, the wanton fury of the king's followers was perhaps that which most hastened the appeal to Louis, the son of Philip Augustus. The Prince having landed, took Winchester in June; at last Salisbury must have seen the hopelessness of the king's cause. At any rate, he now joined Louis and yielded to him his castle of Salisbury. Upon John's death his new master sent him to persuade Hubert de Burgh to yield Dover Castle. Hubert reproached him with the words, "O evil treacherous Earl! and if King John, our lord and thy brother, is dead, he has an heir, thine own nephew, to whom, though all be wanting, thou who art his uncle oughtest not to be lacking, yea, shouldest be another father. How, degenerate and wicked man, sayest thou such things?"*

Whether Hubert's faithfulness to young Henry worked with the Earl or not, he ultimately deserted the French prince, and, like other adherents of the

* Matt. Paris, *Chron. Majora.*, iii. p. 4, Rolls Series.

latter, to give a colour to his political change, he took the cross, and professed to engage in the war in the Holy Land at the bidding of the Papal Legate. Whatever he had suffered in his estates for his disaffection, Salisbury was after this received back, and moreover admitted again to various offices of trust. At this period, if at all, he must have gone to Palestine, for it does not follow that he really entered on the crusade because he took the cross. It is true that so important a chronicler as Matthew Paris * asserts that he was present at the capture of Damietta in A.D. 1219, and distinguished himself during the war by his bravery; but it seems probable that his name has been confounded with that of a Count of Saarbrücken,† and it is possible that some share of his son's prowess against the Saracens later on may have been mistakenly attributed to himself. At any rate, he was back in England by the 28th April in the next year, when the Legate Pandulf laid for him and for his wife two of the foundation-stones of the new cathedral at Salisbury. After the

---

* Matt. Paris, *Chron. Majora*, Rolls Series, vol. iii. p. 49.
† *Dictionary of National Biography:* William de Longespée, by Rev. W. Hunt.

Pope's failure to obtain any firm hold of the government of England, and during Hubert de Burgh's ascendancy, the Earl was a staunch supporter of the national party; as such his name appears in one account * as a ruler of the king and kingdom along with that of the Justiciary on the occasion of the disaffection of the malcontent barons under the Earl of Chester, among the partisans of whom was his former comrade in arms, the mercenary leader Fulkes de Breauté. Not long after the settlement of these domestic broils, there was a threat of war abroad upon the accession of Louis VIII. to the French throne, and in A.D. 1224 hostilities were actually begun by the invasion of Poitou. The next year, therefore, the English king's brother, Richard, Earl of Cornwall, and his uncle, William Longespée, were sent to defend Poitou and Gascony. Their expedition having been successful, in the autumn Salisbury started homewards; he had escaped the difficulties of warfare only to meet worse dangers by sea through rough weather. Whilst

---

* *Memoriale Fratris Walteri de Coventria*, Rolls Series, vol. ii. p. 251. "Comes vero Sarisbiriensis et justitiarius, regis rectores et regni."

in imminent peril of shipwreck, he and his company saw a bright shaft of light playing about some part of the vessel; their fancy changed it into an enormous lighted candle, shielded from the wind and rain by a beautiful maiden, whom Salisbury alone recognised to be the Blessed Virgin; from the day of his knighthood he had ever provided a light to burn before her altar, and that she had come now to succour them, was his consoling explanation of the apparition. Certainly afterwards the ship was driven on the Isle of Rhé, then held for King Louis, where he took shelter in the Abbey of Our Lady there, until, being warned that his refuge was known, he set sail again, and reached Cornwall at Christmas, after a voyage of nearly three months. Unwelcome news met him on his return. Upon a report of his death, Hubert de Burgh had tried to secure the hand of the Countess Ela for his nephew. The Earl was not unnaturally wrath, and went to Marlborough, where the king then was, to complain of the minister's conduct. Henry managed to make peace between them, and Salisbury dined with Hubert. On returning home he fell ill, a consequence probably of the hardships and anxieties of his voyage. Feeling his end near, he sent for Richard le Poore, the Bishop of Salisbury. As the Bishop entered the chamber where he lay, carrying the Host, the Earl flung himself from his bed almost naked before him, and tying an exceedingly harsh cord about his neck, prostrated himself on the floor, continually shedding tears, declaring himself a traitor to the Most High King; nor would he be removed from the place until he had confessed and received the communion of the life-giving Sacrament; and thus in extreme penitence he lasted a few days longer, and yielded his spirit to his Redeemer on March 7th A.D. 1226.* He was buried in the still unfinished Cathedral, where there is a full-length recumbent effigy in armour on a tomb in the south arcade of the nave which is ascribed to him. According to Wendover, while his body was being carried from the castle of Salisbury to the Cathedral, the wax-lights which were borne in the procession along with the cross and incense were not extinguished, in spite of torrents of rain and storms of wind, which openly showed

* Wendover, Hist. Soc. edit., vol. iv. pp. 105 and 107.

that "the so deeply penitent Earl belonged to the sons of light." *

The author just quoted in an earlier part of the same passage calls William Longespée "praiseworthy" (*laudabilis*); Matthew Paris names him in his epitaph on him "the flower of earls." † His life shows little enough to justify such laudation, which must, therefore, be owing not so much to what he did as to what he was. Though often in prominent posts as a commander, he was little more than a brave soldier; he received the royal order, do this, do that, and he did it, taking on himself doubtless the manner in which he should do it, but apparently not considering the reason or result of his master's actions. When his own want of foresight brought him to the verge of ruin, he changed sides, and worked as faithfully among those who but now had been his enemies; and that it was faithfully, is apparent from the trust reposed in him by whatever party he served. Yet he did not fight in the spirit of a soldier of fortune, but as one who, seeing very little of

---

* Wendover, Hist. Soc. edit., vol. iv. pp. 105 and 107.
† *Chron. Majora.*, vol. iii. p. 105, Rolls Series.

his way before him, is determined to do that little to the best of his power. In fact, he was a man of simple probity, and, like many a valiant fighter before and after, in spite of his fierceness, that came to him by inheritance and from the habits of the times, a man of sincere piety. The latter appears not so much in his founding a monastery as in his unfortunate voyage from Gascony, where his calm interpretation of the vision—doubtless some strange effect of lightning—with his confidence of approaching help, denotes that faith in the providence of God that allows no fear with any amazement, and that can only exist in truly religious souls. Moreover, the almost daring appellation of the Charterhouse, Locus Dei or the Place of God, betokens on the part of the founders a trustfulness springing from a deep conviction of the Almighty's merciful acceptance of all offerings of man's love and of all honest human effort after divine perfection, which, if anywhere, was certainly striven after in a Carthusian monastery. Soldier though he was, both William Longespée, and the "most dear lady" Ela, as the chaplain of Lacock Nunnery calls his Countess, might have

HINTON CHARTERHOUSE 217

justly applied to themselves the Psalmist's words which we have placed at the head of this chapter.

The Countess of Salisbury lived several years in secular widowhood, but in the meanwhile was planning the foundation of monasteries for the good of her husband's soul and of her own. Therefore she erected at her own expense, and on one of her own hereditary estates, a house at Lacock in Wiltshire for Augustinian nuns. Having superintended its building, she established them there one morning in May A.D. 1232. On the afternoon of the same day she also established on her manor of Hinton, just across the borders in Somersetshire, a body of Carthusians, these being indeed transferred, as will be related below, from her husband's foundation at Heatherop or Hethrop in Gloucestershire. Upon the report of the Earl's death in A.D. 1226, Ela's hand had been sought, but after his actual demise she appears to have been left in peace; finally, she ended her widowhood herself by taking the veil in her own nunnery; two years later, in A.D. 1240, when she was fifty-three, she became its first abbess. She ruled her flock vigorously, meantime maintaining an assiduously stiff discipline towards herself, and "very devoutly served God" in a life spent in fasts, holy vigils, meditations, and all good works of charity. But cloistered though her existence was, she evidently watched with maternal interest over her children in the world. Her eldest son, William, went on the crusade of A.D. 1248–49; "manfully fighting against Christ's enemies in the Holy Land, suffering continually for the name of Jesus, ending the temporal life to conquer everlastingly in Christ, the athlete of God ascended to the heavenly court in A.D. 1249;" that is to say, he was slain in battle against the Saracens, because upon their overmastering the Christians he refused to flee before them, and was regarded therefore something in the light of a martyr. About the time of his death, his mother is said to have seen him entering heaven from her stall at Lacock, and to have reported the same to her nuns—a very natural dream for the poor Abbess, which she would of course accept as a guarantee of his eternal happiness. Of her other three sons, two rest at Lacock, and the heart of the third, as if to show his affection for her, was also buried there, although, as Bishop of Salisbury, his body was interred in the Cathedral. For eighteen years Ela governed the Abbey; at length, overcome by the increasing infirmities of age, she perceived that "she could not as she would be profitable to her religion," and resigned her post. Released from her duties, she lived till September A.D. 1261, when, in her seventy-fourth year, "possessing her soul in peace, she rested in the Lord," and was "very meetly" buried in the Abbey-choir.*

As for one offspring of the religious fervour of the Earl and Countess of Salisbury, Hinton Priory, the materials for its history are even poorer than in the case of the first Charterhouse. Probably some of the monks came from Witham, others would be brought over from the Continent; but no details whatever remain of the early days of their first establishment at Hethrop. Besides the manor itself, they had the wood of Bradene [——?] and the estate of Chelewurth

* *Cotton. MS.*, Vitellius A. viii., being the Register of Lacock Priory. It is almost illegible owing to damage by fire, but is printed in Dugdale, *Mon. Anglic.*, vol. vi. pt. i. p. 500 *et seq.*, from which the above account of Ela is taken.

(Chelworth or Chelwood, a few miles south of Bristol). To help them to build the monastery, William Longespée, by his will,* made in the middle of Lent A.D. 1225, just before his expedition to Gascony, left them all the profits accruing to him as guardian of the heiress and estates of Richard de Campville until the coming of age of his own heir, the second William Longespée, the husband of his ward. To help them in their services at the altar, he left them also a chalice of gold adorned with beautiful emeralds and rubies, a pix of gold adorned with pearls, two phials of silver, the one gilt and the other plain, and his "grand chapel," or grandest vestments used in his private chapel, namely, a chasuble of red samite, a choir cope of red samite, a tunicle, a dalmatic of yellow taffeta, well worked, an alb with apparels, an amice and a stole, a fanon or maniple, with towels, and all his relics.† Moreover, for the further support of the house he assigned 1000 ewes, 300 rams, 48 oxen, and 20 bulls.

For several years after the Earl's death, the

* Enrolled on the backs of M. 8, Close Roll, 9 Henry III., pt. 1; M. 19, ibid., pt. 2.
† *Excerpta Historica: Illustrations of English History*, by Samuel Bentley.

monks lived on the Gloucestershire manor, but whether not remote enough, or unhealthy, or for some other reason, the place could not supply the requisites of their Order. Upon representing their case to the widowed Countess, she, wishing, by the intuition of God—to use her own expression in her charter—to accomplish what her husband had well begun, gave them in exchange the whole of her manor of Hinton, with the advowson of the church and the park, and all the other appurtenances, and likewise all her manor of Norton (Norton St. Philip), with the advowson of the church, reserving to herself and her heirs, however, all the military services due to her from her tenants in both places. On the last point she made one exception; Richard the Parker held one virgate of land in Hinton by the service of park-keeper, or by military service, which he and his heirs were henceforward to discharge to the monks. She retained to herself and her heirs also the beasts of chase which were without the bounds of the manors. Ela's charter for this grant, which we give at the end of the chapter, was confirmed by Henry III. in A.D. 1227, so it may be presumed that about that date the monks began to build the new Locus Dei at Hinton. The dedication of the monastery was "in honour of God and the Blessed Mary, and St. John the Baptist and all saints." Although not within Selwood, the second Charterhouse was not many miles from the Witham Priory, and like it, was situated amidst well-wooded and undulating ground, but unlike it, was built on the brow of a hill, instead of on more level ground below; a little way off, the river Frome flowed on its course to join the Avon, and no doubt its waters were serviceable to the monks.

Some years passed after the dedication of the house by Ela in A.D. 1232, and Henry III. granted[*] to the religious at Hinton in A.D. 1239 all the liberties and free customs that his grandfather had conceded to the monks of Witham, as well those concerning the election of their priors as those attached to the possession of their estates and freedom from certain dues. An earlier royal charter had also been issued allowing them or their servants to buy the necessaries of

---

[*] Rot. Cart., 24 Henry III., m. 1, dated Westminster, September 7th. For the liberties granted to Hinton on this occasion *vide* the Witham charter of foundation.

their convent, and to sell their cattle and other saleable goods throughout the kingdom free of toll and any other custom.* In A.D. 1245 they received concessions of another kind from Pope Innocent IV.† "Lest any one," he said, "dare within your boundaries to seize a man, commit theft or rapine, kindle fire, slay a man, or molest those going to and coming from your house, no religious may erect any building or acquire any possessions within half a league of the lands you hold." No one was to presume to extort from them tenths for fallow ground, young crops, or food for their live stock. Their priests were to be ordained by the bishop of the diocese, provided he did it freely and without dishonesty, otherwise they might go to any Catholic prelate whom they preferred. Moreover, no bishop or other person was to compel them to go to any synod or strange convent, or to subject them to any secular judgment concerning their substance and possessions, nor unsummoned was to presume to come to their house to treat of the

---

* Rot. Cart., 21 Henry III., No. 5, dated Westminster, 7th June.
† *Excerpts from the Register of the Diocese of Bath and Wells* in Harl. MSS., No. 6965, f. 162.

affairs of the Order or to convoke any public meetings.

After this bull Hinton Charterhouse must have been fully established.

THE CHARTER OF FOUNDATION GRANTED BY ELA, COUNTESS OF SALISBURY.

[Rot. Cart. 12 Henry III. m. 4. "Given by the hand of the venerable father, R. bishop of Chichester, our chancellor at Merwett, (?) 25th May."]

"Universis sanctae matris ecclesiae filiis ad quos praesens scriptum pervenerit, Ela comitissa Sarr' in Domino salutem. Noverit universitas vestra quod dominus meus quondam maritus Willielmus Longespée Comes Sarr' volens construere domum ordinis Chartusiae, per assensum meum et bonam voluntatem, donavit ordini Chartusiae manerium de Athercop in . . . . . et boscum suum de Bradene cum integritate sua, et terram de Chelewurth quam habuit ex dono Henrici Basset, ut ibi manerent tam monachi quam fratres ad serviendum Deo imperpetuum secundum consuetudinem et ordinem Chartus'. Set quia monachi et fratres ad locum ipsum destinati licet stetissent ibi per plures annos non potuerunt invenire in praedictis tenementis locum ordini suo competentem, ego volens intuitu Dei perficere quod praedictus maritus meus bene inceperat, in ligia potestate et viduitate mea post mortem ipsius, et pro anima ipsius, et pro anima Comitis Willielmi patris mei, et pro salute mea et puerorum meorum, et pro animabus omnium antecessorum et haeredum meorum, donavi et concessi et hac carta mea confirmavi ordini Chartusiae in escambium praedictorum tenementorum, totum manerium meum de Henton cum advocatione ecclesiae et parco et omnibus aliis pertinentiis suis sine ullo retinemento inde michi et haeredibus meis: et similiter totum manerium meum de Norton cum advocatione ecclesiae et omnibus aliis pertinentiis suis sine ullo retinemento michi et haeredibus meis; reservatis tamen mihi et haeredibus meis serviciis militaribus omnium illorum qui de me tenent in praedictis maneriis per servicium militare; excepto servicio Ricardi parcarii et haeredum suorum de j virgata terrae quam tenet in Henton, quod servicium pertinebit in perpetuum ad praedictos monachos et fratres, sive praedictus Ricardus defendat praedictum virgatam terrae per custodiam parci vel per servicium militare; et etiam salvis michi et haeredibus meis kaciis forinsecis, quae sunt extra terminos praedictorum maneriorum; Ad fundandam, construendam et in perpetuum sustentandam quandam domum ordinis Chartusiae, in honore Dei et Beatae Mariae et Sancti Johannis Baptistae et Omnium Sactorum in parco de Henton, in loco qui vocatur Locus Dei. Habendum et Tenendum in puram et perpetuam elemosinam monachis et fratris ibidem Deo servientibus secundum consuetudinem et ordinem ecclesiae Chartusiae. Et ego et haeredes mei warantizabimus praedictis monachis et fratribus praedicta tenementa, cum pertinentiis contra omnes gentes, et defendemus eos de omnibus serviciis et consuetudinibus et secularibus demandis; et ut haec donatio, concessio, et confirmatio mea rata et stabilis imperpetuum permaneat, eam praesentis scripti testimonio, et sigilli mei impressione corroboravi. Hiis testibus domino Joscelino Bathonensi, episcopo, domino R. Sarr', episcopo, magistro Edmundo de Abendon, thesaurario Sarr', magistro Elia de Derham, canonico Sarr', Reginaldo de . . . . tunc vic. Wiltesir', Barth de Turbervill, Willielmo Gereberd,

Waltero de Pavily, Johanne Gereberd, Baldwino filio Willielmi tunc senescallo comitis Sarr', Michaele de Cheldrinton, Willielmo de Burneford, Nicholao de Hedinton, clerico, Rogero Lond . . . . . . [et] aliis.*

* The Roll recording this grant is torn where the above gaps occur. Hinton, it will be observed, is spelt Henton, which was the more usual mediæval form of the word. Unless quoting from original MSS. we have preferred to use the modern spelling in the following pages.

CHAPTER II

A LONG CARTHUSIAN SABBATH

> "*Conrad.* For He who feeds the ravens promiseth
> Our bread and water sure, and leads us on
> By peaceful streams in pastures green to lie,
> Beneath our Shepherd's eye."
> —THE SAINT'S TRAGEDY.

FROM the day that this second Carthusian brotherhood were installed at Hinton until the middle of the reign of Henry VIII., they may be said to have enjoyed—to speak after the fashion of a foreign member of their Order—one long "Sabbath," an unbroken "sanctified rest," during which generation after generation of monks adopted their stern "religion."* For that period of nearly three hundred years, the documents extant concerning them, those referring to two or three law-

---

* Heading to chapter ii., in the preceding account of the Witham Charterhouse.

suits excepted, are merely records of a peaceful acquisition of property and privileges, and of an uninterrupted tenure of the same. Indeed, Carthusians lived so retired, and concerned themselves so little with the existence of those without their walls, that usually there was little occasion for the disturbance of their solitude; but now and again, perhaps, some grant would be made to the prejudice of some other party, naturally affording ground for litigation.

Originating in a cause such as that last mentioned may be, in A.D. 1240 a claim was raised by Robert of Norton and Mary his wife against the Prior of Hinton for seven acres of land, with their appurtenances, at Meleham (Mileham), in Norfolk. In so distant a county it seems rather strange that the Priory should have had possessions, and we find no account as to how or when it came by them, nor is there any reference made to them again. The claimants' pretensions were that the land belonged to Mary, having come to her through her former husband, William Fitz Alan of Meleham. The case came on at Oxford, and the Prior appearing neither in person nor by attorney, was amerced for his default, and the judgment was awarded in favour of Robert of Norton.*

The next two suits, the first in A.D. 1246, during the Octave of St. Michael at Bedford, and the second in A.D. 1248, in the Quinzaine of St. John the Baptist at Ivelcestre or Ilchester, are probably fictitious. The former was between Prior Robert of Hinton, plaintiff, and Philip, Abbot of Bordele (Bordsley, Worcestershire), deforciant, of one carucate and forty acres of land in Chyweton and Whytenhull (Whitnel, a hamlet near Wells). The matter was settled by a final concord, in which the Abbot acknowledged the Prior's right, as being of his gift, to hold the land of the chief lord of the fee, for which the Prior gave the Abbot half a mark. The second case was between Robert de la Dune and Agatha his wife, plaintiffs, and the same Prior Robert, deforciant, of seven acres of land in Norton. The Prior finally acknowledged the right of Robert and Agatha to hold it of him by virtue of a deed by which he

---

* *Placitorum Abbreviatio*, p. 118. To be *amerced* is to be punished by a pecuniary penalty, not fixed by law, but appointed at the discretion of the court. An *amercement* differs from a *fine* in that the latter is a definite sum prescribed by statute for the offence committed.

HINTON CHARTERHOUSE 231

had conveyed it to them for a pound of wax to be paid yearly at the Feast of St. Leonard, warranting it to them and to the heirs of Agatha against all men. In return for this, Robert and his wife quit-claimed their right to common of pasture in the Prior's lands in Hinton and Norton.*

Rather curiously, considering the nature of the Carthusian Order, not many years after the foregoing incidents there was issued to the monks of Hinton the first of several licences granted to them at different times, wherein we see them connected with the very secular though necessary occupation of trading. In A.D. 1254 they secured from Henry III. a charter for a fair to be held yearly on their manor of Norton during three days, that is, on the vigil, on the day, and on the morrow of the Feast of SS. Philip and James, with all "the liberties and customs belonging to that kind of fair."† Under the same reign also they had a licence for a similar fair

---

* *Somerset. Pedes Finium*, 31 Henry III., No. 15, and 33 Henry III., No. 25.

† Rot. Cart., 39 Henry III., No. 6, dated at Merton, April 5th and confirmed by Cart. 22 Edward I., No. 48, dated at Westminster, November 24th.

at Hinton during the festival of the Beheading of St. John the Baptist, and the days immediately before and after. The customs mentioned above were the market tolls, including in this case, as the Prior of Hinton owned the soil, stallage, the price for permission to erect stalls, and to keep open any house of business in the vicinity and during the term of the fair, and picage, the price for making holes in the ground for posts. To the Charterhouse also would be due the tolls proper to fairs paid by the vendee, who in return received from the market-clerk* a record of the payment as an attestation of the genuineness of his purchases. Now as the owners of fairs had the monopoly of the trade for the time being of the neighbourhood, it may be imagined that, convenient institutions as that mode of buying and selling may have been in some parts of the country, it was not always to the advantage of the regular tradesmen living near, who did not or could not pay stallage, and were therefore liable to the enforced closing of their shops; thus disputes

* Owing to their exclusion from secular business, the Carthusians would probably have that officer.

HINTON CHARTERHOUSE 233

were likely to arise, and especially where the terms of one fair clashed with those of another, as was the case at Hinton. For among the Hundred Rolls an inquisition is recorded as taken at Bath in A.D. 1273, upon a complaint from the citizens that they received yearly 10s. damage, in consequence of the fair at Hinton being held on the same day (the Beheading of St. John the Baptist) as that granted to themselves, and, moreover, in a place only three leagues from that city. Whether the people of Bath were satisfied in any way for their annual loss or not, the Priors of Hinton were permitted to hold the fair at Hinton without alteration in its time down to A.D. 1345. It was held in some space near the church; a natural consequence of this fact was that the noises, the shouts of buyers and sellers, and "the insolence" of the men resorting to the fair disturbed the divine services in that church. Wherefore, at their own request, in that year Edward III. granted, so that his "beloved in Christ, the Prior and convent of that place," should not be hindered in their devotions, in lieu of the fair at Hinton, that they might hold another yearly at Norton on the day of the Beheading of St. John the Baptist and for the two days preceding. As for the original fair at Norton, in the next year its days of duration, for some reason not mentioned, were allowed to be changed from the eve and the morrow of SS. Philip and James to the day of the festival itself and the two days preceding; and in A.D. 1351 the monks were permitted to extend it to five days, which were the eve and the feast of SS. Philip and James, and the three days preceding. But besides the fair at Norton, in A.D. 1345 a weekly open market, to be held there on Tuesdays, had been granted to the Prior and convent, though, in spite of their experience at Hinton, its site was a certain empty space near the west end of the church. No mention in the charter conferring this licence is made of that given earlier by Edward I., by which they might hold a market there every Friday; so that apparently there were two markets a week at Norton, as the last mentioned does not seem to have been cancelled.*

---

* *The Hundred Rolls*, vol. ii. pp. 120–132; Rot. Cart., 19 Edward III., No. 5, dated at Westminster, 23rd October; Rot.

HINTON CHARTERHOUSE 235

But besides the right of holding fairs on their manors, the Priors of the Charterhouse had other privileges there. In A.D. 1258 Henry III. granted free warren in all their demesne lands in Hinton and Norton to the Prior and convent of Locus Dei and to their successors, so that none without their consent and will might enter their grounds to course or catch anything.* Other privileges are mentioned in the inquisition † of A.D. 1275, to which reference has already been made. The Prior, as well as the Earl of Lincoln, who had property in the neighbourhood, was wont to hold the assize of the beer of Hinton and Norton, and had the right of erecting gallows at both places. On the same occasion the witnesses said that the Prior, to the loss of 12d. yearly to the king, abstained from attending the hundred court of La Berton, to which he ought to be liable for the land of Rodcombe, but according to the charter of liberties granted to Hinton

---

Cart., 17 Edward III., No. 22, dated at Westminster, 18th May; Rot. Cart., 20 Edward III., No. 23, dated at Westminster, 24t November; Rot. Cart., 25 Edward III., No. 10, dated at Westminster, 1st May.

* Rot. Cart., 43 Henry III., m. 1.
† *Hundred Rolls*, vol. ii. p. 138.

Charterhouse in A.D. 1239, he was exempt from such courts.

In A.D. 1279, in the third week after St. Martin's Day, the Prior had by attorney to account for his claim to the view of frankpledge, the right of hanging, and of condemning transgressors to the punishment of the tumbrel or ducking-stool, both at Hinton and Norton. According to the witnesses, the Countess of Salisbury and all her ancestors had enjoyed these liberties, and that after she had bestowed the manors with the rights appertaining to them to the Charterhouse, the Priors until this date had likewise enjoyed them. Therefore the judgment was given in favour of the monks.*

The Charterhouse, however, would receive more tangible profit from the lands which meanwhile, and at intervals afterwards, various benefactors gave up to it. At Westminster, in the Octave of Trinity A.D. 1273, a fine† was drawn between Peter, Prior of Hinton, and Henry de Montfort for a messuage and one bovate of land

---

* *Placita quo Warranto*, p. 700.
† *Pedes Finium*, 1 Edward I., No. 2.

in Iford; this De Montfort acknowledged as belonging, by his gift in frankalmoigne, to the Prior and his church of St. Mary and St. John the Baptist of Hinton,—the Priory church, not the parish church, being meant; in return the Prior received him and his heirs into all future benefits and orisons in his church for ever. Again, for the same grace from Prior Peter, two years later, Henry de Lacy, Earl of Lincoln, and Margaret his wife, conveyed by fine, dated at Westminster in the quinzaine of St. John the Baptist, one knight's fee in "Henton-Chartus" and Norton. This property the convent seem to have let, for in A.D. 1288 an inquisition was taken preparatory to the royal licence for Richard de Dantesy to assign to the community a messuage and a carucate of land with appurtenances in Norton, which he held of them *in capite* by military service, the whole being worth eight marks a year. The Prior and convent had had the messuage and lands and its service in pure and perpetual alms from Henry de Lacy and his wife Margaret, as of her heritage by fine,* levied between the two parties before the passing of the Statute

* *Pedes Finium* for Somerset, 3 Edward I., No. 10.

of Westminster.* A few months later the licence was granted by letters patent to Dantesy thus to return the property.† Some time afterwards, land in Hinton, Norton, and Iford, bestowed on the Charterhouse by the same Earl and his wife, comes into question again. William, the son of John the Parker, and probably the grandson of Richard the Parker, spoken of in the Countess of Salisbury's charter of foundation, had held of the monks 25½ acres of land, 6 acres of pasture, 15d. rent, and half an acre of meadow, with the appurtenances, lying in Hinton and Norton, which were worth annually 10s., and for which the only service he performed was to take care of the Prior's woods, freedom from suits being apparently incident to this duty.‡ The Prior and convent held the estate in frankalmoigne of the Earl and Countess of Lincoln, whose lord was the king. William wishing to transfer them back to the Charter-

---

* Passed A.D. 1275; it was against usury.
† Inquis. post mortem, 17 Edward I., No. 34; Rot. Patent., 17 Edward I., m. 5.
‡ Inquis. post mortem, 33 Edward I., No. 256, where it is mentioned he was never sued previous to this donation, on account of the liberty of the Prior and convent.

HINTON CHARTERHOUSE

house, the royal licence * for him to give and the monks to receive them was issued in A.D. 1304, the Prior having, on his part, to pay into the King's treasury four marks for entering into these lay tenements.†

At that very date Edward I. was completing his second conquest of Scotland, during an earlier period of which he had written from Perth the letters quoted in the first part of this book, soliciting the prayers of both the Somerset Carthusian communities. The same war had occasioned the muster at Carlisle in A.D. 1300, to which the Prior of Hinton had been summoned under the general writ to perform military service against the Scots, because his temporal possessions, according to the return of the commissioners from Somerset, amounted to upwards of £40 per annum.‡ The taxation of Pope Nicholas somewhat earlier tallied with this estimate. The details given in the latter are as follows:—

---

* Rot. Patent., 33 Edward I., m. 2.
† *Abbreviatio Rotulorum Originalium*, p. 142, and also the endorsement of the Inquisition.
‡ *Parliamentary Writs*, vol. i. p. 533.

ARCHIDIACONATUS WELLEN'.

DECANATUS DE FROME.

	Bathon' et Wellen' Temp'.	
Prior de Henton-Cartus'	£4 10 0	Chynton.*
Prior de Henton-Cartus'	12 0 0	Norton Comitis.†
Idem Prior	24 15 0	Henton.

Besides the foregoing, the only other document belonging to the reign of Edward I. is the confirmatory charter ‡ in A.D. 1293 of the right to the fairs on the two manors and of all the other liberties hitherto granted to the monks of Hinton. During the rule of his son they twice received gifts of lands; the first, in A.D. 1308, consisted of one messuage, one carucate of land, and 40s. rent, with the appurtenances, in Hinton and Norton from Stephen Waz; one messuage, twelve acres of land, with the appurtenances, in the same towns from Thomas le Cheseman, and one messuage, three acres of meadow, and a half virgate of

---

* Norton Comitis, Earl's Norton, is, of course, merely another name for Norton St. Philips, as having once belonged to the Earls of Salisbury.

† Chynton is perhaps a misreading for Chyuton, that is Chewton, spelt "Chyweton" in the *Feet of Fines*, 31 Henry III., No. 15, quoted earlier.

‡ Rot. Cart., 22 Edward I., Nos. 47 and 48.

land, with the appurtenances, likewise in the same towns, from John Ganard. The licence for them to accept this property and for the benefactors to present it was dated at Westminster, 6th May, "by the King himself at the instance of the Earl of Lincoln," doubtless the former friend of the Charterhouse.* The second gift † was really for the foundation of a chantry in the Priory Church. The Prior of Hinton having first paid a fine of 20s. to the king, the latter granted that John Sobbury and Roger de Cumpton might give and assign six acres of pasturage, twelve acres of wood, and 12d. rent, with the appurtenances, in Hinton to the Prior and convent of that place, to hold to themselves and their successors for ever, for the maintenance of a chaplain who was to perform the divine services daily in the Priory Church for the benefit of their souls and the souls of their ancestors, and of all the faithful dead; further, that John Sobbury and Roger de Cumpton might concede fifteen acres of land, one acre of meadow, seven acres of pasturage, also at Hinton, which John of Ifford and Cecilia his wife, and

* Rot. Patent., 2 Edward II., pt. 2, m. 9.
† Rot. Patent., 16 Edward II., m. 8, dated York, 30th December.

William his son, and Margery the sister of William, held for their lives, but which after the death of these four tenants ought to revert to John and Roger, to remain instead upon their death to the Prior and convent, in support of same chantry and for the benefit of all the said persons. This was in A.D. 1322; by A.D. 1339 the necessary deaths had taken place, and the monks procured the royal permission to enter upon the land.* Evidently by the middle of the reign of Edward II. the Hinton Carthusians were the chief landowners of their immediate neighbourhood, for in A.D. 1316 the Prior of Hinton, pursuant to a parliamentary writ, is returned as lord of the townships of Hinton Priors with the hamlet of Milford, and of Norton St. Philip with the hamlet of Yatwich, in the county of Somerset.†

A legacy of a small sum bequeathed at this period must not be passed over: one of the items in the codicil to the will of John Hugh, burgess of Southampton, runs thus:—" Item, I will that

---

* Rot. Patent., 13 Edward III., pt. 2, m. 17, dated Kenyngton, 17th October.
† *Parliamentary Writs*, vol. iii. p. 376, No. 12.

my jerkin and cape of motley be sold as best may be, and I leave of the money thence proceeding 2s. 6d. to the monks of Hinton for celebrating one trental for my soul, and the rest I leave to Agnes my wife." *

The Charterhouse, meantime, had found a higher patron in the king. His father had already granted to the Priors and brethren of Witham and Hinton to be quit throughout the kingdom for ever of all aids, tallages, contributions, and customs whatsoever; but Edward II., "out of his more ample grace," on the part of himself and of his heirs, exempted their temporal and spiritual goods from taxation, although those of other religious, by reason of any concession made to the sovereign by the commonalty or clergy of the realm, should be taxed.† But the letters patent were not much heeded by the royal ministers and officers of the revenue, for, in spite of them, they applied to the Carthusians for the payment of

---

* Madox, *Formulare Anglicanum*, No. DCCLXXIII. 426. The will belongs to A.D. 1325. A trental, often called "a month's mind," was the celebration of thirty masses for the soul of the deceased for a month after his death.

† Rot. Patent., 3 Edward II., m. 22, dated Westminster, 8th February A.D. 1309.

taxes, and "grievously" caused them to be distrained, and many a time "disquieted" them for contributions and tallages, until at last, twelve years after the exemption, the Prior and convent of both places complained in A.D. 1321 to the king, who issued more urgent commands to the treasurer and barons of the Exchequer to the same effect, with the further injunction to restore forthwith anything belonging to the monks that might have been seized to the royal use.* Whether the tax-gatherers ceased troubling them or not, the Carthusians were not likely to have much ready money if they followed their Rule, and thus in A.D. 1321, upon a recent Papal exaction of a tenth of the property of the English clergy, of which the Roman Pontiff conceded half to Edward III., the latter issued his permission† that the religious of Hinton might pay their share of the imposition, £71, by degrees, that is to say, ten marks at Michaelmas and ten marks at Easter every year until they should have disbursed the full sum. Later on, in the twelfth year of his reign, Edward

---

* L. T. R. Memoranda Rolls, 15 Edward II., Pasch. rot. m. 59.
† Rot. Patent., 5 Edward III., pt. 2, m. 26, dated at Lincoln, 21st of July.

III. altogether remitted to the Hinton community, for himself and his heirs, the payment of tenths or any other imposition levied from the clergy of England by any Pope or other authority of the Roman Church.* But the monks did not meet with the same leniency in matters of taxation from the king's servants as from the king himself. Perhaps not altogether with disinterested motives, the bailiffs, ministers, and men of diverse towns and places of the country "stupidly" refused their discharge from all the various kinds of burthens granted by Edward's predecessors, and to avoid transgressing the letter of the patents exempting the Charterhouse from payment of imposts, while going against the spirit of them, hit upon the expedient of levying the customs under new names from the Prior and convent and the conventual property. Once more the brethren appealed to the royal patron, with the consequence that he issued in A.D. 1345 a charter confirming the former exemptions, and forbidding

* Rot. Cart., 1 Henry V., pt. 1, No. 13, makes mention of this patent of Edward III., which was dated at Northampton, 20th July, and confirms it, amongst others.

any one to trouble them again by exactions, however much it might be thought proper to levy the usual taxes under new names.*

Some years later, the Hinton Carthusians were annoyed, for other reasons, by another class of men in the royal employ.† The Black Death had been the cause of difficulties at Witham; in like manner, the younger community did not escape from its influences. The plague had indeed carried off a large part of their servants and workmen; and other men, some of them tenants of the Charterhouse, who were wont to make the wool from the conventual sheep into the cloth for the monks' dresses, and to do other services for the brethren, after the passing of the Statute of Labourers, for fear of being sued, dared not any longer work for them, on account of the large salaries and rewards that their religious employers thought it just to give them. Some of them, according to the representations of the Prior to the king, had been brought

---

* Rot. Cart., 19 Edward III., No. 2, dated Westminster, 26th October.
† Rot. Cart., 1 Richard II., No. 20, supplies the materials for this paragraph, where it quotes two grants by Edward III. in A.D. 1355 and A.D. 1359.

before the justices of the county and roughly treated because they had remained in the service of the monks. As shown elsewhere,* workmen of all kinds were absolutely necessary to the maintenance of a Carthusian establishment, whose members might not personally go forth to seek the necessaries of the household. Edward fully understood this, and taking the "pitiable state" of the monks under these circumstances into consideration, granted that they might retain in their service whom they would of their tenants for whatsover wages were agreed on between the latter and themselves, and further that neither they nor those whom they employed were for the future to be sued for any fines or forfeitures due to the crown by reason of the Statute of Labourers. On the same occasion licence was also given for the lay-brethren and servants of Hinton Charterhouse to trade freely in the skins of the beasts of the convent tanned on the premises, or in other skins purposely bought and likewise tanned in their own tannery.

The Prior at that time or soon after was probably John Luscote, in whose life the pestilence

* Chapter iv., in the preceding account of Witham Charterhouse.

may be reckoned as an indirect factor. The story of the foundation of the third and most famous Charterhouse is well known — how the Black Death worked such havoc among the people of London that there was difficulty in burying their bodies; how Ralph Stratford, the Bishop, bought, enclosed, and consecrated for a burial-ground "No man's land," building a chapel on it for funereal services, to obviate the difficulty; how next year, following his example, Sir Walter Manny bought a plot of ground adjoining, and caused him to consecrate it for the same purpose, thus between them affording the resting-place within a twelvemonth for 15,000 dead; and how in A.D. 1371 the worthy knight founded in that place the Charterhouse of the Salutation of the Blessed Virgin Mary, as a completion of his pious and charitable act. The year before, no doubt in contemplation of Manny's foundation, which may then have been begun to be built,* a General Chapter of the

---

* Dugdale gives A.D. 1371 as the date of the foundation of the London Charterhouse. Father Doreau (*Henry VIII. et les Martyrs de la Chartreuse*) gives the year before, doubtless because the Chapter of A.D. 1370 appointed Luscote Rector there preliminary to his priorate.

Carthusian Order had met, and had constituted the English houses into a separate province for the first time, they having been hitherto visited by French Priors. At this Chapter John Luscote, who had been Prior of Hinton for some time, and had grown weary of the government of his brethren, was among those who sought the *misericordia* or discharge from office. His superiors granted his desire as regards Hinton, but while there his capacity for ruling and his aptitude for business had probably shown themselves, and he was appointed Visitor to the new English Province, and because naturally the Rule could not exist in its integrity in the embryo Charterhouse of London, being appointed its head, he received, as was usual in such cases, the title of Rector. However much Dom Luscote yearned for the seclusion of his own cell, he put his heart into his work, and looked after the completion of the building. As soon as the Charterhouse was finished he was installed as Prior; thereafter for nearly thirty years he watched over the welfare of the community, receiving his discharge at last not from an earthly superior, but from death in A.D. 1398.

Long afterwards, nearly a century, in fact, the London Carthusians supplied a Prior for Hinton, and once again, still later, a Prior of Hinton became head of the house in Smithfield; but for the present we must leave this new home of St. Bruno's English sons.

By the charter of the Countess of Salisbury, the Priors of Hinton received the advowsons both of the church of Hinton and of Norton; but apparently they afterwards lost them through some lapse, or parted with them for some reason or other. Perhaps the possession of the advowsons was more trouble than they were worth; at any rate, at Hinton there were quarrels between the convent and the Rector, which were likely enough to occur at Norton also. In A.D. 1262, Joceline, Bishop of Bath, had had to settle a controversy between Gilbert de Sarum, Rector of the church of Hinton, and the Prior and convent about three virgates of land, with their appurtenances, formerly belonging to the church demesne, and about the great and small tithes issuing from the demesne of the Charterhouse, and those issuing from twelve virgates of land in the villenage of the monks.

a century, in fact, ...
...ed a Prior for Hinton.
..., a Prior of Hinton be-
...se in Smithfield; but for
... ... leave this new home of
...nglish sons.
... charter of the Countess of Salisbury,
the ...rs of Hinton received the advowsons
...of the church of Hinton and of Norton;
but ... ...ly they afterwards lost them through
... ... with them for some reason
... ... possession of the advow-
... ...le than they were worth.
... Hinton there were quarrels
... ...vent and the Rector, which
... ...gh to occur at Norton also.
..., Joce... Bishop of Bath, had
a ... ...versy between Gilbert de
... church of Hinton, and the
...bout three virgates of land,
... ...es, formerly belonging to
... ...nd about the great and
sa... ...m the demesne of the
Chart- ... ... issuing from twelve
virga... ... villenage of the monks.

HINTON CHARTERHOUSE CHURCH, EXTERIOR.

By way of satisfaction to both parties, it was ordained that the Prior and convent should have the whole of the demesne land, with all its appurtenances, free of all tithes for ever; that they should hold in perpetual farm the church of Hinton, paying fifteen marks yearly to the Rector and his successors. Also they were to have the dwelling once attached to the rectory, on the condition that they first built and finished a house for the use of the rectors in a space near the church containing twenty perches in length and eight perches in breadth. The Rector and his successors, on the other hand, were to keep this house in repair at their own expense, and also the chancel, to supply all books, ornaments, and other necessaries for the services of the church, and sustain all burdens, ordinary and extraordinary, contingent to the rectory.* Not a hundred years after this settlement, the advowson of the church at Hinton was held by the Bishop of Bath and Wells as belong to the See. In May A.D. 1342, the king having previously licensed Ralph Shrewsbury, the then Bishop, to hand it over

---

* Harl. MS., 6965, ff. 104, 105.

to Master William de Littleton, Precentor of the Church of St. Andrews, Wells, to hold of him by the service appertaining, granted Littleton, being then in peaceful seizin of it, to concede it to the Prior and brethren of Hinton.* The next step for the monks to gain the advowson was to apply to the Bishop for his permission for the appropriation.† They put before him their poverty, how their hilly arable lands were very stony, how their water-mills brought them in slender profits, how certain heavy pensions they had to pay on some of their property exceeded its real value, and how their possession of the patronage of Hinton would help them. The episcopal consent was given in due form at Ilchester the 11th of December A.D. 1344. By it, however, a yearly pension of 6s. 8d. was reserved to the use of the cathedral of Wells, and another of 40d. to the Archdeacon of Wells, instead of the profits which, during a vacancy, would have gone to that See before the possession of the living by the monks.

* Rot. Patent., 16 Edward III., pt. 1, m. 16. The Church of St. Andrews is the Cathedral.
† Harl. MS., 6966, ff. 170-172. The church in the Register is called the *Ecclesia de Henton Monachorum*, either in consideration of their past or future ownership of the living.

At the same time, it was ordained that the Vicar, as the parish priest of Hinton had now become, in consequence of this appropriation of the living by an ecclesiastical corporation, should have all and every kind of the small tenths, with all dues to the altar from the crops, and all oblations belonging to the church, and £4 sterling yearly from the Prior and convent, and for fuel two waggons of wood or 3s. sterling, and one waggon of straw; that the religious, at their own expense, were to build for him a suitable house near the church, in a space as large as the former rectory, within six months, the expenses for the repairs of which house, as well as all ordinary and extraordinary burdens contingent to the living, except the tenths, he himself was to pay for the future;* and also that they were to rebuild the chancel, and find the necessary books and ornaments, which afterwards the Vicar must supply. As for the choice of a Vicar, the Precentor of Wells for the time being was to nominate two proper men, of whom the Prior and convent must elect one for the Bishop's approbation.

* The two pensions to the See of Wells were to be paid by the monks, not the Vicar.

HINTON CHARTERHOUSE CHURCH, INTERIOR.

repairs of
extraordi-
at the
and
find
ter-
choice
for the time
men, of whom
one for t[he]

See of Wells

On the same day, May 16th, A.D. 1347, that Edward III. licensed Master Littleton to give the advowson of Hinton to the Charterhouse, the king issued other letters patent about the church of Norton St. Philip to the effect that, whereas, by royal permission, Ralph, Bishop of Bath and Wells, had conceded the advowson to Walter Rodeney in exchange for eight marks rent, with appurtenances in Woky and Westbury, the said Walter, having full and peaceful seizin thereof, might assign it to the Carthusian Prior and brethren of Hinton, and that the latter might receive it, paying the same amount of rent to the Bishop.* For some reason this licence took no effect, and in October three years later, another was granted for the Bishop to give the advowson to the monks.† Yet even so late as A.D. 1377 these patents were not fully carried out. At that date, upon request of, and upon payment of one mark by, the Prior and convent of Hinton, the king gave a new licence to John, Bishop of Bath and Wells, to grant the advowson of Norton Church to John de la Mare of Nony (Nunney), Knight, John Panes of

---

* Rot. Patent., 16 Edward III., pt. 1, m. 15.
† Rot. Patent., 19 Edward III., pt. 2, m. 2.

MISSION FROM THE INTERIOR.

NORTON ST. PHILIP, EXTERIOR.

Wyk, John Bury, parson of Whatele (Whatley), and Robert Kayner, parson of Lullington, in exchange for the manor of Wodewyk and its appurtenances, so that these persons when once in possession might give the advowson to the Prior and brethren afterwards.* Probably after this the right of presentation to Norton St. Philip really belonged to Hinton Charterhouse;† but as for the manor of Wodewyk, the Bishop does not appear to have had seizin of it, since by a mortmain licence bearing date July 21st, A.D. 1392, we learn that John Panes of Wyk still had an interest in it,‡ though neither the priests nor the knight had retained theirs. The shares

* Rot. Patent., 51 Edward III., pt. 1, m. 30.
† In his *History of Somerset*, Collinson, bearing in mind that there was some connection between the Charterhouse and Norton St. Philip Church, says that in the south aisle of the latter "lies the effigy of one of the religious of Hinton Abbey, who is supposed to have rebuilt the church; her hands are uplifted in a suppliant posture and at her feet there is a dog." In this statement he makes two mistakes; the Charterhouse never was from first to last an abbey; the religious of Hinton were certainly not women. Moreover, this figure is not that of a woman at all; it is clad in a close-fitting and rather long surtout, with the hat or cap of a man, and is furnished with a knife or short dagger in its belt.
‡ Panes and the other owners of Wodewyk perhaps held it of the Bishop, as by Inquisition of 1 Henry V. the convent of Hinton held it of the then Bishop of Bath and Wells, as part of his manor of Hampton.

of the latter were then held by two other clergymen, Richard Cook and John Wodeford, who with Panes received permission by that instrument to transfer the manor and the advowson of its church to the Prior and convent of Hinton Charterhouse, and to their successors for ever.* The living itself, however, was not appropriated to the monastery, as was the case with that of Hinton, for there was still a Rector of Norton in A.D. 1442.†

Meantime the temporal possessions of the monks had been increasing. In return for prayers and daily masses offered up in the Priory Church for the king and for himself, both during life and after they should have "migrated from this light," John Talbot, on the grant of the usual licence,‡ gave them two messuages with appurtenances in Bristol, which he held of the

* Rot. Patent., 16 Richard II., pt. 1, m. 17.

† *Vide* the witnesses in Prior Richard's lease of that date. The value of the Church of Norton in A.D. 1291 was £10, and that of Hinton £9. 9s. 3½d. (*Taxatio P. Nicolai*).

‡ Rot. Patent., 33 Edward III., pt. ii. m. 17, dated Westminster 30th July. Talbot held the property in "free *burgage;*" *burgage* was the tenure of land or houses in a borough, equivalent to free socage in the country; *socage* was tenure of property on condition of fixed services, especially that of suit to the lord's court, or soken. (Bishop Stubbs: *Select Charters*.)

HINTON CHARTERHOUSE 257

Lady Philippa, queen of England, for the term of her life, and after her death of the Lord King and his heirs, in chief and in free burgage, for the rent of 3½d., their value being 16s. This was in A.D. 1359. Three years later, on Ascension Day, an inquisition * was taken at Norton St. Philip preparatory to the licence granted afterwards † for Giles, parson of the church of Norton St. Philip, to give two messuages, one carucate of land, 26s. 4d. rent, with the appurtenances, in Zatewick (Shapwick?) and Lullington; for John Talbot to give one messuage, twelve acres of land, and three rods of meadow, with the appurtenances, in Norton St. Philip; for William of Farlegh and Agnes his wife to give one messuage, fifty acres of land, and seven acres of meadow, with the appurtenances, in Whoweford (———?) and Stanrewyk (Standerwick); for Master Nicholas de Iford to give a messuage, four cottages, and one carucate of land with appurtenances in Freshford and Wodewyk; ‡ for

---

* Inquis. Post-mortem, 33 Edward III., No. 65 (2nd numbers).
† 28th June.
‡ In the patent he gives five messuages, four cottages, a mill, and two carucates of land in Freshford, Wodewyk, Overwestwode and Netherwestwode, Chyne and Anenchyne.

R

Walter de Rodeney * to give his manor of Pegelynch, and one carucate, two virgates of land, and twelve acres of meadow, with the appurtenances, in Wodebarwe (Woodbarrow), Ekewyk (East-Wick), and Whittokesmede (White Oxmead), to the Prior and convent of Hinton, to have and hold for ever in part satisfaction of the lands and tenements of their own or alien fees, which by a patent † of March 7th in the same year they were allowed to acquire to the amount of £20 yearly, and by another to the amount of £100 yearly, with the exception of tenements held of the king in chief. All this property was held of various persons for different services, some of it indeed being of the monks' own fee, and were altogether worth £23 *per annum*.‡ They did not enter into possession of it immediately; on November 20 A.D. 1374, other letters patent § were issued at their request, that the same tenements might be conceded to them by

---

* In the patent he and his wife Petronilla give three carucates and twelve acres of meadow.
† Rot. Patent., 36 Edward III., pt. 1, m. 24.
‡ Inquis. Post-mortem, 36 Edward III., pt. 2, No. 60 (2nd numbers), and Rot. Patent., 36 Edward III., pt. 2, m. 42.
§ Rot. Patent., 48 Edward III., pt. 2, m. 49.

NORTON ST. PHILIP, INTERIOR.

… … … ……
… … … … …
… … … … … chil-
… … … … of … …
… … … … … a knight's

… different … … marks of
… brothers … … …, received
… of Edward III., this was an
a yearly hogshead of wine, to be
… from the royal butler for the
… r ever, in return for which
… welfare of the kin…

*, 36 Edward III pt. 2, m. 20.

INTERIOR.

John de la Mare of Nunney, Knight, John Panes of Wyk, Henry of Ford, John of Bury, parson of the church of Whateley, William of Westbury, parson of the church of Rode, and Robert Kayner, parson of the church of Lullington, then holding them.

A portion of the remainder of the sum of £25, to which the purchase of lands by Hinton Charterhouse was limited, was supplied also in A.D. 1362 by Giles, the parson of Norton again, who conceded to the Prior and brethren two messuages and twenty acres of land and half an acre of meadow, with appurtenances, in Norton St. Philip, of the value of eight shillings *per annum*, that he had held of them by the service of a twentieth part of a knight's fee.*

A grace of a different nature the monks of Hinton, like their brothers at Witham, received during the reign of Edward III.; this was an allowance of a yearly hogshead of wine, to be received at Bristol from the royal butler for the time being yearly for ever, in return for which they were to pray for the welfare of the king,

* Rot. Patent., 36 Edward III., pt. 2, m. 20.

and of Queen Philippa, and of their children while living, and for their souls when dead, and the souls of the king's progenitors sometime kings of England.* This perpetual gift, made 1st November A.D. 1363, was renewed by each of the successors of Edward III. as regularly as the other grants by charters and letters patent were confirmed.

The next benefaction to Hinton Priory occurred under Henry IV. In A.D. 1407, John Wyking and Isabella Tanner, who, as we have seen, also favoured the Carthusians at Witham, assigned to the religious at Hinton, after the purchase of the king's licence for 100s., two tofts, thirty acres of ground, and four acres of wood with the appurtenances in Le Hope and Wells, in yearly value 26s. 8d., which they held for the service of 8½d. annual rent of John Soundenham and Agnes his wife, and of William Nyer and Johanna his wife, as part of their manor of Milton: the latter held the property of the Bishop of Bath and Wells as belonging to his Church of St. Andrews of Wells. The purpose of the donation was to supply a lamp

* Rot. Patent., 37 Edward III., pt. 2, m. 25.

to be burnt always at high mass before the high altar of the Priory Church.*

In the first year of the next reign the monks received land for the last time from private persons.† On that occasion Walter Hert, clerk, assigned to them a messuage, forty acres of land, six acres of meadow, with the appurtenances, in Freshford, Somerset, which he held by military service of themselves as of their manor of Wodewyk, which they held of Nicholas, Bishop of Bath and Wells, as of his manor of Hampton, for 12d. rent; also $4\frac{1}{2}$ acres of wood, and one acre of pasturage, with the appurtenances, in Westwood, Wiltshire, which he held of the Abbot of St. Swithin's, Winchester, for a yearly half-pound of cinnamon to be paid at Michaelmas. Walter Hert and another clerk, John atte Water, together conceded a messuage, eleven acres of land, one rod of meadow land, with the appurtenances, in Freshford, which was to revert to them after the deaths of William Kees of Freshford and Agnes his

* Inquis. ad quod Damnum, 8 Henry IV., No. 13; Rot. Patent, 9 Henry IV., pt. 1, m. 31, dated at Westminster, 4th October.

† Rot. Patent, 1 Henry V., pt. 4, m. 33; and Inquis. ad quod Damnum, 1 Henry V., Nos. 23, 24, and 25.

wife, and which being part of the same manor of Wodewyk, they held of the Prior and convent for 3s. yearly rent. All these messuages, lands, meadows, pastures, and woods were worth 23s. per annum.

Besides the foregoing there is one more record* concerning the property of Hinton Charterhouse, this being the confirmation by Henry VI. in A.D. 1442 of a lease granted by the Prior three years earlier. By his "indented charter," as the deed of conveyance is called in the king's letters patent, "Richard, late Prior of the house of the Place of God of the Carthusian Order," let to John Fortescue and Isabella his wife, and Margery, formerly the wife of John Jamys and the mother of Isabella, the whole messuage in Philip's Norton in which Margery then lived, with the adjacent yard and garden, so much as was enclosed by the stone wall, along with the whole messuage and its adjoining croft and garden, situated at the southern end of the town, and then occupied by John Boucher at the Prior's pleasure; and also the croft "called Bennett's croft,"

* Rot. Patent., 21 Henry VI., pt. 2, m. 33, dated at Westminster, 12th February.

and four acres of land in the field south of the said town, and four acres in the field to the north of it, according to the bounds of the said eight acres newly set, with all such gates, easements, and common of pastures as the conventual tenants had had hitherto at the Prior's will; to have and hold to themselves and to the heirs male of John Fortescue and Isabella lawfully begotten for ever for the yearly rent of 13s. 4d., to be paid in equal portions at Easter, the Nativity of St. John the Baptist, Michaelmas, and Christmas; and if John and Isabella died without male heirs, all the above tenements on the death of Margery were to return to the Prior and his successors. In testimony of which the Prior on his part set the convent seal, and John and Isabella and Margery on their part set theirs; the witnesses being John Long, clerk, Rector of Norton, John Wyste, Patrick Tarmonger, John Troyes, John Fyssher, and others, the deed was dated in the Chapterhouse of Hinton, Tuesday next after the Feast of St. Hilary, in the nineteenth year of Henry VI.

Notwithstanding all these donations and grants of liberties and privileges, somehow the monks had not grown rich, apparently not even possessing property quite sufficient for their support. But in A.D. 1445 they received a valuable addition to their income. Henry II. had allowed fifty marks yearly, half the amount being paid at Easter and half at Michaelmas, to the Grande Chartreuse, the Carthusian house over the sea in Savoy, as the patent of Henry VI. calls it. Some of the later kings granted the same allowance by their letters patent; but the parent community, taking into consideration the poverty of the Prior and convent of God's Place at Hinton, restored all these letters through their Proctor to the king to be cancelled, to the intent that the fifty marks should be paid yearly to the last-named house, instead of to themselves. Henry VI., then, on the 8th of November A.D. 1444, issued letters patent granting the same sum of fifty marks to the Prior and convent of Hinton, " existing on his patronage," and to their successors in frank-almoigne. That is, they were to receive £14 at Easter and Michaelmas in equal portions from the subsidy and alnage of cloths sold in the county of Wilts at the hands of the farmers and occupiers for the time being of the said subsidy and alnage, and £9. 6s. 8d. from the Prioress of Ambresbury from the issues of her own bailiwick in the said county, in equal portions at the same two terms, and the remaining £9 from William Zouch and his heirs from the farm of the Hundred of Calne in Wiltshire, and from a certain mill there, during the life of Sir Walter Hungerford, but after his death the whole sum was to be drawn from the subsidy and alnage of cloths sold in the county. For some reason the letters patent were not valid, and the Prior of Hinton had to get them cancelled and obtain new ones. The latter, issued for Prior William Marchall, the 19th July next year, granted the same amount in the following divisions:—£14 from the subsidy and alnage of cloths sold in Wiltshire and in "New Sarum," to be received from the farmers and occupiers at the time being of the subsidy, in equal portions at Michaelmas and Easter; £4. 6s. 8d. in equal portions at Michaelmas and Easter from the Sheriff of Wilts; and £15 from the fee-farm of the Hundred of Calne in Wilts, and from a certain water-mill, with its appurtenances, in Calne, at the hands of Sir William la Zouche of Totnes, and his heirs, during the life of Sir Walter Hungerford, and after his death the whole sum was to be received from the alnage of cloth sold in Wiltshire.* In the exceptions to the Act of Resumption of Henry VI.† in A.D. 1450, there is a special mention among those in favour of "the Priour and Convent of the house of the place of God of Henton" of the "L. marcs to be takyn yerly to theym and to zeir successours for evermore of the subsedie and awnage of sale clothes in the counte of Wiltes, and in the towne of Newe Salysbury," as also of the annual gifts of wine to them and to the other houses of the Order, "severally graunted" of the king's "almesse, to be takyn and had by ye hondes of our Boteler of England for the tyme beynge." Upon the accession of Edward IV., the monks had the annuity of fifty marks once more assured to them by new patents ‡ given at Westminster, July 20th, A.D. 1461, 13s. 4d. being paid into the treasury for the re-issue of the grant, which was made to the then Prior, Dom William Hatherlee. In the preamble we learn that their possessions had greatly fallen into decay, and that much of

---

* Rot. Patent., 24 Henry VI., pt. 1, m. 32.
† *Rolls of Parliament*, vol. v. pp. 186b, 304a.
‡ Rot. Patent., 1 Edward IV., pt. 4, m. 4.

the yearly value of their property, which they had been accustomed to receive, was now to a great extent lost to them. The reasons are not given; but a probable cause was the Wars of the Roses, which would affect even the Somerset Carthusians more or less directly in their temporal welfare by impoverishing their tenants, and in other ways in which war is always a drag on the prosperity of individuals.

Considering that at this period the minds of all ranks, from the highest to the lowest of the nation, must have been chiefly occupied by the continual strife between the Houses of Lancaster and York, it is not unnatural to find after this date no record of any endowment or emolument to the Charterhouse until years later, after peace had been long re-established, and very shortly before the peace of all English monks was disturbed for ever.

Meanwhile the life of the religious of Hinton generation after generation ran on in the grooves set for them of old by St. Bruno and the early Priors of the Grande Chartreuse, and, as at Witham, along an almost hidden way. Before the close of the century we have a glimpse of two of the monks. Of these, Dom Edmund Storer or Storan had made his profession in the London Charterhouse, and being appointed Prior there by a General Chapter of the Order in A.D. 1469, had ruled his brethren till A.D. 1477; he then retired to his own cell, but its solitude was subsequently interrupted by his holding the same office at Hinton for a time, though, when his death took place in A.D. 1503, he had been spending his last days once more in perfect seclusion and silence.*

A few years before him, perhaps while he was Prior there, Dom Stephen of Hinton must also have died. The story of this monk, just at the period where modern history is reckoned to begin, upon the eve of the Reformation seems almost an anachronism. If it has any real foundation, with its strange savouring of the mediæval legend, it does but show that life in the monastery, however varied by incidents, however different in individual cases, is spiritually the same, that upon certain kinds of minds in all ages it must produce the same effect. Dom Stephen at the end of the fifteenth century was an ecstatic visionary, like many a religious recluse in the

* Dom Lawrence Hendriks: *The London Charterhouse.*

centuries before him. A foreign Carthusian, Petrus Dorlandus, living about the same time, gives the account of his vision; the author's language is somewhat sensuous, and suggests a meeting between some mortal with a goddess in Greek or Roman mythology, rather than that of a holy man and a saint, and in it much of the simple quaintly pious tone of the earlier Christian legends is lacking; nevertheless his words show how, even amid the din of arms resounding through the England outside their monastery walls, it was still possible for these "servitors of the celestial court" to so abstract themselves from all secular thoughts as to be haunted by "rich ideals ... by day and night," * until these last became part of their very life. Stephen, the monk of Hinton, was in fact an illustration of the words Charles Kingsley puts in the mouth of Conrad, the monk of Marpurg in the thirteenth century :—

"Dost thou long
For some rich heart, as deep in love as weakness,
Whose wild simplicity sweet heaven-born instincts
Alone keep sane? . . . . .

---

* *The Saint's Tragedy*, act i. scene 2.

. . . . . .   Then go—
Entangled in the Magdalen's tresses lie;
Dream hours before her picture, till thy lips
Dare to approach her feet, and thou shalt start
To find the canvas warm with life, and matter
A moment transubstantiate to heaven." *

The following is a slightly abridged translation of what Dorlandus says in his Chronicle of the Carthusian Order † "of the admirable Stephen" and his devotion to the Blessed Mary Magdalene:—

We have seen a house in England near to the town of Hinton, in it flourished a certain monk of rare piety named Stephen; he thought, he slept, he dreamed of his well-beloved, and was transported in spirit to the top of a very beautiful mountain, where he saw a garden full of roses and violets, and diapered with all sorts of fair sweet-smelling flowers, as if it had been a paradise of delights. As he was proceeding to admire the place, he met a wondrously beautiful

---

* *The Saint's Tragedy*, act i. scene 2.
† Book V. chap. vi. The author in this part of his work is giving anecdotes of the different houses of the Order illustrative of the sanctity of the members. For the date of Dom Stephen's death (*ante* A.D. 1500) *vide* Add. MSS. Nos. 17092, 17085.

lady, from whose face streamed forth rays of sunlight, and from whose head the hair hung like golden glory. Breathing out an ambrosial odour, she shone in garments of silk and gold-wrought fabrics, that set forth the exceeding beauty of her heavenly figure; she accosted him with "God keep thee, my lover, Stephen!" but he, astonished at her splendour, threw himself at her feet, but recognising his saintly patroness, took courage to speak to her.

Stephen. God preserve thee also, O very sweet among women, O my light, O heart of my soul, O fire of my heart!

Magdalen. I know thy affection very well, Stephen; but what wouldst thou of me?

Stephen. That I may be like that Stephen who, after many sins, was taken back into favour. As thou hadst pity on him, kind lady, do as much for me, by effacing the anger and indignation of the Great Judge towards me, and restoring me to His grace.

Magdalen. I desire this with all my heart.

Stephen. Go, my very debonair one, to the throne of His grace, for thou wilt easily obtain what thou prayest in my behalf.

Magdalen. Thou speakest truly, for I and all the saints pray the Great God for the safety of the faithful.

Stephen. I doubt not this, my holy mother, but since I love thee above all the others, saving the Virgin Mother of God, honour me, I beseech thee, by being my special patroness.

Magdalen. Then thou deemest me the most able to help thee with the Lord?

Stephen. Yea, I find none fitter, save the Sacred Virgin.

Magdalen. What thinkest thou of the other saints?

Stephen. I think well of every one of them, but thou, my beloved, thou art my safety, my guardian, my mother, my patroness, my all!

Magdalen. Why hast thou chosen me for patroness, among so many saints?

Stephen. Because thou hast pierced my heart, and thy love has been praised by my Lord's own mouth, since He became the consoler of thy soul, thy Brother, thy Spouse, thy Friend.

Magdalen. Hast thou any other reason?

Stephen. We know from Holy Scripture thou wast a sinner, and having washed thy sins in thy tears, didst throw thyself at the feet of Jesus Christ, which emboldens a sinner like to me to ask thy favours.

Magdalen. Thy wisdom is praiseworthy, my Stephen; for it is I, it is I, I say, who have this pre-eminence above all the saints, of being the advocate of poor sinners; this I won when lamenting my wickedness at the feet of the Lord. But what wouldst thou have me do for thee?

Stephen. That as thou didst recall this sinful Stephen of Flanders * to thy grace, so thou wilt satisfy me with thy love.

Magdalen. Thy request is pleasant to me; be comforted then, and be strong, and thou shalt find grace in time and opportune help.

Stephen. O words sweeter than honey! O my most pious lady, since it has pleased thee to speak to the heart of thy servant, I would make some offering to thee, could I find aught worthy of thy deserts.

---

* In the notes to the book added by Theodorus Petreius, who also wrote much on the Carthusians, it is related that a certain Dominican was so encouraged by the pardon of Stephen of Flanders through the Magdalen's intercessions, that he remained in the habit of his Order, instead of giving it up, as at first inclined.

Magdalen. The promise of your heart I receive joyfully; if thou givest this I am content, for outward gifts are to be scorned.

Stephen. What inward gift am I to offer thee?

Magdalen. Rejoice heartily for my blessedness and in my privileges, be glad at having found an advocate in me, and of all this thou shalt receive this fruit, that, obtaining pardon and grace through my intercession, thou shalt therefore have with me eternal glory, joy, and rest.

Hardly had she uttered these words than the Magdalen disappeared from Stephen, who, upon coming to himself, was greatly comforted.

CHAPTER III

BROKEN PEACE

"Are your minds set upon righteousness, O ye congregation; and do ye judge the thing that is right, O ye sons of men?"—Ps. lviii. 1.

HE ecstasy of Dom Stephen brought him comfort. Perhaps, even then within the walls of Hinton Priory there was another visionary enthusiast to whom wild dreams brought much discomfort and sorrow. This monk, the Vicar of the Charterhouse, Dom Nicholas Hopkyns, is not discovered to us upon his knees before some saintly image of his fancy, but in the unhappy position of an unwilling witness against a friend. The innocent cause of the first disturbance of the peace of the convent, and an innocent factor in the death of that friend—the Duke of Buckingham—his memory years afterwards was evoked by Sir Thomas More in warning to Elizabeth Barton to keep

ENTRANCE TO THE TOWER OF HINTON PRIORY CHURCH ON THE WEST.

r
d
ures, I am
us upon
his fancy,
a unwilling
ent cause of
he convent,
in the death of that
of ingham—L nem
was ed by Sir
Elizabeth Barton t p

close her revelations of the future, especially "from worldly men, who receive poyson of everythynge."* For, like the Maid of Kent, along with great piety, Dom—or, to use the earlier form of the word—Dan Hopkyns thought himself in the possession of the fatal gift of prophecy, and it was this that brought him into near connection with the first tragedy of the reign of Henry VIII.

Buckingham, in rank, in wealth, by blood and connections, the first subject in the kingdom, had to confessor this Vicar of a poor country Charterhouse. As early as May 9th, A.D. 1508, there was some kind of intercourse between Buckingham and the Priory, for at that date he records a fee "to a servant of the Prior of the Charterhouse at Henton, called Hoxton;"† this perhaps was the time when his friendly relations with the community began. Hopkyns, if not in office, would be there at least as simple monk, and as such would appear before the great man along with the rest. Buckingham was not wholly free from superstition; the evident piety and earnestness of

* *Calendar of State Papers of Henry VIII.*, vol. vi. No. 1467, which is a letter from one of Cromwell's correspondents, and makes mention of that of More to Elizabeth Barton.

† *Calendars of State Papers*, vol. iii. pt. 1, No. 1285.

Dan Nicholas would be all the more enhanced, therefore, in his eyes by his reputed gift of prophecy, and he chose him from among his brethren to be his director. The mind of the monk was naturally much occupied with so important a spiritual son; moreover, he did not altogether approve of the doings of Henry; quite as well as the latter he knew Buckingham's proximity to the throne, and maybe, in hoping better things from his knowledge of the Duke's character, and perhaps from his own influence over him, his wish was father to the thought that he would soon become king, and he dreamed over this desire in his hours of silent meditation in his cell until it became to him not a probable but a positive reality of the near future. A dupe of his own imaginations, it was almost a matter of course that he should reveal his visions of things to come to the subject of them. If Buckingham actually believed his confessor's prophecy that he should be king, beyond listening to him he entered upon no treasonable course; so that the poor monk's speech or silence concerning the hidden matter of the succession had really little influence on his fate. Henry determined to endure no rival to the crown; as was the case with the Poles at a later crisis, the Duke might be in his way, and must therefore die. That "the Chartreux friar" had

> " . . . . fed him every minute
> With words of sovereignty,"
> (*Henry VIII.*, act i. sc. 2),

and that he had hearkened to him, was sufficient pretext for the judicial murder.

But besides the dangerous topic of his accession to the throne, the monk frequently discussed other matters with the Duke, more in keeping with the ordinary duties of a confessor. Thus he wrote to him the following undated letter,* which doubtless received a favourable answer, as the request conveyed in it was granted:—

Nicholas Hopkyns, Vicar of Hinton Charterhouse, to the Duke of Buckingham.

"My moste syngler and gracyouse lorde in god. I your poore and worthy oratour desyrose of yowre noble gracys prosperyte, whych owr lorde gode omnipotent of his infynizte mercye and goodnes continually conserve from all my-

---

* *State Papers of Henry VIII.*, vol. iii. pt. 1, No. 1277.

sauenter and parell as wele in this myserable worlde as yn the celastyall worlde to cum, whereas is perdurable ioy ineffable, attempte now to wryte on to your gracyouse hynes, trustynge and also bysechynge yowr noble grace to accepth my cheritable stryvynges as yowr noble grace has done here byfore. And whereas y now with fervent charryte am moved to be desyrouse of yowr noble gracys cheryte, I byseche your lordys grace to condescende on to my desyrouse petycyon, for as mych as hit is to the augmentynge of godes seruyce, and specyally as y do feyfully truste hit wylbe yn tyme cumynge to the grett comforte of our smalle cumpaney and place. there is now with vs a poore chylde of xiiii yere of age, whych is vertuously dysposyd, intendynge to be of owr hooly relygyon when allmighte god send tyme lawfull onto whom for the vertue and grace that y dayly se in hym y owe grette fauour, wherefore yf hit myght please yowr noble good-nes to doo yowr almesse vppon hym, fyndyng hym to his grammer tyl he be ful xxti yere, whych with owzte dowzte y truste veryly ye shall haue of hym a good and a vertuose relygyose man, and also a trew and truste bedman, and moreouer awfter my confydente felynge y beleue hit shalbe to yowr lordes grace as cherytable dede byfore allmighte god, and as wele accepth as euer was dede of cheryte by yowr noble gracys power donne, as knowyth Jhesus which be euer your protector, and at his moste pleasure be onse yowr lordes grace conductor onto owr poore place. Amen.

"Wryten at Charterhowse Henton,
    "By your symple and vnworthy oratour,"
        Dan Nychas Hopkyns, *Vycar*.

[Add.]:—1. *Illustrissimo in Christo Domino Domino Edwardo Duci Buckingame tradatur haec litera cum honore.*

[In another hand]:—2. *To the ryght honorable and his singular good lord my lord.*

[Endorsed]:—*Dan Nicholas Hopkyns of the Charterhows of Henton to the Duke of Buckingham.*

After the Field of the Cloth of Gold, the Duke, who had been present, though disapproving of Henry's amicable relations with the French king, had retired from court and occupied himself at home in innocent amusements and employments, amongst which was care for the well-being of this "poore chylde."

The boy, "little Francis," was then being brought up for a scholar at Oxford, under the charge of the Prior of St. John's of Jerusalem. In Buckingham's money accounts for A.D. 1520-1521 there are several references to him, his clothing and other necessaries, his amusements, and his illnesses, in which, from a sore throat to the "yellow jaundice for twenty-four days," he was by no means neglected;* thus:—For shaving his head, 1d.; a pair of gloves, 2d.; a pair of shoes, 6d.; a pair of hose, 10d.; a silk girdle, 6d.; for healing his head and neck, 12d.; for writing-paper, 1d.; pen and ink-horn, 2d.; for washing his petticoat sundry times, 3d.; mending and dry scouring his Kendal coat, 6d.; a shirt, 20d.; walking shoes, 8d.; "for a hen at shrovetide for Francis to sport himself with the childer, 7d.;" a bow, 6d.; shafts, 3d.; strings, shooting-glove, and brace, 3d.; and for a reward, 30s.; for attendance on him during the twenty-four days of jaundice, the expense was 4s. Not long after these outlays on himself the lad lost his protector.

While Buckingham was busying himself in the

* *Calendar of State Papers*, vol. iii. pt. 1, No. 1285 (5).

country with his ward, with making religious offerings to shrines, training horses and dogs, and attending to his garden and domestic affairs, the king was resolving his death. If the Duke never plotted treason, he was careless, and had dropped words not only against Wolsey, but against Henry; he was haughty also, and took no special trouble to retain the royal favour. To realise the heinousness of his conduct in these days of more than free speech is difficult, and pity only can be felt for him, and indignation alone is excited against the king, who, after examining the three witnesses—Dan Hopkyns, crazy with his hallucinations and with fear at the evil which these were now likely to cause, Knyvet the surveyor, and Delacourt the chaplain of the Duke, both prejudiced against him—without finding more traces of treachery in any dealings of his victim than words such as any might utter about a policy or ministers disapproved of by them, "is convinced that Buckingham will be found guilty and be condemned by the Lords," and "for the matter" is going to summon a Parliament.

These words, from a memorandum written on the back of a private letter by the secretary,

Pace,* are too suggestive of an intention to find the Duke guilty.

Buckingham was summoned to London on April 8th, A.D. 1521. The Vicar of the Hinton Charterhouse was sent for days previously; after his examination, along with Delacourt he was taken to the Tower to await the Duke's arrival. In the above-mentioned notes Pace added that Arthur Pole, the Duke's cousin, had "been expelled the court," and had asked Lord Leonard Grey to write about the imprisonment of Buckingham, and that Grey refused, but finally went with his request to the brethren at Hinton.† Partly in consequence no doubt of this application to the monks, but chiefly on account of their Vicar's connection with the accused, a careful search was ordered in the Charterhouse for any letters or information throwing light on the Duke's alleged treason. The proctor had been dispatched to London with Hopkyns apparently, and had been detained there for some reason, much to the inconvenience of the convent. The latter must have been extremely

* *Calendar of State Papers*, vol. iii. pt. 1, No. 1204.
† Ibid. "Ivit tandem ejusdem rogatu ad *H.* fratres" in the memoranda; Dr. Brewer interprets the "H" as Hinton.

uneasy just then with suspicions of treason resting on them, and in the letter* written by their Prior Henry on May 13th to the Earl of Worcester, giving a report of the inquiries ordered, which he appears to have been permitted to make himself, and requesting the return of "our brother proctor," they show not a little anxiety to wash their hands in future of so unlucky a prophet as Dan Hopkyns.

Henry, Prior of Hinton Charterhouse, to the Lord Chamberlain (the Earl of Worcester).

IHC.

"My dutye to yowre Right honorable grace with all hymble subjection and reverens premised certifying the same, that where I had a strayte commandment of yowre noble grace to make a diligent inquisicion of all letters prejudiciall to owre most noble and gracious sovereyn Lord the Kynges good Grace or any maner of thynge that shulde turne contrarie to his noble astate

---

* *State Papers of Henry VIII.*, vol. iii. pt. 1, No. 1276. Dan Hopkyns's letter recommending "the poore chylde" to Buckingham perhaps was enclosed in this, which would account for its second address to the Lord Chamberlain, written, moreover, in the same hand as that of Prior Henry's letter.

that oughte to be shewide by any of my brethern that it myghte cum to the true knowlege of yowre goodnes by writynge. Wherefore Lowly I beseche yowre grace to accept my poore diligens. Insomuch that I have chargid my brethern with the same commandment that I was chargid with nothynge to consile or to hyde that shulde turne to the Kynges displesure or hurte. Ande moreover all the letters that we may fynde or the effect of the same I have sende upp with this present writyng. And such of owre brethern as have harde and knowne more of Dan Nicolas Hopkyns woordes then I, I have causid them for my discharge and theyrs to write theyre maters with theyre owne hands and put thereto theyre namys for the true testification and for the Avoydans of the Kynges grace displesure. Therefore I umbely beseche yowre noble grace to make instans and labour for us that we may have no more besynes or troble abowghte this mater, but that he may bater the fawte that is fownde culpabill and nott we that are inculpabill. And that it myghte please the Kynges noble grace and his gracious concell that owre brother proctor may cum home to vs agayne and that owre brother Dan Nicolas Hopkyns maye be sent to sume other place of owre religion, there to be punisshed for his offenses as long as shall please the kynges noble grace. And in soe doynge ye shall bynde us the more to be the kynges continuall orators and yowrs to Allmyghty god for the good preservation of yowre moste noble and gracious Astates.

"Writen at the Charterhowse Henton the xiii daye of Maii

By the handes of yowre poore bedysman

HENR', *prior vnworthy*.

"And for a more large testification of the trowghthe of this my simpull writyng conteynyd in this letter above rehersid, I have causid all my brethern to subscribe theyre namys with theyre owne handes."

Dan Hwe Lakoq.
Dan Thomas Wellys.
Dan Robert Frey.
Dan Anton Ynglych.
Dan thomas Flatcher.
Dan Wyllyam Stokes.
Dan Nycholas lycchefeld.
Dan John Hartwell.

[ADD.]:—*To the right honorable, his singular good lord, my lord Chamberlayne.*

[ENDORSED]:—*The Prior of the Charterhows of Henton letters to my lord Chamberlayne.*

This letter from the Prior was written on the very day of Buckingham's trial. As for the Duke's connections with the Vicar of the Charterhouse, it was alleged against him * that on the 24th April A.D. 1512 he sent John Delacourt, then his chaplain, from Thornbury to Hinton Charterhouse to Nicholas Hopkyns, who pretended to a knowledge of future events, and who having made Delacourt swear secrecy, bade him inform Buckingham that he should have all, and that he should endeavour to obtain the love of the community,† and that this he knew by the grace of God; all which Delacourt reported the same day to the Duke, who ordered him to keep it secret. That upon Delacourt taking letters from the Duke in July, the monk repeated the message. That next year, on Henry's invasion of France, Buckingham again sent letters to Hopkyns desiring to know the event of the war, and whether James of Scotland would enter England; in the reply to which was prophesied the king's death without issue male of his body. That on the

---

* *Calendar of State Papers*, vol. iii. pt. 1, No. 1484 ii.
† The "commonalty," that is ; *vide Henry VIII.*, act i. scene 2, Thornbury, in Gloucestershire, was the Duke's seat.

16th April A.D. 1514, the Duke himself went to Hinton Priory and put various treasonable questions to Father Nicholas, who told him that he should be king of England; to which Buckingham answered that he would in that case be a good prince; that Father Nicholas said he knew it by revelation, and advised him to obtain the love of the community. That the Duke on this gave then and there to the Priory an annuity of £6 for a tun of wine, and £20 for the carriage of water to the convent, of which he "traiterously" paid down then and there £10, and at separate times to Father Nicholas £3; 40s.; 1 mark; and 6s. 8d. That on the 20th March A.D. 1518, the Duke visited Father Nicholas again, who again told him he should be king, and Buckingham told him he had done well to make Delacourt keep it secret under seal of confession, for if the king knew it he (Buckingham) should be altogether destroyed. That in the year before, the Duke had sent another chaplain, Gilbert, to Hinton to request Father Nicholas to send him word of anything he should hear about himself, to which the monk answered that before the Christmas following there should be a change, and Buckingham should have the rule of all England. The depositions of Knyvet, the cousin and surveyor of Buckingham, detailing the conversation "at the Rose within the parish of Saint Lawrence Poultney,"* repeat the same prophecies of Dan Hopkyns. As for the confessions of the latter himself, they supported the foregoing so far as he admitted that the Duke granted the monastery £6 a year for the wine and £20 for the conveyance of water, of which he paid £10. In Buckingham's accounts the Duke records payment† on 25th March A.D. 1519 of 100s. to his "ghostly father at Henton," which might also refer to the sums mentioned as given at divers times to the monk.

After the reading of the depositions, which had been taken unknown to himself before he had received the sudden orders to come up to London, at the Duke's own request the witnesses were produced, but he was neither allowed to cross-examine them nor to bring forth any evidence in his own favour. His denial, or rather different version, of some of the charges against him, is contained in the damaged faded frag-

---

* *Henry VIII.*, act i. scene 2.
† *Calendar of State Papers*, vol. iii. pt. 1, No. 1285.

T

ment in his handwriting among the Cotton MSS.,* entitled "Ans[wers made by me the Du]ke of Bukingham beffore Sir Thomas Lovell,† knyght, one of the Kynges moste honorable concell, towching such wordes as was between me and my gostly ffader callyd th[e] wycar-generall of Hynton." According to this paper, the summer before Henry went to Calais, Dan Hopkyns wrote to the Duke asking him to let him see him, or at least a trustworthy chaplain of his. "Whereupon," continues Buckingham, "bycause he had bene longe my goostly ffader, thynking that he coold have infformyd me off sum wrongs that I had doon, or elles in some materes off pyte, I wrote ... and schewed hym that I myght not cum to hym, and prayd hym to wryte it to me, or elles to schewe it to Master Delacourt." Instead of doing either, the Vicar preferred to wait till the Duke could come to him. A fitting opportunity occurred later, when Henry was departing for France, and on the occasion of the Duke's confessing before leaving England.

---

* Cotton. App. xlviii. f. 109.
† The Constable of the Tower.

When Father Nicholas heard that Buckingham was about to join the king, "he sayd [that he was very] glad thereoff: ffor . . . the Kynges grace [would] wyn gret honor ther, and that whe [should] all cum home save ageyne; but that the Scotts schuld make sum trobyl. And then he sayd iff the kyng off Scotts came [into this realm, he] schuld nott goo home ageyn; and I . . . axyd him wheder he had knowledge thereoff [by] prophesye; and he seyd, naye, but seyd to [me] Ex Deo habeo." Then entering upon the question of the king's children, he "sayd I pray God hys issue may co[ntinue] ffor I ffer gretly God ys not contentyd [that] he makyth not restytucion according to the Kyng [his father's will] ffor he herd no man speyk thereoff; and he charchyd me upon my allegiance towards hys Grace, to adwyse hys concell to make restitution." So far as this paper is preserved, there is not a vestige of treason in it, but it may have gone on to give some account of other interviews that might serve as a kind of confirmation of the reports of the witnesses. Lord Herbert in his History of Henry VIII., for instance, relates that at another time the Duke visited Hopkyns, with his son Lord Stafford and the Earl of Westmoreland, and that the Carthusian then said that some of Buckingham's blood should hereafter prove great men; and that afterwards Hopkyns again sent to the Duke to ask him for a contribution to defray the expenses of making a conduit for the Priory, according to his promise, because £10 formerly given to the monks by him had all been spent.* The Duke's answers, the only attempt at a defence that he could make, as is well known, weighed nothing with his judges. Sentence was passed on him, and on the 17th May he was executed.

"Yet the tragedy ended not so, for though George, Lord Abergavenny,† after a few months' imprisonment, was, through the king's favour, delivered, yet Hopkyns, after a serious repentance that he had been the author of so much mischief, died of grief." Where the last days of bitter sorrow ended for "that devil-monk,"‡

* Dr. Brewer's *Reign of Henry VIII.*, vol. i. p. 393, in the footnote. Recently water was observed springing out of the ground in the lawn at "Hinton Abbey," which upon examination was found to proceed from a leak in a conduit said to be that in question at the Duke's trial.
† The Duke's son-in-law. ‡ *Henry VIII.*, act ii. sc. 2.

as Shakespeare cruelly called him, whether at Hinton or some other Charterhouse, or in prison even, Lord Herbert,* who gives this information, does not say. Complete seclusion, utter obliteration of his personality from men's minds, must have been the broken-hearted prophet's desire; this thenceforth from all sides seems to have been accorded to him.

Meanwhile the little cloud like a man's hand had arisen out of the sea, the precursor of the storm that was to overwhelm English monkdom. From their seclusion the Carthusians of Hinton were watching it with anxious eyes as it came floating over from the Continent to their own land. While the king was winning his title of "Defender of the Faith," a servant of his own, who was also to employ his pen against the German reformer, had there put on the habit of the Order.

John Batmanson, sometime Prior of Hinton Charterhouse, must have immediately succeeded Prior Henry. Of his varied life, with its strange combination of the religious and secular, almost

* *Life and Reign of Henry VIII.*, p. 207.

nothing is known; of his writings, with one exception, only the titles are preserved. In September A.D. 1509 a commission was issued to Sir Robert Drury, Sir Marmaduke Constable, and Dr. John Batmanson, as ambassadors to Scotland to take the oath of James IV., in confirmation of the lately renewed treaty between him and Henry VIII., for deciding the mutual disputes of the two countries by arbitration and not by war. Somewhat later Batmanson and John Sanchare sent home a notarial attestation of the Scotch king's oath, which four years afterwards he broke in so treacherous a manner by entering England suddenly during the absence of his brother-in-law in France.* In A.D. 1509, also, Dr. Batmanson and his fore-mentioned colleagues were commissioners for the Marches of Scotland.† Later his name occurs in a rather unexpected connection for that of an ecclesiastic, although it was not unusual to employ the clergy in matters entirely foreign to their profession. In

---

* *Cal. State Papers*, vol. i. Nos. 467, 488, 548, 714.

† *Ibid.*, pt. 2. "The King's Book of Payments" records money due to them as such.

March A.D. 1514, and again the next year, a commission of *Oyer and terminer* for certain cases of piracy was issued to him in conjunction with the Earl of Surrey, the High Admiral, and Christopher Middylton, Bachelor of Law, commissary and deputy of the Earl.* From that date for a few years no more is heard of him until he appears in the field of religious controversy. It may then be presumed that about that time he entered Hinton Charterhouse as postulant, there to devote his learning in writing books of devotion and theology. One hears of no regrets for the active life that he had left, so different in all ways from that henceforth to be passed in the "solitude," but only that he was "assiduous in reading and in meditation of the Holy Scriptures," and, in fact, proved an exemplary monk. His literary productions were not for the exclusive use of the community.

In March A.D. 1519 the New Testament of Erasmus with his annotations had been republished at Basle. His bitterest enemy, Edward Lee, persuaded Father Batmanson to write against

* *Cal. State Papers*, vol. ii. pt. 1, No. 235.

the work. In May next year, Erasmus wrote to Fox, Bishop of Winchester, lamenting the controversy stirred up against him by Lee, the latter's share in it being likely to damage his own reputation. "He has," he continued, "suborned a Carthusian of London, John Batmanson by name, I think, a young man as appears by his writings, altogether ignorant, but vain-glorious to madness."* The great writer was perhaps piqued by the insignificant monk, of whom elsewhere there were higher opinions; that he knew nothing about him is clear, for, besides his doubtful language concerning him, he supposes him to belong to the Charterhouse in Smithfield,—a very natural mistake, as that was the only community of the Order with which the foreign Reformer was likely to be acquainted. The Carthusian's youth at that period was somewhat by-past also, if, as there seems little reason to doubt, he was indeed the same person as the above-mentioned commissioner. That he was unskilled in controversy is possible, but if he were so ignorant as Erasmus represented him, Lee would scarcely have singled him out to

* *Epistola*, lib. 12.

assist him. Soon after Dom Batmanson was writing against the errors of the more formidable German reformer. The king had begun to compose his book in support of the Pope in A.D. 1518; Luther's treatise *De Captivitate Babylonica* reaching England in April A.D. 1521, had caused him to hasten the completion of his work, that appeared a few months later. Luther's virulent answer, though calling forth no reply from Henry, who preferred to maintain a dignified silence, was not allowed to pass by some of his subjects. His vituperations against the English sovereign and those of the latter's then opinions challenged loyalty to the monarch and fidelity to Catholicism alike. Sir Thomas More stooped to enter the lists against him, employing language unhappily as coarse and violent as his own. Whether Father Batmanson followed in More's steps, or whether his book "Against certain Writings of Martin Luther" was a refutation of his errors generally rather than a personal attack on his opponent, is not discoverable from the title, which is all that is left of it. In A.D. 1523 Hinton Charterhouse received a new Prior [*]

[*] *Dictionary of National Biography.*

in this literary inmate of its walls, and was ruled by him for about seven years; during that time, or at any rate during that period of his life spent with his Somerset brethren, he also wrote the treatises or books entitled, *On the Song of Songs, On the Proverbs of Solomon, On the Words of the Gospel, " Missus est Angelus," On the Identity of the Magdalen in the Gospels, On the Child Jesus amidst the Doctors at Jerusalem*, and *On Contempt of the World*. Either during his office, or later on in the London Charterhouse, he drew up some instructions for novices, supposed to be contained in the Cotton MS. Nero A. iii. fol. 139, from which much information concerning the Order may be obtained.*

On becoming Prior of Hinton, Dom John Batmanson also became Assistant-Visitor of the English Province of Carthusians. In an age when monks generally had lost their early reputation for learning, he may have been esteemed, at least by his own Order, and in A.D. 1529, he was removed to rule the more important Charterhouse in Smithfield. Shortly before he left for London,

* *Vide* chap. ii. in the preceding account of Witham Charterhouse.

the Hinton community received the last addition to their wealth scarcely ten years before their dispersion. In the reign of Henry III. an Augustinian Priory of Canons had been founded in Wiltshire, at Longleat, on the site of which Sir John Thynne built the magnificent house still occupied by his descendant, the present Marquis of Bath. This Priory of St. Radegund of Longleat, or Langelete according to the earlier spelling, in A.D. 1529 was appropriated to Hinton Charterhouse; the mortmain licence* for Lawrence, Cardinal Bishop of Salisbury, and Peter Stantour, Esquire, "patron or founder of the house or priory," to assign it with all its lands, tenements, churches, advowsons, rents, reversions, services, and every right appertaining to John the Prior and the brethren of the House, the Place of God, of Hinton of the Carthusian Order, is dated June 10th of that year. The reason given for this appropriation is that the Priory, through the sloth and negligence of its inmates heretofore, was "almost destroyed," and so neglected as regards its internal affairs, that the canons had dwindled

* Rot. Patent., 21 Henry VIII., pt. m. 27, given in Rymer's *Fœdera*, tom. xiv. pp. 297-298.

to a number too small for the performance of divine worship after the ancient institutions of the house. As for the amount of property which the Hinton monks were thus allowed "to appropriate, incorporate, consolidate, annex and unite," this will appear in the valuation made by the King's orders of all the possessions of the Charterhouse. The only other mention of bequest or gift to the monastery during Dom Batmanson's rule was in A.D. 1528, when Sir William Compton left to it and to the Charterhouse of St. Anne's Coventry bequests for obits.*

Of Prior John's government of his brethren there is nothing to be said, except that he exercised care in admitting subjects, and was not anxious to carry out the principle to the full of killing the body in order to save the soul. A few months before he left Hinton, a religious of the London Charterhouse, "Dan Halnath" wrote from Axholme to Dom William Tynbygh, the then Prior of the Smithfield monastery, to ask to be allowed to return thither, or else to go to Sheen, in which house he had offered to submit to a two years' probation; he thought the Prior of

* *Calendar of State Papers*, vol. iv. pt. 2, No. 4442.

Sheen would have taken him, but was prevented by the Priors of Axholme and Hinton; but he did not explain the objections of the latter. Father Batmanson was perhaps then at Axholme in his capacity as Assistant-Visitor, and thus naturally interfered; his reasons were doubtless good, if, as is not unlikely, this man is Dan Hales, whose Christian name, Alnett, had such various spellings, and of whom we have given an account elsewhere.* The querulous tone of the letter seems also to point to the identity of the monk, and it scarcely seems probable that in one house there were two Carthusians with such similar names. If he might not go to Sheen, he added, he desired to be sent to Witham, where were several cells vacant, or, as a last resource, to Bevall, for "I love to be southward and I hate bondage,"—a statement, coming from one of his Order, showing traces of indiscipline of mind quite sufficient to prejudice against him the author of the instructions to novices.† Batmanson evidently felt that those

* Chapter v., in the account of Witham Charterhouse.
† *Calendar of State Papers*, vol. iv. pt. 3, No. 5191, is the abstract of this letter. The Prior of Sheen at that time was Dom John Jonbourne, the Provincial Visitor to whom Dom Batmanson was assistant.

who could or would not conform to the harsh rule had best put off the habit. While he was Prior in London, a member of that community, Dan John Norton, felt the solitary silence of his cell so oppressive that he almost became insane and threatened suicide. Father Batmanson wisely discharged him from the Order, after which he became "a canon in the West Country, and did very well."* A certain Andrew Bord, a monk in priest's orders, also belonging to the same convent, who never could "live solitary" and "intrusyd" in a close air could never have his health, if not discharged had a dispensation during his priorate to quit the "religion" along with two others for a time at least.†

Dom John Batmanson ended "the angelic life he led among men"‡ in the London Charterhouse on the 16th November A.D. 1531. Three years before him, Dom Thomas Spenser, a monk of Hinton, and likewise an author, had died in that Priory. He is said to have been the son of Leonard Spenser of Norwich. From his early

---

* *Calendar of State Papers*, vol. vi. No. 1046.
† Ibid., vol. ix, Nos. 11 and 239.
‡ Pits, *Relationes Historicæ de Rebus Anglicis*.

years being addicted to learning, and especially to piety, he became a Carthusian at Hinton, "whence for a time he receded to Oxford (as several of his Order did) to improve himself or to pass a course in theology." Upon returning to Hinton, he wrote a *Commentary on the Epistle of St. Paul to the Galatians*, and a *Trialogue between Thomas Bilney, Hugh Latimer, and William Repps*, neither of which works are extant in print or manuscript in England. The Trialogue, no doubt, set forth the arguments on the side of the New Learning, as represented by Bilney and Latimer, against those of the old school of Churchmen, of whom Repps (or Rugge) was a close adherent, who, at that time a monk, being afterwards promoted to the See of Norwich, was one of the bishops who opposed the Acts of Parliament of A.D. 1547–1550, allowing communion in both kinds to the laity and the marriage of priests, and confirming the new liturgy, and enforcing other points obnoxious to Roman Catholics. As for Spenser himself, "he gave up the ghost, after he had spent most of his time in the severities belonging to his Order," in A.D. 1529, and was buried in the monastery at

Hinton, "leaving behind him a most rare example of piety."*

Prior Batmanson and Dom Spenser had written in the cause of the Papacy; the very year of the former's death, A.D. 1531, the king, by extorting the acknowledgment of his supremacy from the clergy, began those series of acts—of which the suppresion of the monasteries was not the least important—which led to the English schism. Soon enough after that date, Hinton Charterhouse found itself fallen upon "evil days and evil tongues." The submission of the clergy, the passing of the first Act of Annates and of the Act of Appeals, and the marriage with Anne Boleyn, following in so swift a course, might well disquiet the minds of thinking men. How these events disturbed the peace of Edmund Horde, then Prior of Hinton, has been related already in the earlier part of this book, and how also one evil tongue among the Somersetshire brethren seemed to be doing his best to bring the heads of the two houses into discomfort. But how that

---

* *Wood's Athenæ Oxonienses*, edit. by Bliss, vol. i. p. 54. Spenser had made his profession in the Charterhouse in Vaucluse in the South of France.

HINTON CHARTERHOUSE

same Prior yielded his trust into the hands of the spoiler remains to be told.

Before we close this chapter we subjoin a list of the Priors of Hinton whose names have survived. As in the list of those of Witham, the date prefixed is not that of the commencement of their rule, but that at which they were known to be presiding over the community.

THE PRIORS OF HINTON.

A.D.
1246–49. Dom Robert.
1272–75. Dom Peter.
Before 1370. Dom John Luscote.
1403. Dom Thomas Wyne or Wynne.
1440. Dom Richard.
1445. Dom William Marchall.
1461. Dom William Hatherlee.
About 1477. Dom Edmund Storan or Storer.
1482. Dom Thomas Torburigenaci (?), died.
1513–21. Dom John.
1521. Dom Henry.
1523–29. Dom John Batmanson.
1529. Dom Edmund Horde, probably succeeded.

The following list of monks, with the dates of their deaths, is taken from Additional MSS. Nos. 17092 and 17085, mentioned in the first part of this book :—

A.D.
1472. Dom John Clerke, a professed monk of Hinton.
1473. Dom Richard Dixtan, a professed monk of Hinton.
1473. Dom William Marschell, made his profession in the House of Bethlehem at Sheen, and became Prior of the House of the Place of God, after he had been Vicar at Sheen.
1480. Dom John Spaldick, Vicar of the Place of God, priest.
1482. Dom Thomas Torburigenaci, late Prior of Hinton.
1482. Dom John de Nicca, Vicar of the Place of God, priest.
1483. Dom Thomas de Gatton, a professed monk of the Place of God, Hinton, priest.
1484. Dom Kicze, a professed monk of Hinton, priest.
Before 1500. B. Stephen.
1529. Dom Thomas Spenser, a professed monk of the Charterhouse of Vaucluse, in the province of Burgundy, before he went to Hinton.

Two or three of the surnames are difficult to recognise as English, especially since they do not appear in any form in the English records of the House. They are spelt here as in the MSS.

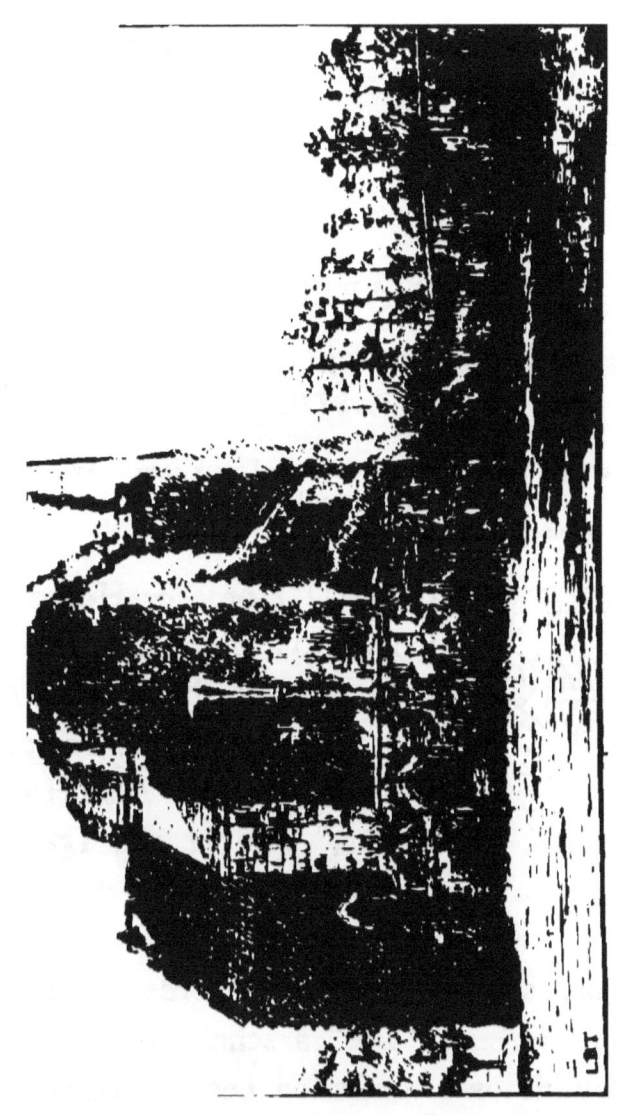

CHAPTER IV

THE SCATTERING OF THE SHEEP OF THE PASTURE

"Now they break down all the carved work thereof with axes and hammers ... and have defiled the dwelling-place of Thy Name, even unto the ground."—Ps. lxxiv. 7–8.

EDMUND Horde or Hoorde belonged to a Shropshire family of that name; for his brother, Alan Horde of the Middle Temple, is without doubt the "Alan Hoorde, gentleman, of London," who in A.D. 1541 was bound in a recognisance of £100 for the appearance before the Privy Council of a kinsman, John Hoorde, son of Richard Hoorde, esquire, of Shropshire, and "late" a scholar of Eton, who had by his own confession been concerned in a robbery committed there.* Dom Edmund in

---

* *Acts of the Privy Council*, vol. vii. ed. by Sir Harris Nicolas. Mr. Archbold in a note to p. 84 of *The Somerset Religious Houses*, states Alan Horde and Edmund to have been half-brothers, referring to *The Genealogist*, New Series, vol. ii. p. 46, and *Misc.*

EXTERIOR OF THE CARTHUSIAN CHAPTER-HOUSE, HINTON.

A.D. 1528 was the Procurator (or Proctor) of the London Charterhouse; as we hear of no intervening Prior, he must have succeeded Father Batmanson at Hinton in the next year. He too was esteemed for his learning and virtue among his brethren. At the last, he surrendered his Priory at the unjust demand of his temporal master; nevertheless, as regards the last quality attributed to him, the opinion of his fellows was hardly wrong. He ruled the House of God's Place in such a "day of trouble, of perplexity from the Lord of Hosts in the valley of vision and of breaking down of walls," as no monks had seen since heathendom had given place to Christendom, but he strove to rule it as one knowing fully the sacred trust committed to him. From the beginning to the end of his priorate, he tried conscientiously to serve God and honour the king, a task most difficult when the king was breaking with the holy traditions of the past, and

---

Geneal. et Herald., New Series, vol. iv. p. 138. Both these references supply only the descent of the Hordes from Alan the Bencher of the Middle Temple; in the first, the monk Edmund is not mentioned at all, and in the second named work, p. 140, only incidentally in the quotation of Alan's will, where he is distinctly spoken of as "my brother Dr. Horde."

when the mighty King of kings Himself was permitting this prince of the earth to guide the English Church out of the grasp of Rome by such strangely evil ways.

Henry's attitude as regards the Pope did not meet with Prior Horde's disapproval so much as those of his acts that were illegal both on the side of religion and on the side of justice. His dream, that the blabbing Dan Peter of Witham divulged to Lord Stourton, was characteristic of him; he sees the nobles of the realm drawing "the queen's grace that now is," Anne Boleyn, up to "a stage royal;" wishing to obey the king, he puts out his hand to help her up; his conscience suddenly pricks him that this is "in prejudice to the law of God and Holy Church." Does not the place upon the royal stage belong of right to the broken-hearted Katherine, who has been put away without a cause? "God defend that ever I should consent to so unjust and unlawful a deed!" he exclaims. So in actual life it cannot be doubted that he condemned the injustice of the divorce, while at the same time, after that step was irrevocable, he was quite as willing to swear to the Act of Succession as other upright men of the kingdom. Unlike some of the best and noblest of his fellow-subjects, the Oath to the Act did not present apparently any difficulty to him on account of the disavowal extracted especially from the clergy and monks of the authority of the Bishop of Rome in England. Probably the Prior's influence weighed sufficiently with the monks of Hinton to cause them to subscribe to the Oath without much coercion on the part of the royal commissioners, for the correspondence of the latter record no complaints against them. The "certeyn profession in wrytyng," mentioned in his own letter of September A.D. 1534 to the king, can hardly mean any other document than the subscription of the convent to the Act.

The Prior of Hinton Charterhouse to Henry VIII.

"Please it yowr maiestie to vnderstende that I have ben enstructyd by master Layton of yowr gracis pleasure concernyng the subscrybyng and sealyng of a certeyn profession in wrytyng, whych I have sent vnto yowr grace wyth as trew and feythfull hart and mynd as any yowr gracis subiect lyuyng, most humbly besechyng yowr grace appon my knees to accept the same. And thus have I don frely and frankly of very zele and feythfull harte, whych I ow yowr graciouse maiestie and the trueth, whych duryng my lyfe I woll sett forth fortifie and defend agaynst almen accordyng to my bounden duetie, and also dayly pray for yowr prosperus estate, from yowr poore howse the charterhowse at Henton the fyrst day of Septembre.

"By yowr humble subiect and Bedesman the Prior ther."

[ADD.]:—*To the Kynges maiestie.*
[ENDORSED]:—*The Priour of Henton to the kyng.*

All due allowance being made for the excessively humble language in which men of the lower ranks under the Tudors were accustomed to address those of more exalted position than themselves, there is an honest ring in the tone of Dom Horde's correspondence. Evidently he did not hide his opinions, yet he managed to retain the respect of the Order in England, and even of those members of it that were still surviving in the London Charterhouse, which was the very

* *State Papers of Henry VIII.*, vol. vii. No. 1127.

hot-bed of Romanism. As there was so much difficulty in shaking the fidelity of that community to the Pope, Cromwell sent John Whalley to take from them such books as those containing the statutes of Bruno and "suche lyke doctors." The agent, according to orders, perused the books in every cell, and reported to his chief the state of the inmates' minds. Three or four monks refused to forsake their opinions, and the rest trusted much in the Prior of Hinton, "Dr. Howrde," for whom it would be necessary to send. "Somone of thiese olde preachers," he added, "might preache unto them every weke, and I thinke they wille sone be at appoynt." A little more than a month later, on July 9th, A.D. 1535, Archbishop Lee wrote, amongst other matters, to suggest to Cromwell to employ Horde in a similar way. "As there are in every house some weak simple men of small learning and little discretion," the Prior of Mountgrace advised him "that Dr. Horde, a Prior of their religion, whom all the religious esteem for virtue and learning, should be sent to all the houses in the realm. They will give him more credence and rather apply their conscience to his judgment than to any other, although of greater learning, especially if some other good father be joined with him." In August, Lee wrote again, stating that the Prior of Mountgrace requested that Dr. Horde might be sent there to "allure" some of his simple brethren, for, because of their confidence in him, this would do more good than any learning or authority. It does not appear, however, that Cromwell thought it worth while to call for the services of the Prior of Hinton, of whom indeed it may well be doubted whether he would consent to the performance of so unfair a work as the coercion of the consciences of his brethren, for that was what that business of "alluring" them would probably amount to.*

Meanwhile, the Act of Annates having been passed and ratified by the king, the royal commissioners some time during the earlier part of this same year had been to Hinton to survey the property of the Charterhouse. In spite of their poverty of less than a century ago, the following particulars from the Valuation † will

* *Calendar of State Papers*, vol. viii. No. 778, and No. 1011, and vol. ix. No. 49.

† *Valor Ecclesiasticus*, vol. i. p. 156 *et seq.* The place names, as in the Witham valuation, have been left in the spelling of the original.

show that the monks, what with their profits from the alnage and their rents from the Longleate Priorial estates, by this time were drawing a by no means inconsiderable income, and somewhat indeed above that of the other Somerset Carthusians.

ARCHDEACONRY OF WELLS
DEANERY OF FROME

THE PRIORY OR CHARTERHOUSE OF HENTON

Declaration of the extent and yearly value as well of all possessions, Temporal as Spiritual, to the same Priory house and its other Benefices belonging within the Deanery in that place . . . . by the reverend Father in Christ and lord John the Bishop and the other Commissioners of the Lord King in the time of Edmund Horde, Prior of the same place.

HENTON

	£	s.	d.
Value in rents from the tenants free and customary, from the demesne land after xxijs. vjd. deducted for the fee of John Boneham, Esquire, the steward there. Perquisites of the court and other casualties there with the sale of wood and fines of land there	lxxij	xvij	ii

MUDFORD

	£	s.	d.
Value of rents of all tenants there .	—	cxv	—

LE FRARY

	£	s.	d.
Value of rents there yearly .	—	lxiij	—

HINTON CHARTERHOUSE 315

Iford

	£	s.	d.
Value of assized rents yearly besides the deduction of xxxvjs. a certain yearly payment to the Prior of St. Swithun's, Winchester	—	lxxj	vij

Norton

Value of rents of free and customary tenants from the demense land after xxs. deducted for the fee of the bailiff Morgan Philips. Perquisites of the court and other casualties there with lxs. profit from the fair, and fines of land there	lij	xix	iiij

Fresford

Value of assized rents yearly there.	iiij	xiij	iiij

Wodewik

Value of assized rents yearly there.	—	lxx	viij

Lutecom'ys Myll

Value of rents or farm of the mill.	—	lxx	—

Peggelege

Value of assized rents of all the tenants of Sheweston and of the farm of the manor or demesne land and Perquisites of the court and other casualties there yearly and fines of land there.	xxxv	xix	iij

Whittockysmede and Ettewyke

Value of assized rents there yearly.	iiij	xj	iiij

Hopp'

Value of assized rents there yearly.	—	xl	—

Lem'eslond

	£	s.	d.
Value of assized rents there yearly.	—	vj	—

Oldeford

Value of assized rents there yearly.	—	xiij	iiij

Greneworth with Whitnell

Value of rents of demesne land there remaining in the hands of the Prior to the use of the House, as shown by four lawful and honest men	xiij	vj	viij

Com' Wiltes

Returns from the ulnage of woollen cloths after xls. deducted in fee to Ambrose Dancy, bailiff or collector of the same	xxxj	vj	viii

Westwode

Value of assized rents there yearly.	—	xxxvij	viij

Rewleigh *juxta* Farlegh

Value of assized rents there yearly.	—	xiiij	—

Lungleate with Lullyngton and Bekyngton

Value of rents of free and customary tenants there yearly, and of the farm of the demesne lands after the deduction of iiis. iiiid. annual payment to the Abbot of Glastonbury for certain land of his there, xxvjs. viiid. for the fee of Walter Hungerford, knight, steward there, and xxs. fee of Thomas Tucker, bailiff there	xxj	xvj	viij
Perquisites of the court and other casualties there, and fines of land there			

HINTON CHARTERHOUSE

The sum of the whole value of the possessions was £262. 12s., but out of this amount there were certain pensions to be paid yearly.

	£	s.	d.
To the Cathedral Church of Wells	—	xj	viij
To the Archdeacon of Wells for the Church at Norton	—	iij	iiij
To the same for the Church at Hinton	—	ii	vi
To the Vicar of Norton	—	liij	iiij
To the Prior of Sheen, Rector of Chewton	—	xl	vi
To the Dean and Chapter of Salisbury	—	xx	—
To the Marquis of Dorset for land in Greneworth and Whitnell	—	xxviii	ij
To a certain chaplain for celebrating the divine services at Longleate	—	cxiii	iiii

And thus after all deductions there remained clearly £248. 19s. 2d.

The commissioners for taking the ecclesiastical survey had been appointed in January; on the 31st of that month, Cromwell also had his commission from Henry, as supreme head of the Church, for a general visitation of the monasteries. Early in the year, Prior Horde incurred the powerful secretary's displeasure, possibly in connection with either or both of these two matters; the tone of the letter written on March 17th suggests, however, another cause of the unfriendly attitude of the vicegerent. In his latter capacity being charged to reform the Church, Cromwell ordered the clergy everywhere to preach the new doctrine of the royal supremacy, and perhaps enjoined the Prior of Hinton to do so especially, as he was considered as a man of authority by the Order; to this the worthy monk was likely to show "vntowardness" sufficient to call for strong remonstrances, if not more, from the king's vicar-general. Upon reflection, after a certain interview with the latter at Sir Walter Hungerford's house, Dr. Horde appears to have thought it wiser to have an explanation. Of their correspondence on the subject the following letter is still extant in the Public Record Office :—

Prior Horde to Cromwell.[*]

"After moste humble recommendatyons with dwe reverence to yowr honour, this is to gife moste meke thankes to yowr maistershippe for yowr goodnes toward me, whiche I perceive by yowr gentle letters sende to me bi the wourshipfull fader of Shene, whiche wer to my excellent comforte, for bi them I did perceyve evidentlie

---

[*] *State Papers of Henry VIII.*, vol. viii. No. 402.

that thinge, whiche I ever supposid and trustid yn, that is that the olde benignite whiche I have fownde in yow towarde me in tymes paste is not vttrelie extincte, but that alle suche wordes as hit pleasid yowr maistershippe to speke to me at Sir Water Hungerforthe is place rose vpon my vntowardnes in certaine thinges whiche ye willed me to do concerning the kynges maiestie. And that in other maters I may yet have sum truste of sum sparke of yowr favowr, which is more to my comforte then I kan expresse bi writynge, for the whiche comforte if there were in me any qualites or hability to do you seruice I wolde be glad to do hit to the vttermoste of my little powr soo ferforth as shuld beseme a poore Religious preste to do to a man of yowr honour with myn assured dailie praier to the blessid trinite longe to preserve yowr maistreshippe in grace and honour. ffrom the Charterhowse of Henton the xviith daie of Marche

"By yowr assuryd bedsman the Prior ther."

[ADD.]:—*To the Right honorable his especyall good master the kinges secretarie.*

[ENDORSED]:—*The Prior of Henton.*

This letter, however, besides giving no promise to perform those "certain things concerning the king's majesty," expresses a very cautiously worded desire to serve the king's secretary, so that Cromwell may well have doubted as to whether he could employ the Prior's influence, and whether indeed it would not be best to keep his eye on him as an obstacle to his proceedings. At any rate, Andrew Boorde, the London Carthusian, of whom there was a mention in the last chapter, in writing to him in the following June from abroad to give notice of certain "synystrall" matters against Henry, adds a postscript begging him "to be good friend to the Prior of the Charterhouse (in Smithfield) and to Dr. Horde, the Prior of Hinton," of which the meaning must be that Cromwell was still inclined to frown on "the poor religious priest."* Between the sober conscientious Dom Edmund Horde and the restless rather light-hearted monk Andrew, who, according to some accounts, was the original "Merry-Andrew," there evidently existed a warm friendship, formed no doubt while the Prior of Hinton was the Proctor of the

* *Calendar of State Papers*, vol. viii. No. 901.

House of the Salutation in London. The following confused but characteristic letter to the latter is without date of any kind; but if it does not belong to the period of his life when he was hoping to be "dispensed with the religion" by Prior Batmanson, must belong to A.D. 1535 when Boorde ceased to be a monk altogether.

Andrew Boorde to the Prior of Hinton.

"Venerable father, perardyally I commend me vnto yow with thanks, &c. I desyre yow to pray for me and to pray all your conuent to pray for me, for much confydence I have in your prayers, an yff I wyst that master prior of London wold be good to me I wold se yow more soner. pray yow be ware off I am nott able to byd the rugorosyte off your relygyon, yff I myth be sufferyd to do what I myth with outt interrupcyon I can tell wat I had to do, for my hart is euer to your relygyon and I love ytt and all the persons ther as Jesus knowth who euer kepp yow.

"youres for euer A. BORD."

[ADD.]:—*To the ryght venerable father prior of Hynton be this byll deliueryd.**

---

* *State Papers of Henry VIII.*, vol. vii. No. 730.

Only a few months after Boorde's commendation of him to Cromwell, Prior Horde and his convent must have been interrupted by the agents for the monastic visitations, for they were in that part of Somerset in August.* Among the "Remembrances" of Cromwell this year, the words "Of the Charterhouse of Henton" occur, without any explanation; the correspondence of Layton and the other visitors do not mention it; but it is quite possible that, though they found nothing to report against it, he was already planning the downfall of the Priory.† But whatever the meaning of Cromwell's note, although Horde said he yet had "some trust of some spark" of his favour, it is clear that the "benignity" of the Vicar-General towards himself was not sufficient to cause him to be employed in the king's concerns; for an agent in Yorkshire, on the 13th July A.D. 1536, writing from Mountgrace Charterhouse, wrote: "If a commission were issued to Dr. Horde, one of their religion"—he had just mentioned the Prior and convent of Mountgrace—

---

* Witham was visited in August.
† *Calendar of State Papers*, vol. ix. No. 498; *cf.* Father Gasquet, *Henry VIII. and the English Monasteries*, vol. ii. p. 301.

"and one joined with him, there would be no stop, and all of that Order in the north parts will be inclinable. Your mastership cannot do a more charitable deed than to win such a simple sort with mercy."* We find no such commission issued, though it is possible that it was not Cromwell's fault, but owing to the Prior's own scruples.

Some weeks after the penning of this letter from Yorkshire there was the rising in Lincolnshire, followed by the more important rebellion known as the Pilgrimage of Grace, which led to the dissolution by attainder of many of the monasteries. By this time Henry and Cromwell were well versed in all sorts of artifices by which they could conform the minds of both the religious and the secular to their will. To enable the king to grasp all the booty to be derived from the possessions of the former, there remained only the business of forcing the monks to surrender their houses. The watch set by the royal commissioners for the suppression to deter any anticipation of their fate has been touched upon elsewhere. At Hinton, as at Witham during this period, the Prior was forced to accept a steward of his estates

* *Calendar of State Papers*, vol. xi. No. 75.

at Cromwell's nomination; in both cases Sir Walter, afterwards Lord, Hungerford by his own desire was appointed;* he, or another member of his family of the same name, was holding the same kind of office for the property of the Hinton Carthusians at Longleat, Lullington, and Beckington when the valuation of A.D. 1535 was taken. Not much later, either just before and in contemplation of the speedy suppresion of the Charterhouse, or just after the event, Cromwell received a similar application from a certain Sir Henry Longe, who had been at one time Sheriff of Wiltshire, "to be his grace's farmer to the house of Henton within the county of Somerset." "The king's visitors be in these parts now," he writes, "to suppress divers houses. I had never nothing of his grace, and I am much more charged now than ever I was; unless the king's grace be good and gracious unto me, I shall be fain to give over mine house and to get me into some corner."†

The "king's visitors" were Tregonwell and Petre. In January A.D. 1539, after dissolving the

---

* *Calendar of State Papers*, vol. xiii. pt. 2, App. 4.
† *R. O. Cromwell Correspondence*, xxiv. 5, quoted in *The Somerset Religious Houses*, by Mr. W. A. J. Archbold.

monastery at Keynsham, they went to Hinton, because it "lay best" in their way, as they wrote to Cromwell on the 26th. Immediately on their arrival they told the Prior the cause of their coming, and used such means and persuasions as they thought most meet to make him surrender. Horde's answer, they reported, in effect was, "that if the king's majesty would take his house, so it proceeded not of his voluntary surrender, he was contented to obey, but otherwise his conscience would not suffer him willingly to give over the same." But after further talk he desired to delay until the morning his final answer. The next day, however, although they used "the like diligence in persuading him" as they did before, "he declared himself to be of the same mind he was yesternight, or rather more stiff in the same." "In communication with the convent," the visitors continued, "we perceived them to be of the same mind the Prior was, and had much like answers of them as we had of the Prior (three excepted which were conformable). And amongst the rest one Nicholas Baland, monk there, being incidentally examined of the king's highness's title of supremacy, expressly denied the same, affirming the Bishop of Rome to be the vicar of Christ, and that he is and ought to be taken for supreme head of the Church." The Prior, no doubt alarmed at the consequences of this declaration both to Baland himself and to the rest of the community, excused the monk by showing them that he "hath been in times past and yet many times is lunatick." For once Cromwell's agents, perhaps really giving credit to the apology, restrained their usual severity, and "(not putting him in any fear) . . . let him remain" until their master's further pleasure should be known therein. Petre and Tregonwell had other business to dispatch, and as they would be back in the neighbourhood later, they determined to defer working further on the sturdy consciences of the community, lest, as they added, "the other Charterhouse, taking example by this, will not conform themself." *

Prior Horde's brother, Alan, the Bencher in the Middle Temple, also, either upon his own motion, or because called upon to do so by the king or Cromwell, counselled submission, with

* R. O. *Cromwell Correspondence*, xliii. 74, quoted in *The Somerset Religious Houses* in full and with the original spelling.

the result that Dom Edmund sent him the following answer:—

Prior Horde of Hinton to his Brother Alan.

JH̄US.

"In Owr Lord Jhesu shall be yowr Salutation. And where ye marvelle that I and my brotherne do nott freely and voluntarilie geve and surrendure upe owr Howse at the mocyone of the Kyns Commissionars, but stonde styffle (and as ye thynke) obstenatelye in owr opynion, trulye Brothere, I marvelle gretly that ye thynk soo; but, rather that ye wolde have thought us lyghte and hastye in gevyn upe that thynge which is not owrs to geve, but dedicate to Allmyghte Gode for service to be done to hys honoure contynuallye, with other many good dedds off charite whiche daylye be done in thys Howse to owr Christen neybors. And consyderyng ther is no cause gevyn by us why the Howse shall be putt downe, but that the service off Gode, religious conversacion of the bretherne, hospitalite, almes deddis, with all other owr duties be as well observyde in thys poore Howse as in eny relygious Howse in thys Realme or in Fraunce; whiche we have trustyde that the Kynges Grace wolde considere. But by cause that ye wrytte off the Kyngs hye displeasure and my Lorde Prevy Sealis, who ever hath byn my especialle goode Lorde, and I truste yett wyll be, I wyll endevere my selffe, as muche as I maye, to perswade my brotherne to a conformyte in thys matere; soo that the Kyng Hynes nor my sayd good Lorde shall have eny cause to be displeside with us; trustyng that my poor brotherne (which know not where to have them lyvynge) shall be charitable looke uppon. Thus owr Lord Jhesu preserve you in grace. Hent' x die ffebruarii.

"E. HORD.

"To hys brother Alen Horde in
 Medylle Tempulle, *dd.*" *

Ten days later the commissioners wrote from Exeter still asking Cromwell what they should do about Hinton, but the conclusion of the Prior's letter to his brother shows that, perceiv-

---

* Cott. MS. Cleop. E. iv. f. 270, printed in Ellis's *Original Letters*, 2nd Series, vol. ii. p. 130.

ing there was nothing to be got by resistance except the royal anger, leading probably to imprisonment or worse, he had resolved to "conform" himself and his brethren, as the best and wisest course for all alike, though sorely against his conscience. On the 31st of March, accordingly, in the presence of Tregonwell, he and the convent signed the deed of surrender in their chapter-house. The wording of the deed is exactly the same as that of Witham. The seal attached is rather broken; it is in brown wax, and represents the Transfiguration of our Lord. Christ Himself is standing, His whole figure surrounded with glory, which behind His head is concentrated into the form of a cross; above Him is the dove, and the prophets kneel on either side, and below them are the three disciples in an attitude of adoration. The very badly impressed legend round the broken margin, according to the *Monasticon*,* was SIGILLUM . DOMUS . LOCI . DEI . DE HINTON . ORD̃IS . CARTUSIẼSIS.

* Vol. vi. pt. 1, p. 4. Dugdale there says that the subject of the seal was "the intention of the foundress, who dedicated the Priory to the honour of the Blessed Virgin Mary, St. John the Baptist, and All Saints."

The signatures are in the margin :—

per me Edmund
    hord', *priorem*
per me Robertum Frey
p me Wilhelmū Coke
p me Thomā Fletcher
p me Wylhelmū Reynolds
per me Wilhelmū Burforde
per me Henricū Bowmā
per me Joħem Bagecross

per me Robertū Nelynge
per me Robertu Sauage
    Harry Gurnay
    Nycholes balland
p   Robert' Skameden
p me Thomā Helyer
per me Jacobū Marble
per me Hugonē Lakoq
per me Joħes Chābleyn

That the name of the reputed crazy monk Nicholas Balland—as he spelt it himself—should appear along with those of the other subscribers to the deed is not surprising, considering the terror under which the religious throughout England were then labouring. He had not changed his opinion concerning the Pope's supremacy during the weeks that had elapsed since the king's visitors were last at Hinton, but to refuse his signature meant the loss of his pension, and could go no way towards saving the Priory. A few months later, when the profane axes and hammers were already raised against the walls of his monastery, we have a glimpse of him haunting its neighbourhood like the ghost of its vanished holiness. "On the iiijth day of June last past," writes Sir Walter Hungerford to Cromwell, "came before me one John Clerke of Henton in the county of Somerset, weaver, and Roger Prygge, a Wiltshire fuller," who "showed me as they both were drinking in the house of one John Elyott in the town of Henton aforesaid, came into them one Sir Nicholas Balland, priest, late monk of Henton, and then he began, among other communications, to reason of the Bishop of Rome's authority, and said in hearing of them and others openly, in the house aforesaid, that he would not take the king's highness to be supreme head under God of the Church of England, but only the Pope of Rome, which should be taken and noted in his heart during his life, and so would he die in that opinion." The witnesses brought the monk to Hungerford, who kept him in his house until he should hear from Cromwell how to dispose of him otherwise; the said priest, he added, "hath byn dystracte out of hys mynd, and as yet is not much better."* Whether, upon this plea or not, Dom Balland received no extra ill-treatment on account of his utterances on the supremacy, he was granted a pension with the rest of the

* *State Papers of Henry VIII.*, vol. xiv. pt. 1, No. 1154.

community, which he was still taking when Cardinal Pole drew up his list. When the opportunity offered, he returned to the old conventual life, and on the accession of Elizabeth followed Prior Maurice Chauncy to the Continent.

The following list of monks, including the lay-brethren, with the annuity and gratuity of each, is taken from the patents in the Augmentation Office, Miscellaneous Book, No. 233, f. 242.

	Annuity.	Gratuity.
Prior Edmund Horde.	£44 0 0	£11 0 0
Robert Frie	6 13 4	0 33 4
William Cooke	6 13 4	0 33 4
Thomas Fletcher	6 13 4	0 33 4
William Reynolds	6 13 4	0 33 4
William Burford	6 13 4	0 33 4
Henry Bowman	6 13 4	0 33 4
John Bachecroste	8 0 0	0 40 0
Robert Nelynge	6 13 4	0 33 4
Robert Savage	6 13 4	0 33 4
Henry Corney [or Gurnay]	6 13 4	0 33 4
Nicholas Baland	6 13 4	0 33 4
Robert Scamanden	6 13 4	0 33 4
Thomas Helyer	6 13 4	0 33 4
Jacobus Marble	6 13 4	0 33 4
Hugh Laycocke	8 0 0	0 40 0
John Chambleyne	6 13 4	0 33 4
Robert Russell	0 40 0	0 10 0
Robert Legge	0 40 0	0 10 0

Robert Lightfote	£0 40 0	£0 10 0
William Robynson	0 40 0	0 10 0
William Howe	0 40 0	0 10 0
John Calert [or Skalerd]	0 26 8	0 6 8

The patents for the Hinton and Witham monks were drawn up in the same form. Stevens in his *Supplement to the Monasticon** has translated that for the Prior thus :—

"Henry the VIII., by the Grace of God, King of England and France, Defender of the Faith, Lord of Ireland and Supreme Head of the Church of England upon Earth; To all to whom these presents shall come Greeting. Whereas the late Monastery of Carthusians of Hinton is now dissolved, whereof Edmund Horde was Prior at the Time of the Dissolution, and long before. We being willing that a reasonable yearly pension or suitable promotion should be provided for the same Edward, for his better Exhibition, maintenance and support. Be it therefore known to you that We, in consideration of the premises, of our special grace, and of our certain knowledge, and mere proper motion, by the advice and consent of

* Vol. ii. p. 245.

the Chancellor and Council of the Court of Augmentations, of the revenues of our crown, have given and granted, and by these presents, do give and grant, to the same Edmund a certain annuity, or yearly pension of forty-four pounds sterling, to be had, enjoyed, and yearly received, the same forty-four pounds by the said Edmund and his assigns from the Feast of the Assumption of the Blessed Virgin Mary last past, to and for the term of the said Edmund's life, or till such time as the said Edmund shall by us be preferred to one or more ecclesiastical benefices, or other suitable promotion of the full value of forty-four pounds, or better, as by the hands of the Treasurer of the Revenues of the Augmentations of our Crown, for the time being, out of our Treasure, which shall chance to be in his hands of the said Revenues; as by the hands of the Receivers of the Profits and Revenues of the said late Monastery, for the time being out of the same profits and revenues, at the Feast of St. Michael the Archangel, and the Annunciation of the Blessed Virgin Mary, by equal portions. And further, of our more ample grace, we have given, and for the aforesaid consideration, do grant to the aforesaid Edmund Horde eleven pounds sterling, to be had by the same Edmund of our gift, to be paid by the hands of our Treasurer aforesaid, out of the Treasure aforesaid, or by the hands of the said Receiver out of the profits and revenues of the manors, lands, and tenements of the said late Monastery. There being no express mention made in these presents of the true yearly value, or of the certainty of the premises, or of any one of them, or of other gifts or grants by us made to the said Edmund before these times; or any statute, act, ordinance, proviso or restriction to the contrary had, made, ordained, or provided, or any other thing, cause, or matter whatsoever, in any wise notwithstanding. In testimony whereof, we have caused these our Letters Patents to be made. Witness, Richard Riche, Knight, at Westminster, the twenty-seventh day of April, in the thirty-first year of our Reign.

"DUKE ——

"*By the Chancellor and Council of the Court of Augmentations of the Revenues of the King's Crown, by virtue of the King's Warrant.*"

But besides the pensions to the monks, there were certain other annual payments that Henry VIII. disbursed in connection with the late priories of Hinton and Witham. Thus we find recorded 26s. 8d. paid to Thomas Brownynge, Vicar of Norton St. Philip, being part of the yearly sum of 53s. 4d. which the Prior and convent of Hinton had agreed that he should receive; and 106s. 8d. due to Richard Drynkwater, chaplain of Longleat, as the annual stipend granted to him by letters patents under the convent seal on the 10th May A.D. 1529; also 53s. 3d. and 36s. 8d. to William Horde and to Richard Pynnock respectively, both pensioners of Hinton Priory. To the chaplain, Richard of Cheddar, was paid £7. 10s., out of his salary of £10, as agreed on in A.D. 1382 by the Prior and convent of Witham at that date; and to Elisha, chaplain of Witham, 70s. towards the £7 due to him annually from the Prior and convent there. These payments were made the first year after the suppression.* The name of William Horde occurs among the disburse-

---

* Augmentation Office, Ministers' Accounts, 30-31 Henry VIII., No. 224.

ments of the Augmentation Office now and then in subsequent years, as does that of a certain William Davies, but of the others we lose sight. At the beginning of Mary's reign, according to Pole's pension-book, there were only three of the religious of Witham drawing their pensions; but from the other Somerset Charterhouse the monks Henry Bowman, Nicholas Ballande, Thomas Hellier, Robert Savage, Robert Frye, Robert Nelling, Thomas Howe, John Bachecroste were all receiving theirs.* Under the head of "Henton late Monastery," the same book records annuities to—

	s.	d.
Richard Pynnocke	36	8
Morgan Phillipes	36	8
Richard Pope	30	0
Thomas Stanter	36	8
William Davies	40	0
Hugh Shorte	20	0
William Horde of London	53	4
William Davyes	26	8

As for the fate of the monks, as usual, we can find little or nothing about them after the Suppression. Dom Balland went abroad and died in

* *The Somerset Religious Houses*, pp. 135-140, and p. 153.

A.D. 1578. Prior Edmund Horde may have found shelter among his own kindred; there is a mention of him in the will* of his brother, Alan Horde, then living at Ewall, in Surrey; the latter died on the 25th January A.D. 1553. Among the items in his testament is the bequest of, besides more substantial property, "plate which my brother Dr. Horde gave" him, to Edmund, his second son, and perhaps the monk's godson. It would be interesting to know whether this plate had belonged to Hinton Charterhouse, and whether the Prior had managed to secrete it, as other religious were accused of doing. Of the other monks not mentioned in the pension-book, those who had not died were perhaps abroad. During the temporary restoration of the Carthusians at Sheen under Queen Mary, a certain Dom Fletcher joined Chauncy's community, but it is unknown whether he was Father Thomas of Hinton or Father Robert of Mountgrace, as his Christian name is not mentioned in the narratives referring to that period; he died before the second dispersion of his brethren, but his memory

* *Miscellanea Genealogica et Heraldica*, New Series, vol. iv. p. 140.

lived on in the place long after their departure. In A.D. 1571, Sir Francis Englefield, who happened to be dining with Prior Chauncy while he and his monks were dwelling in St. Clare's Street, Bruges, related "that his tenants in England had written unto him that they dwelling near Sheen heard for nine nights together the monks that Father Chauncy had buried in Sheen to have sung service with lights in the church; and when they did of purpose set ladders to the church walls to see them in the church, suddenly they ceased. And they heard Father Fletcher's voice, which every one knew, above them all."*

This ghostly reminiscence of the English monks singing the old service in their own land, where the new order of things had brought and was bringing so many changes in ritual as well as in doctrine, is a fitting close to the history of the Carthusians of the Priory of God's Place.

As for the Charterhouse itself, barely two months passed before destruction came upon it on its being surrendered into the king's hands. Tregonwell, who took the surrender, sold a part of the monastery almost at once to Sir Walter

* *The London Charterhouse*, by Dom Hendriks.

Hungerford; but while the latter was absent for some reason or other in London, Sir Thomas Arundel, coming to survey the property, "sold and despoiled, and quite carried away a great part of the church and other superfluous buildings," which he had bought; not through ill-will apparently, but through a misunderstanding. Hungerford persuaded Cromwell to dispatch a letter to stay such proceedings any further. But when Sir Walter visited the Priory, he found it "so defaced and spoiled," he wrote again to Cromwell, "that it is and will be to my great loss, if you be not my good master to direct your letters unto him [Arundel] to make me recompense for the same." "He hath surveyed the demesnes of the monastery after such sorts and rates as no man will take them; as for me, I am not able to pay the rent, but if I shall pay it of my own lands." The king's liking for plunder was shared by his subjects. This same letter supplies information which may partly account for the scarcity of documents belonging to Hinton. "The last Prior's back-door of his cell has been broken up by one Harry Champneys of Orchardleigh, in Somerset, and others.

In the cell the king's grace's evidence lay, and what they have taken away of the evidence it is to me unknown. When I went to see after I reached home, the door of the evidence was broken and the evidences ruffled, and among them a confirmation and grant under one of the king's grace's noble progenitor's great seal, which seal was half broken off." Sir Walter ended by requesting Cromwell "to be a mean" for him to the king for the fee-farm for himself and his heirs of "the manors of Hinton and Philips Norton, with the appurtenances and the demesnes of the house of Hinton itself, Longleat, Buttonsmill, Greeneworth, and Iford, for as I perceive my old friend Sir Harry Long doth make friends to have it from me. My good Lord, all the said lands lyeth within a mile of my poor house of Farleigh, saving Greeneworth and Longleat, wherefore I beseech you to be good Lord unto me."*

Ultimately, however, Sir Walter Hungerford did not receive any more of the property of the

---

* *State Papers of Henry VIII.*, vol. xiv. pt. 1, No. 1154. Buttonsmill is presumably that which in the *Valor* as printed appears by the name of "Lutecom'ys Mill."

late monastery, though part of it came into his family some years later. The value of the estates of the Priory according to the Ministers of the Augmentation Office was as follows :—

County of Somerset.

	£	s.	d.
Henton and Midford—Rents of certain lands and tenements, &c.	17	18	0
Frayre—Assized rents	3	1	8
Charterhouse Henton — Farm of the Grange, &c.	51	8	6
Henton Priory—In the same place	7	11	8
Iford, Westwod, and Rawleigh, near Farleigh—Assized rents	7	17	8½
Norton St. Philips—Assized rents	27	12	8
Norton St. Philips—Farm of the house or Grange	22	4	4
Fresheford and Woodurke—Assized rents	9	10	0
Ladcombe—Farm	3	10	0
Puglege with Shewiscombe—Assized rents	8	3	1
Whittokesmede—Assized rents	4	11	2
Puglege—Farm of the manor	26	13	4
Puglege—Perquisites of the court	0	1	11
Hope—Assized rents	2	0	0
Lemondslonde—Rent of one tenement	0	6	0
Buckelande—Rents, &c.	0	4	0
Grenewerit with Whitnell—Farm of the manor	10	0	0

Wiltes and Somerset.

	£	s.	d.
Returns from the alnage	33	6	8
Lullyngton, Bekyngton, and Longlete—Rents of the free tenants	0	4	6

	£	s.	d.
Lullyngton, &c.—Assized rents	7	7	10
Bekyngton and elsewhere—Assized rents	7	13	0
Lullyngton—Farm of the manor	2	13	4
Lullyngton—Farm of the rectory	1	0	0

County of Wilts.

	£	s.	d.
Longlete—Farm of the demese lands	2	19	0*

The site of the Charterhouse was granted in A.D. 1546 to John Bartlett, *alias* Sancock, and Robert Bartlett, and the other estates from the 31st to the 38th year of Henry VIII. to various other persons. The monastic buildings, as at Witham, had small chance of a long existence. The first attack on them by Sir Thomas Arundel was followed by the stripping of the lead from the roofs of the church, cloisters, bell-tower, and other erections of the late Priory. Richard Walker, the plumber, received 40s. for melting down the whole amount of 33 pigs of lead procured thus at Hinton, weighing 16 fodders, the rate being 2s. 6d. the fodder.† The same roll of accounts of the Ministers of the Augmentation Office that gives this information

---

* Dugdale, *Mon. Angelic.*, vol. vi. pt. 1, p. 5. Abstract of Roll, 31 Henry VIII., in the Augmentation Office.

† A. O. Minister's Accounts, 30–31 Henry VIII., No. 224.

makes no mention of the sale of bells or other materials at Hinton, though it records the profits arising in this way from Witham and the other Somerset monasteries, which seems to be from some oversight.

The destruction of the roof would soon bring about the decay of the whole fabric, but rough hands were early laid on it. The Bartletts sold it to Matthew Colthurst, whose heir in Elizabeth's reign in his turn alienated it to a member of the Hungerford family; and in later times it passed to owners of yet another name. One of the first masters of the place used the monastic buildings as a quarry to erect a fine house for himself in the handsome style of the last half of the sixteenth century; it is still standing, a conspicuous gabled dwelling on the road from Frome to Bath, and bears a reminiscence of its origin in its erroneous name of *Hinton Abbey*. The ground about the house is uneven with stones and traces of the old buildings under the grass, and indeed has been known to give way with the crumbling of the ruins buried beneath it. So early as the date of Leland's *Itinerary*, to judge by his language, the greater part of the former Priory was non-extant. "From Farley," he wrote, "I ridde a mile of by woddy ground to a graung great and well builded, that longed to Henton Priory of Chartusians. This Priory stondith not far of from this graung on the brow of an hille abouth a quarter of a mile from the farther Ripe of Frome, and not far from this place Frome goith ynto Avon. I rodde by the space of a mile or more by woddes and mountaine grounde to a place where I saw a rude stone waulle hard on the right hond by a great lengthe as it had beene a park waulle. One sins told me that Henton Priory first stode there; if it be so, it is the lordship of Hethorpe that was given to them for their first habitation." * This "graung" was presumably the granary, that was still in existence in A.D. 1791, according to Collinson, as well as what he calls "the chapel and ante-chapel and the charnel-house."† A charnel-house had no place in a Carthusian establishment, and there is nothing now among

* Leland, *Itinerary*, vol. ii. p. 34.
† *History of Somerset*, vol. iii. p. 366. The ante-chapel is the part of a chapel that lies between the western wall and the choir-screen, corresponding in a cruciform church to the transept. *Vide* Parker's *Glossary of Architecture*.

the remains which could suggest such a building. His chapel and ante-chapel are what tradition, without doubt correctly, calls the chapter-house. The latter occupies the ground-floor of a large tower adjoining the site of the Church,* that of the monks, to judge by the length of the south wall, of which the direction eastwards may still be traced in the grass that grows less richly in the thinner soil that hides the stones of its foundation. Entrance to the chapter-house was on the west by a door now reached from the open, but originally reached probably from a cloister or another part of the Church, as there are marks of some contiguous building on the wall above it. On the right of this door there is an entrance to this covered space in front of it, from presumably the south cloister, the signs of this again being visible on the outside of the south wall of the tower. The chapter-house, or more properly in this case chapter-room,

* Hinton Charterhouse was founded years after that of Witham, and it may be that here the earlier rule of an entirely separate church for the lay-brethren was discontinued, and, as in the London Charterhouse, they may have had merely a portion of the one church especially devoted to them. The modern Carthusian church is thus divided into the monks' choir and the lay-brothers' choir, which are partitioned off from one another.

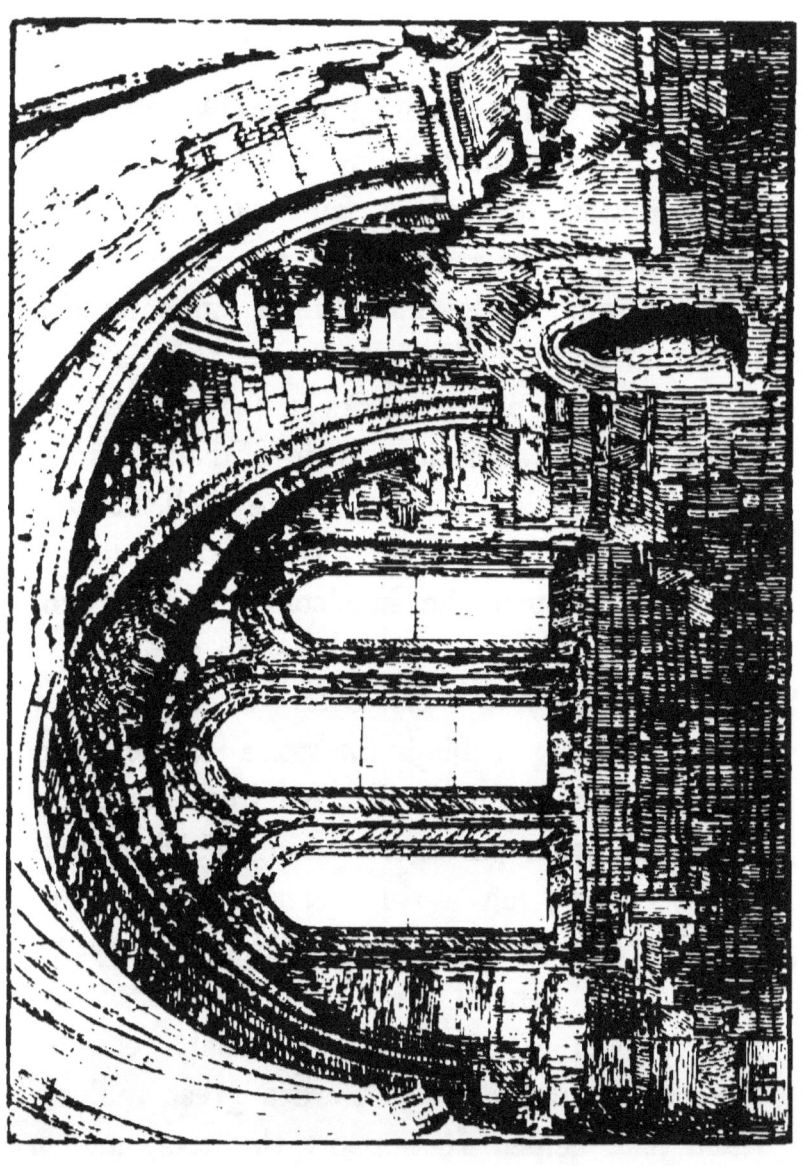

HINTON CHARTERHOUSE

is a chamber stone-vaulted much like Witham Church, being a short oblong in shape; the light was admitted through a fair-sized window of three lights on the east, and by two other longer and narrower windows of single lights on the north and south. The place of the altar is even now discernible by the marks in the wall left on the removal of its reredos. As in Witham Church, there is a double piscina, with the shelf, according to some authorities, used as a credence-table; but this is much the handsomer of the two. Opposite in the north wall there is a recess, probably an ambry, the places for the hinges and fastenings being visible in the stone. Close to the entrance a door on the left led from the chapter-house into a passage, entering which, immediately on the left again was a wider door to the Church, now partially blocked, as may be seen in the general view of the ruins of the Priory given in this book. The only relics of the interior of the Church are a great vaulting shaft that helped to support the roof, and a recess, perhaps another ambry or a sedilia, in its south wall. The passage just mentioned now ends in an outer doorway; close to it are the

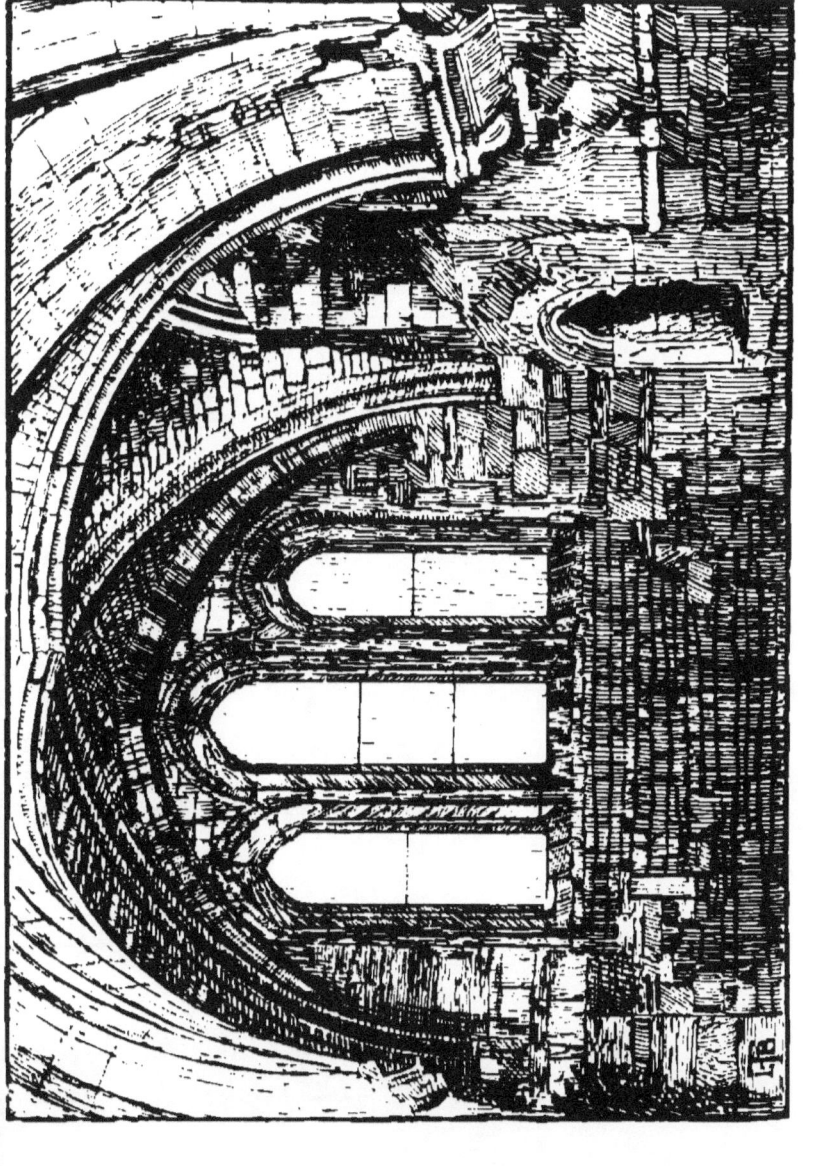

INTERIOR OF THE CARTHUSIAN CHAPTER-HOUSE, HINTON.

　　　　　　　　ts
　　　　　　　　be
　　　　　　　.. the
　　　　　　　ries of
　　　　　　vaulting
　　　　　', and a
　　　　　.lin, in
　,　　　　d now
to it ... the

stairs of the tower. On the first floor is a room also vaulted with stone, lighted by three windows once fitted with glass; in the recess of each is a seat or a shelf; the flooring has disappeared and one treads on the uncovered vaulting of the chapter-house underneath; possibly this, as is said, was the monastic library, though its position makes that doubtful. Beyond it, exactly over the east end of the chapter-house, is a loft fitted for a dove or pigeon house There is also on this floor a smaller room lighted by two little windows that have been merely glazed. The highest storey consists of a rather ruinous landing and a spacious loft, also arranged for doves.

The only other extant building is some yards to the west of the tower: it is partially shut off from the Church by a substantial wall entered by an arched gateway; it consists of a ground-floor and upper storey. The chamber below is the reputed refectory, but it is ill-lighted, and the stone-vaulted roof is supported in the centre by a row of three columns, which would leave little clear space for a table and the requisites of a dining-room. At one end of it there is an entrance to a smaller room with a large fireplace; from this there was egress to a covered way, which, no longer existing, used to lead to the Church, says the tradition, and which may have been part of one of the cloisters. From the ground-floor of this building an outside flight of steps led to the upper room, guessed to have been originally a dormitory.

It was a fitting imagination of the inhabitants of Hinton Abbey that led them to hear the singing voices of the departed monks about the house as if their spirits had followed the consecrated stones of their church when these were carried away to build it. The site of their own house, where they offered up so continually their praise and prayer, is covered with grass, and the beasts of the field trample over the once holy ground. The neighbouring chapter-house—and among the Carthusians this is a chapel—though yet almost intact, went through a desecration as bad or worse. When the Blessed Lord emptied Himself of His glory and first appeared before the eyes of those whom He came to redeem, it pleased Him to be born in a stable. After the storm of the Reformation men grew forgetful of what was due to that glory, which He assumed again on His Ascension, and of what was owing to that Divine humility, and the place once dedicated to His honour was turned into a stable. Though still occupying it for secular purposes, the present owner is more reverent in his use of it, and, except for the pitched and drained floor, the signs of the older abuse have been removed. Little light falls through the perforated zinc with which the spaces of the windows have been stopped; after the bright daylight without, the eye, attracted by the groined vaulting and the carved piscina, is impatient of the gloom to which it must become accustomed before it can follow the details of the architecture; but the gaze soon takes in the secular objects there, and the floor that horses or cattle trod, and the darkness only seems in keeping within the walls of the last remnant of the Place of God, where the light and warmth of religious devotion have long since been extinguished.

IN HINTON CHAPEL HOUSE.

T A THULAN

 ' to that glory, which
 His Ascension, and of
 Divine humility, and
 ted to His honour was
 Though still occupying
 the present owner is
 House of it, and, except for
 d and floor, the signs of the
 abuse have been removed. Little light
 through the perforated zinc with which the
 windows have been stopped; after
 light without, the eye, attracted
 vaulting and the carved piscina,
 the gloom to which it must be
 accustomed before it can follow the details
the architecture; but the gaze soon takes in
the secular objects there, and the floor that horses
or red, and the darkness only seems to
 the walls of the last remnant of
 , where the light and warmth
 have long since been extinguished.

PISCINA IN HINTON CHAPTER-HOUSE.

CHAPTER V

A PLEA FOR THE CARTHUSIANS

> "Sæculi sordes fugit et prophanat
> Et suam vitam, nihil ista curat,
> Dulce nil Christo sine, nil amœnam,
>   Cartusiano.
> Veste procedit cito nuptuali,
> Obviam sponso manibus intentes,
> Lampades gestans, oleo decoras,
>   Cartusianus." *

THE history of the Charterhouses of Witham and of Hinton is typical of that of all the English monasteries of the Order. The establishment of the convent, attended by more or less interesting incidents, is in every case followed by the same gradual increase

---

* From a poem in praise of the Carthusian Order by Sebastian Brant of Strasbourg. It is printed in the *Chronicle of the Sacred Carthusian Order* by Peter Dorlandus. For the sake of some of our readers we give the following free translation of these two verses:

"He flees the impurities of the secular world, and does violence to his own life: he takes no care for this; nothing is sweet without Christ, nothing pleasant to the Carthusian.

"In the wedding-garment the Carthusian quickly goes forth to meet the Bridegroom, with outstretched hands bearing the lamps properly fed with oil."

of property, the same uneventful life down to the end of the Middle Ages, the same lack among the monks of men eminent for their learning or writings or as theologians, or for extraordinary sanctity (though for individuals to be in advance of the rest in saintliness, which was almost an inherent quality of the Order, it might be difficult); then at last come the days of persecution and destruction, which, as regards the Carthusians, was but the sweeping away of special bodies of "bedesmen." This being so, it may not unnaturally be asked, of what use were these monks? That question, put in the present practical and material times, means, what tangible visible good did they work for their fellow-men? how did they benefit either their contemporaries or posterity? Granted that they contributed almost nothing to the intellectual improvement of their countrymen, at least they did contribute somewhat to the bodily welfare of the latter. The statutes of the Order commanded them to give their superfluous goods to the poor, and Witham and some other Charterhouses that were well off could easily have afforded to do "many good dedds off charite" to their "Christen neybors," which Prior Horde of Hinton considered among the duties of the Carthusians. Monasteries, it has been often said, and even reproached against them, as if it were their only benefit to mankind, were the asylums and harbours of refuge to the broken-hearted and those who had felt too much the world's buffetings. But the Charterhouses could very rarely have been put to such a use; life within their walls was too stern to be a very consolatory form of religion. To one sorely smitten with sorrow, the solitariness of the cell, if endurable at all, afforded such ample opportunity for brooding over his griefs, that it could not be long in making him literally a prey to them. To live the Rule perfectly, as St. Hugh was reminded before he entered La Grande Chartreuse, the Carthusians must be as hard as the rocks in their first solitude. By this it was not meant that he should become inhuman. The good Bishop of Lincoln manifested in his own person how it was possible morally to kill self, and yet to attain to an almost perfect standard of Christian charity to others. He who would follow St. Bruno must be able to use his full energies; not only his physical, but his mental powers would be more or less severely tried by the continuous efforts at prayer, and, to use the language of the monks, by the spiritual warfare against the flesh; and "grief is proud and makes his owner stoop," by incapacitating him in mind as well as weakening him in body sometimes, and taking from him, for a time at least, the capability of application to any work. But to men of another stamp these monasteries might be salutary asylums. When our ancestors felt keenly on any topic, they sometimes expressed their feelings in strong actions, and if their deference to the Church did not often allow their religious emotions to appear in such extravagant forms as after the upheaval of old ideas by the New Learning, yet they did occasionally get into trouble with ecclesiastical authorities. To those possessed with a flagrant desire of showing their unbounded zeal in extraordinary ways, the Carthusian manner of devotion would be a safety-valve for their fervour which might lead them to unwise courses, and in such, the difficult novitiate would soon prove how much was true religion and how much was short-lived excitement.

But to understand the true work of the Order

depends upon belief in the efficacy of prayer and worship. St. Bruno and his spiritual descendants did but literally carry out the command "Watch and pray." And faithful watchmen they were to the last in England; not even the evil pens of Cromwell's infamous agents of destruction could write a single bad word against their character, though many indeed were the complaints against their conscientious steadfastness. Sebastian Brant * said what was as true of the English as of the foreign Charterhouses:

> "Degener nunquam fuit ordo visus
> Cartusianus"

("The Carthusian Order was never seen degenerate"). Now and then, indeed, they would tend to grow somewhat lax in some details of rule, but the system of supervision was so excellent that these faults would soon be espied and rectified; for the strict obedience demanded of the Carthusian not only of necessity maintained him in the difficult path to perfection that he had chosen, but also if he fell, almost forced him

---

* See note at the beginning of this chapter. With this quotation may be compared the well-known saying in reference to the Order, that it was never reformed because never corrupt: "*Cartusia nunquam reformata quia nunquam deformata.*"

on his feet again. Obedience was the life of the Order, and herein lay its strength and its power of reforming itself and of retaining the form that St. Bruno gave to it. And so in England at least, from the first day of their inauguration at Witham, where Henry II., stained with Becket's blood, set them to watch and pray for him and the country, until the last day of their silent existence here, when Henry VIII., stained more deeply with sin, turned them adrift, they were regarded as the faithful orators of the nation. The Carthusian holiness was scarcely attainable, the stern loneliness of the Carthusian rule hardly endurable, by ordinary Englishmen, but from king and subject the Order met with reverence. But it may be asked, what was there in the Carthusians to cause Edward I., the chief feature in whose character was not religious devotion, as well as Henry II., to appeal to their prayers, especially when engaging in an arduous venture?* Other monks could pray, and at that date, moreover, some other monks were still obedient followers of the various rules of their Orders. Giraldus

---

* The reference is to his demand for the prayers of the monks of Witham and Hinton.

Cambrensis, the contemporary of St. Hugh, in his *Speculum Ecclesiæ*, or *Mirror of the Church*, contrasts them most favourably with the Cistercians. This passage, amounting almost to a panegyric, though short, and now defective, owing to the original manuscript having been damaged by fire, affords a good idea of St. Bruno's system.

A large part of the *Speculum Ecclesiæ* has for subject the degeneracy of the Cistercian Order, once not the least holy, and certainly among the most popular, in England, which in part was the very reason of their growing worldliness, which the historian so much laments. "Would," said he, "that they strove less eagerly to collect and accumulate vain sums of money and transitory possessions, and cease to join fields to fields, and granges to granges." Their wealth, indeed, they spent, he added, in works of charity and in "the obsequiousness of hospitality;" but how much better it would have been, and more wholesome, to control their expenditure and outlays in the manner of the Carthusians, rather than endlessly to extend their communities and congregations, and their lands and possessions, in consequence of which they had so many cares as to how to feed their large establishments, and how to keep up hospitality, and so many anxieties arising from lawsuits and their own insatiable cupidity, that they were hardly able to look after the salvation of their own souls. "Since the purpose moulds every action, since it is the will and resolution that marks a service, it is not the habit of any monks, but their mind that saves them; for not in a deep tonsure or a round, not in the crown covered with hair, not in a loose cowl is safety, but rather in the innermost heart, in sincere devotion and true intention, not in outward appearance, but in the inward life." "The way and fashion once was for the monk and any religious man to give himself up to die to the world and to live to God; but in modern days, love growing too cold in the evening of the world, the custom and fashion through a perverse change is, as we say lamenting, to live in the world, and, indeed, to live to the world and to die to God." After thus inveighing against the lack of real devotion among the Cistercians, the author described how the Carthusians, on the other hand, took care to cut off everything superfluous and unbecoming their religious state " with the pious sickle of control;" how they limited their communities to a certain number of monks as well as of lay-brethren; how they prescribed certain measurements for their lands, and held all their other possessions in moderation and temperance; how, happily resolving to choose the better part, they had enough to do in giving their labour and energy to sacred meditation and contemplation. Then, after relating the history of St. Bruno's foundation of the Grande Chartreuse, fifteen years before that of the Cistercian Order, he detailed some of the Carthusian peculiarities, as, for instance, their rejection of linen and dressing in coarse clothing made from skins, the prohibition to eat flesh or things cooked in fat, which was not allowed even in cases of illness. "In their cells they eat upon bare tables, that is, without napery, but on feast-days, when they eat in the refectory, tablecloths are spread. Both the monks and the brethren wear the hair-shirt, except when devoting themselves to labour. They may not drink except at meal-times, unless by the Prior's grace and dispensation. Each monk has his own little gate opposite the cloister leading towards the meadow, from which he may not go forth, but only use to look from; for one foot, not two at once, may any one extend beyond his little gate." "They never use candles nor lamps in their cells, but every one has his own little fire on his hearth." The whole monastery is surrounded by a wide and deep moat and a good wall, including the church also. Their estates, about seven miles in circuit, are enclosed by ditches or open boundaries. As for their hospitality, according to their moderate resources they receive guests and feed the poor, but they would far rather take in a number of the poor than of the rich. They place before their guests most liberally in the way of food whatever they eat themselves, but they supply the needs of neither horses nor grooms. Moreover, they do not attract a crowd of paupers to their gates; thither ribald folk running about from place to place, mere idle livers, are not wont shamelessly to bring themselves as if they were veritably penniless. "As may be read in the book of their Institutions, not far from their houses are towns in which there are many poor—true paupers, and not pretended—who lead a miserable life in the depth of penury; of whom some have fallen from plenty to the last stage of want and beggary, but some are invalids, unable by force of long disease to move from their beds and chambers; to them for their sustenance they (the Carthusians) cause to be brought whatever remains from their own poverty."* Nor is it surprising that the Carthusians are not hindered by such throngs of guests in their hall, or such crowds of poor at their gates, as their Cistercian brethren, considering that they retire into arid and wretched places, bare and uncultivated solitudes and rough ground, purposely to serve God only and to save souls, and not to hunt the favour of men. "It is to be added also, for the increase of perfect religion, and to augment the praise of the Carthusians, that if any of their estates or possessions are taken away from them, the loss is so bearable that they endure it with equanimity. But if, on the other hand, their very house itself suffers a too unusual detriment, they show the damage

---

* Giraldus refers here to the scanty income that the Charterhouses allowed themselves, and probably to the earlier name of the monks, "the Poor of Christ."

and injury received to the patron or founder of their house, or to the bishops of the diocese, if the former perchance fails, so that through either of them it may be rectified, and what has been taken from the house restored without labour of their own, or without causing them to dispute with any one else."* "Oh! how much more satisfactory and more salutary for those who have wholly renounced secular cares and deeds, according to the religious example of these men, in fleeing and retiring afar off to quit betimes the unquiet and insignificant possessions of a moment, rather than, by seeking one's own shamelessly and insisting on it with strifes, to incur publicly, and in the presence of worldlings, the spots and black blemishes of mundane solicitude and secular ambition." †

Centuries later than Giraldus the Order's former prestige had not died not. In A.D. 1534 the Vice-Chamberlain, Sir John Gage, perceiving

* One of the rules was that the Carthusians might not appear in person in lawsuits, because this would have involved them in secular affairs.

† *Speculum Ecclesiæ*, Distinctio iii. caps. xix., xx. This book is vol. iv. of the Works of Giraldus Cambrensis in the Rolls edition. In this passage the sentences directly translated only are set between inverted commas.

the growing profligacy of the king and court, expressed his intention of joining the Carthusians, provided that his wife would consent, as their mode of existence still seemed the best way to perfect holiness. Sir Thomas More, also, a man of practical Christianity as he was, aspired to an ascetic life in a Charterhouse.

But why this continuous respect? once again we hear it asked. The answer lies in the frequently quoted sentence of St. Bernard, "*Otiosum non est vacare Deo, sed negotium negotiorum omnium*" (to be occupied with God is not idleness, but the business of all businesses); for no other monks so fully carried out the sentiment therein expressed. The slightest acquaintance with mediæval literature suffices to make manifest the extremely personal worship of those times. The Blessed Trinity was indeed a living reality to men then; the language of their devotional writings, deeply reverential as was the spirit that animated it, was as familiar as if addressed to a well-beloved friend, whom, separated from them by some ordinary circumstance, they would see again. In those days there was an extraordinary earnestness in all that men thought and did, so that they could easily appreciate and reverence the ardent devotion of the Carthusian, who spent himself in an exclusive service to that adored and Divine Friend. The Carthusian life had nothing, humanly speaking, to show for it; but to the believer in prayer it was not waste of time, being indeed one long form of prayer. Nor was it selfish. Some, it is true, and the founder himself is an example, betook themselves to their solitude as a shelter from secular temptations and difficulties, and as affording exceptional opportunities for the sole occupation of working out their own salvation. But in many cases the adoption of St. Bruno's habit was an act of love. It was more; it was a supreme act of love, fulfilling an ideal of self-surrender so awful that it is little wonder if the Order, though winning an acknowledgment of its holiness, could win no place in the heart of the nation. The saints while on earth may be beloved; the saints in heaven are only approached through the awe and mystery of heaven, and these monks, it would seem, were already half-way to the far-off country. Martyrdom is a high sacrifice; but it is a question whether to give up all that makes life worth having be not a higher, for it is a sacrifice of longer agony, a living death. In common with the monks of other Rules, the Carthusian, in taking the irrevocable vows, literally left house, and brethren and sisters, and father and mother (and even, it is to be feared, wife and children occasionally), and lands for Christ's sake. Yet he gave more than they, for to them the chance was still open to distinguish themselves as preachers, and as teachers through the medium of books, and to gain through the medium of their intellectual gifts a power in the world of letters at least; but even this privilege and solace of the ascetic life he laid down on the altar of his solitude; preaching was forbidden to the son of St. Bruno, and learning must be for him strictly a means to the spiritual perfection of himself and his brother recluses.

It was in the spirit of the Magdalene, who poured out the precious ointment on the person of her Lord instead of spending the price of it on the poor, that the Carthusians made, without regard to the possible good they might do for their fellow-men, a free-will offering of themselves for the service of God, the supremely Beloved alone. The purpose that they fulfilled was to inculcate a lesson on the world; their mode of teaching it contained exaggerations; but since man ever perceives most clearly what is presented to him in an exaggerated light, exaggeration may have been useful, especially when the tumults of much war and the perpetual din of arms in the strife of might against right so often led him to forget to listen to the voice of righteousness. The lesson that they set forth was that God has the first claim above all human beings to the highest love, and that to give that love rightly must entail sacrifice—no new lesson indeed, but that which beyond all other Orders they realised.

INDEX

ABEL, Father Robert, of Mountgrace, 188
Abergavenny, George, Lord, 292
Adam, Brother, St. Hugh's biographer, 78, 81
Adam, Master, the Scot, 71–75; becomes a Carthusian at Witham, 71; his writings, 72–74
Ainard, a lay-brother of Witham, 21
Albert, Prior of Witham, 71, 77
Alexander III. changes the form of penance for Becket's murder, 6
Alexander V., 106
Alnage of cloths in Wilts, grant out of, to the Hinton monks, 264–266, 316, 342
Ambresbury [Amesbury], 206
—— Prioress of, 264
Animals, St. Hugh's fondness for them, 52
Annates, Act of, 138, 304, 313
Antwerp, the Carthusian Prior of, appointed to visit the English province, 110
Appeals, Act of, 304
Appleby, Lincolnshire, 206
Ap Rice, 153
Arundel, Sir Thomas, 340, 343
Asteley, Thomas, 99

Aston, manor of, in Berks, 103–104, 114, 140, 144, 192
Atte Water, John, 261
Augustine's, St., Bristol, Abbot of, 141
Aumare, Robert de, 89
Avalon, *vide* St. Hugh and William of
Avon river, 222, 345

BAILIFFS of Witham Charterhouse, 140–145; of Hinton, 314–317
Bakster, Dom William, of the London Charterhouse, 121
Balland [Baland], Dom Nicholas, a Hinton Carthusian, 325–326, 330–332, 337
Barker, Dom Thomas, of Mountgrace Charterhouse, 123, 124, 126
Bartlett, John, *alias* Sancock, 343
—— Robert, 343
Barton, Elizabeth, 148–149, 275
Basileus, Prior of La Grande Chartreuse, 50
Basle, 295
Basset, Henricus, 224
Bath, 77, 233, 344
Bathe, Thomas, 102
Batmanson, Dom John, 293, 299,

300; his secular life, 293-295; his literary works, 295-298; enters Hinton Charterhouse, 295; becomes Prior there, 297; becomes Prior of London Charterhouse, 298; his government of his monks, 300-302; his death, 302; mention of, 304
Beauflour, Geoffrey, 98
Becket, St. Thomas, 6, 653
Beckford, William, Lord Mayor of London, 196
Beckington, Somerset, 316, 324, 342
—— Bishop of Bath and Wells, 112, 113, 199
Bedford, 230
Bekynton, John of, 97
Bellomont, Robert de, Earl of Mellent and Leicester, 102
Benedict XIII., 106
Bernard, St., quoted, 18, 363
Bible, a, taken from Winchester by Henry II. for the Witham monks, restored by St. Hugh, 59-60
Billerica, a grange, 143, 195
Bilney, Thomas, the reformer, 303
Black Death, 94, 246, 248
Bocking, Father, 148
Boleyn, Anne, 133, 137, 154, 304, 309
Boneham, John, Esquire, steward, 314
Bord [Boorde], Andrew, a London Carthusian, 302, 320; letter from, 321
Bordele [Bordsley] Abbey, 230
Boucher, John, 262
Bouvines, battle of, 209
Bovo, Prior of Witham, 10, 71

Bracton, Henry de, 85
Braddeley [West Bradley ?], 141
Brant, Sebastian, quoted, 351, 355
Brewham, 6
Bristol, 101, 141, 193, 259; grants to Witham and Hinton Charterhouses of tenements there, 97-100, 256
Brownynge, Thomas, Vicar of Norton St. Philip, 336
Bruges, the Charterhouse of, 184, 188; the English Carthusians settle in the town, 189
Bruno, St., founds La Grande Chartreuse, 4-6; his rule, 32 *et seq.*
Bruton, 83
Buchelande, 342
Buckingham, Duke of, 275; his intercourse with the Hinton monks, 276-292; his execution, 292
Bugett, Robert, 145
Burges, Henry, 142
Burton, Dom William, a Witham Carthusian, 122
Bury, John, parson of Whatley, 99, 100, 254, 259
Byrche, Helie [Elisha], the chaplain of Witham Friary, 145, 336

CAJETAN, Cardinal, 190
Calais, 290
Calne, Wilts, 265
Camden, his *Britannia* on Witham, 7-8
Campville, Richard de, 218
Caneford, salt from the manor of, 105
Canynges, Agnes, 98
—— John, 98

INDEX

Canynges, William, 98, 99
Carthusian Order founded, 4; introduced into England, 6; its rules, 31-44; the vow, 42; constitutions of the General Chapter of, 107-110; the English Houses constituted into a separate province, 249; sanctity and purpose of the Order, 351-356
Cemetery at Witham, 113-114
Champneys, Sir Harry, 340
Chantries at Witham and Hinton, 98, 241-242, 256
Chapelle, the Prior of the Charterhouse of, 111
Chapter-house of Hinton, 263, 346-348
Charterhouse, a, described, 15-18; the word explained, 54, 118
Charterhouses—
    Axholme, Isle of, 124, 300, 301
    Beauvale, 127-129, 301
    Coventry (St. Anne's), 126, 185, 300
    Hinton. *See* under Hinton
    Mountgrace, 123, 124, 125, 312-313, 322, 338
    Sheen, 121, 148, 150, 186, 300, 338, 339
    Smithfield, London, 120, 121, 123, 124, 126, 132, 150, 165, 177, 247-250, 268, 296, 298, 300, 302, 308, 311, 320, 346
    Witham. *See* under Witham
Charterhouse-on-Mendip, 82
Charterhouse-Witham [Witham-Friary, or Witham], 3, 142, 143, 145, 192, 193, 194; the church there, 3, 19, 198-200

Chartreuse, La Grande, 5, 7, 9, 12, 34, 41, 42, 48, 49, 109, 184, 264, 353, 359
Chauncy Dom Maurice, 158, 184; Prior of the restored Carthusians, 186; goes abroad with some of them, and establishes the Sheen Anglorum, 187-189; dies, 190; mentioned, 332, 338, 339
Cheddar [Cedderford], 27, 87, 88
—— or Cheddre, Robert, 97, 98, 99
—— William, 98, 99
Chelworth, 219, 224
Cheseman, Thomas le, 240
Chester, Earl of, 212
Chewton [Chyweton, &c.], 230, 240, 317
Chilthorne - Domer [Chelterne - Dummer, &c.], 100, 142, 193
Cistercian monks, 357-362
Clerke, John, 331
Cliffe, Dom John, a Witham Carthusian, 187
Clifford, Ludovic de, 103
—— Rosamund, 204
Clink [Clynck], in Somerset, 141, 192
Colthurst, Matthew, 344
Compton, Sir William, 300
Constable, Sir Marmaduke, 294
Cook, Richard, 256
Copinger, the confessor of Sion, 158, 159
Corcelle, Roger de, 6
Coumbe [Combe], William of, 97, 99
Cromwell, Thomas, 130, 133, 134, 138, 150, 151, 153, 155, 157, 159, 162, 165, 166, 167, 169, 178, 179,

2 A

312, 313, 317, 318, 320, 322, 323, 324, 326, 328, 331, 340, 341
Cumpton, Roger de, 241

DAMIETTA, capture of, 211
Dancy, Ambrose, 316
Dantesy, Richard de, 237, 238
Dedications of Witham and Hinton Charterhouses, 23, 222
Delacourt, John, chaplain of Buckingham, 282, 287, 288, 290
De la Mare, Sir John, 254, 258
De Montfort, Henry de, 236, 237
Derby, John, 97
—— Walter, 100
Devizes, Richard of, 77; his Chronicle dedicated to Fitz Henry, a monk at Witham, 78
De Vitré, Eleanor, 206
D'Evreux, Walter, Count of Rosmar, 206
Doreau, Father, his description of a Charterhouse, 15–18
Dorlandus, Petrus, 269; quoted, 270–274
Dorset, Marquis of, 317
Dover, 208, 210
Draper, Thomas, 140
Dreux, Robert, Count of, 209
Drury, Sir Robert, 294
Dryburgh Abbey, 71
Drynkwater, Richard, chaplain of Longleat, 336
Dune, Agatha de la, 230
—— Robert de la, 231

EAST-WICK [Ettewick, &c.], 258, 315
Edith, wife of John the Fisher, 92–94
Edmund, Earl of Cornwall, 89

Edward I., 356; his grants to Witham and Hinton Charterhouses, 87–89, 240, 243; his letter to them, 89–91, 239
Edward II., grants of, to Witham and Hinton monks, 243, 244
Edward III., grants of, to Witham and Hinton monks, 94–100, 244–247, 254, 259
Edward IV., payments to, for confirmation of grants, 115, 266
Einard, a Carthusian lay-brother, some time of Witham, 39–41
Ela d'Evreux, Countess of Salisbury, foundress of Hinton Charterhouse, 205, 206–208, 213, 217–219
Elizabeth, Princess and Queen, 137, 187
Ely, Isle of, 210
Elyott, John, 331
Englefield, Sir Francis, 338
Erasmus, 295–296
Erlestoke, Thomas, parson of Fisherton, 100
Erpingham, Sir Thomas, 103–104
Eton, 307
Ewall, Surrey, 338
Exeter, 328
Eynsham, Council of, 50

FAIRS and markets, granted to the Hinton monks, 231–234
Farlegh, Agnes of, 257
—— William of, 257
Farleigh, 341, 342, 344
Feltham, Somerset, 192
Ferrand of Flanders, 208–209
Fisher, Bishop John, 151, 177
Fisher, John the, 92–94

INDEX

Fisherton, 100
Fitz Alan, William, 229
Fitz Henry, Robert, some time Prior of St. Swithun's, Winchester, a Carthusian at Witham, 77–81
Fitz James, Nicholas, 144
Fitz Jocelin, Reginald, Bishop of Bath, 10
Fitz Rolf, Turstin, 6
Fletcher, Father, of Mountgrace or of Hinton, 188, 338–339
Font in the chapel at Witham, 20, 113–114
Fontel-Gyfford, Wilts, 141, 192
Fortescue, Isabella, 262–263
—— John, 262–263
Fox, Bishop of Winchester, 296
Fox, John, a London Carthusian, 158, 184, 185
Francis, a protégé of Hinton Charterhouse and of the Duke of Buckingham, 279–281
Freeman, John, the royal goldsmith, 197
Freshford, 257, 261, 315
Frome, 85, 97, 140, 344
—— river, 222, 345
Fry, William, 141
Fulkes de Breauté, 209, 210, 212

GAGE, Sir John, 362
Ganard, John, 241
Gernefeld [Yarnfield, &c., Somerset], 85, 86
Giffard, John, 194
Gilbert, chaplain of Buckingham, 288
Gilbert de Sarum, Rector of Hinton parish church, 250–253

Giles, parson of Norton St. Philip, 257, 259
Giraldus Cambrensis, 111, 356; quoted, 357–362
Girard, a Witham lay-brother, 21–22
Glastonbury, Abbot of, 316
Grace, Pilgrimage of, 156, 323
Gregory XIII., 106
Greneworth, 316, 317, 341, 342
Grenoble, 45
Grey, Lord Leonard, 283
Guigo I., fifth Prior of La Grande Chartreuse, Customs of, 34, 35

HACSTON, John, 97
Hales [Halys], Dom Alnett, of the London Charterhouse and of Witham, 120, 123, 124, 126, 301
Hampton, manor of, 255, 261
Harrys, David, 142
Hatherlee, Prior William, 266
Heatherop [Hethrop], in Gloucestershire, 217, 345
Henry, Prior of Hinton, 284, 293; letter from, 284–286
Henry II., 12–14, 21, 54–56, 59, 62, 67, 81, 89, 204, 206, 264, 356
Henry III., 210, 213, 221; grants of, to the Witham and Hinton monks, 82–89, 222, 231, 235
Henry IV., 260
Henry V., grants of, 101–104
Henry VI., grants of, to the Witham and Hinton monks, 105, 114, 262, 264–266
Henry VIII., supreme headship ceded to him by the clergy, 119; marriage with Anne Boleyn, 133, 134; dissolves lesser monasteries,

156; mentions of, 139, 148, 165–197, 276–291, 293, 297, 309, 317, 320, 323, 333, 336, 356; letter to him, 310

Herbert, Lord, 293; quoted, 291–292

Herdeburgh, Thomas, 99

Hert, Walter, 261

Heyles, John, 103

Hidon [Hydon], a grange, 142, 193, 195

Hinton Abbey, 344, 349

Hinton [Charterhouse-Hinton], the church of, 221, 233, 250–253, 317; land in, 231, 237, 238, 240; manor of, 221, 225–227, 232, 233, 235, 236, 240, 314, 341, 342

Hinton [Henton] Charterhouse, 31, 90–91, 115, 134, 135, 169; called Locus Dei, or the Place of God, 216; the Carthusians removed from Hethrop to Hinton, 217; bequests from William Longespée, 220; situation of the monastery, 222; foundation charter, 224–227; privileges of the monks, 235–236; the priory church, 237, 260, 340, 347; the Prior summoned to the muster at Carlisle, 239; a legacy to the monks, 243; the monks troubled by royal ministers and the Black Death, 243–247; growth of their property, 230–267; their poverty remedied by a grant out of the alnage, 264; their relations with Buckingham, 276, 283–286; their new conduit paid for by the Duke, 288, 289, 292; Priory of Longleat appropriated to them, 299–300; they surrender their monastery, 329; the conventual seal, 329; list of monks' signatures, 330; the destruction and sale of the site and of the property, 339–344; the ruins, 344–350

Hopkyns, Dom Nicholas, Vicar of Hinton Charterhouse, and confessor of the Duke of Buckingham, 275–280, 282, 283, 284, 285, 289, 290–293; his letter to the Duke, 278–280

Hopp [Hope, Le Hope], 260, 315, 342

Hopton, family of, 8
—— Dorothy, 195
—— Ralph, grantee of Witham Priory, 193, 195, 196, 198
—— Sir Ralph, 196

Horde, Alan, 307, 326–328, 338
—— Edmund, Proctor of the London Charterhouse, Prior of Hinton, 134–136, 175, 307–314, 317–323, 325–328, 332, 333–335, 338, 353; letters from him, 310, 318, 327
—— Edmund, son of Alan, 338
—— John, 307
—— Richard, 307
—— William, 336, 337

Houghton, Prior John, of the London Charterhouse, 150, 176, 186

Hoveden, Roger of, 204

Hoxton, a servant of Hinton Charterhouse, 276

Hubert, Bishop of Salisbury, 85

Hubert de Burgh, 210, 212, 213

Hugh of Avalon, St., 9; departs

INDEX

from France and arrives in England, 10-12; re-establishes the monks and builds the monastery at Witham, 12-23; date of his death, 31; his earlier monastic life, 49-54; his influence over Henry II., 55; his rule at Witham, 55-60; elected Bishop of Lincoln, and his fitness for the office, 60-66; his visits to Witham, 66-68, 74; his opinion of Rosamund Clifford and of the dignity of womanhood, 203-205; mentions of him, 146, 147, 353, 356
Hugh, Bishop of Grenoble, 4, 10, 11
—— of Southampton, Agnes, 243
—— John, 242-243
Hungerford, family of, 344
—— Sir Walter, afterwards Lord, 167, 168, 265, 316, 318, 319, 324, 331, 339, 341
Huse, Prior John, of Witham, 130, 132; letter from, 130
Hychemans, Tristram, Proctor of Witham, 167, 179, 187, 188
Hyde Monastery, 75

Iford [Ifford], land in, 237, 238, 315, 341
—— Cecilia of, 241
—— John of, 241
—— Master Nicholas of, 257
—— Margery of, 242
—— William of, 242
Ilchester [Ivelcestre], 230, 252
Innocent IV., grant of, 223

James IV. of Scotland, 287, 291, 294

Jamys, John, 262
—— Margery, 262-263
Jews mourn at St. Hugh's funeral, 66
Joceline, Bishop of Bath, 226; settles disputes between the Charterhouse and Rector of Hinton, 250-251
John, Bishop of Bath and Wells, 254, 255
—— Don, of Austria, 189
—— Prince and King, 9, 30, 65, 208, 209, 210
—— Prior of Witham, 88
John's, St., Prior of, London, 141
—— —— Oxford, 281
Jonbourne, Dom John, Prior of Sheen and provincial visitor, 121-127
Joseph II., Emperor, 191

Katherine of Arragon, 137, 309
Kayner, Robert, parson of Lullington, 255, 259
Kees, Agnes, 261
—— William, 261
Keynsham, monastery at, 325
Kingsley, Charles, quoted, 269
Kington [Kyngton], Warwickshire, 140
Knyvet, surveyor of the Duke of Buckingham, 282, 289

Lacock Abbey, 207, 216, 217, 218
Lacy, Margaret de, 237, 238
Ladcombe, 342
Latimer, Hugh, 303
Layton, Richard, 151, 159; letter from him, 164; letters to him, 159, 160, 163

INDEX

Lee, Edward, 295-296, 312, 313
Leland, the antiquary, quoted, 7, 344-345
Lemondeslonde, 316, 342
Lincoln Cathedral, 18, 62
Lincoln, Henry de Lacy, Earl of, 235, 237, 238, 241
Little Malvern Court, Worcester, 191
Littleton, Master William, 252, 253, 254
Livery, grant of a, by the Prior of Witham, 92-94
London, 209, 248, 283, 289
Long, John, Rector of Norton, 263
Longe, Sir Henry, 324, 341
Longespée, William, Earl of Salisbury, founder of Hinton Charterhouse, 204; account of his life, 206-217; his son William, 218, 220
Longleat [Langelete], 299, 316, 317, 324, 336, 341, 342, 343; Priory of St. Radegund of, 299
Louis, son of Philip Augustus, 210, 212, 213
Louvain, 189
Lovell, Sir Thomas, 290
Lullington, 255, 257, 316, 324, 342, 343
Luscote, Dom John, of Hinton, first Prior of the London Charterhouse, 247, 249, 250
Lutecom'ys myll, 315, 341
Luther, Martin, 119, 297

MAIDEN-BRADLEY, 102, 141, 192
—— leper hospital there, 84
—— the Canons of, 85-87

Maiden-Bradley, the Prior of, 141
Malet, Ralph, 13
Man, Prior Henry, of Witham, 120, 140, 146-150, 157, 158, 159
Manny, Sir Walter, 248
Marchall, Prior William, of Hinton, 265
Marlborough [Marleburgam], 30, 213
Marshall, Father Robert, of Mountgrace, 188
Marston, Somerset, 141, 145, 192
Mary, Queen, 183, 184, 186, 187, 338
Maurienne, Count of, 9
Maximus, St., cell of, 47, 48
Mechlin, 190
Mendip Hills, 7, 82, 101, 195
Mershton, John of, 97
Middylton, Christopher, 295
Milbourne, 85
Mileham [Melcham], Norfolk, 229
Milford, 242
Milton, manor of, 260
Monks of Witham and Hinton, 117-118, 306; pensioned, 178-179, 332-333, 337
Monksham [Monkisham], an enclosure, 89, 143, 192
Montalembert, Marquis de, quoted, 43
More, Sir Thomas, 149, 151, 177, 275, 297, 363
Moreland, Somerset, 142
Morian, Richard, 198
Morvell, William, 194
Mudford, 314, 342
Mulleward, Walter, 99
Mychell, Prior John, of Witham, 158, 159, 174, 179, 187

INDEX

NEEL, Robert, 102
Nevers, Count William of, 6
Newbury [Nueburye], in Berkshire, 142, 144, 192
Nicholas, Bishop of Bath and Wells, 261
Nieuport, 190
Northairy, 13
Norton, St. Philip [Norton-Comitis or Earl's Norton], the church of, 221, 234, 254-256, 257, 259, 263; land in, 230, 231, 237, 238, 240, 257, 259, 262; the manor of, 221, 225, 231, 234-236, 240, 242, 257, 315, 341, 342; the Vicar of, 317, 336
Norton, Dom John, a London Carthusian, 302
Norton, Mary of, 229
—— Robert of, 229, 230
Nottingham, Thomas, 98
Nunney [Nonney de la Mare], 7, 254, 258
Nyer, Johanna, 260
—— William, 260

ORCHARDLEIGH, Somerset, 340
Otto IV., Emperor, 209
Oxford, 124, 147, 229, 281, 303
—— Earl of, 195

PACE, the royal secretary, 283
Pandulf, the Legate, 211
Panes, John, of Wyk, 254, 255, 256, 259
Paris, 190; the Prior of the Chartreuse there, 106
Paris, Matthew, 211, 215
Parker, John the, 238

Parker, Richard the, 221, 225, 238
—— William the, 238
Parkminster, St. Hugh's Priory, 191
Pascal quoted, 38
Patrick, Earl of Salisbury, 206
Peers or Perys, Dom Richard, of Witham, 121, 127, 130; letters from him, 121, 127
Pegelynch [Peggelege, &c.], 315, 342
Pensions for the Carthusians and for persons connected with the two Charterhouses, 333-337
Peter, St., Archbishop of Tarentaise, 53-54
Peter, Prior of Hinton, 236-237
Petre, Doctor (Sir William), 157, 169, 178, 324-326
Philip, Abbot of Bordsley, 230
Philip Augustus of France, 208, 209, 210
Philip III. of Spain, 190
Philippa, Queen, 257, 260
Philips, Morgan, 315, 337
Pisa, Council of, 106
Pole, Arthur, 283
—— Cardinal, 185, 186, 332, 337
Préaux, Abbey of, 102, 104
Priors of Witham and Hinton, lists of, 116, 305
Privy Council, 307; order of, concerning monks' pensions, 180-183
Prygge, Roger, 331
Pynnock, Richard, 336, 337

QUARRE, a grange, 143, 195

RALPH, the sacrist of Winchester, 78
Rasing, Roger, 194
Reading, Abbot of, 142

INDEX

Reims, 4
Rentals of Witham and Hinton Priories, 192, 342
Repps (or Rugge), William, Bishop of Norwich, 303
Resumption, Act of, by Henry VI., not prejudicial to Witham and Hinton, 114, 115
Retclyffe Church, Bristol, 141
Rewleigh juxta Farleigh, 316
Rhé, Isle of, 213
Richard I., 206, 207, 208
Richard II., grants of, 100-101
Richard, Earl of Cornwall, 212
Richard le Poore, Bishop of Salisbury, 214
Richard, Prior of Hinton, lease of, 262-263
Richards, Dom, a Coventry Carthusian, 185
Richmond, Friars Observant of, 150
Robert, Prior of Axholme Charterhouse, 125
—— Prior of Hinton, 230-231
—— Prior of Witham, 81
—— Prior of Wormley, 88
Rochester, Sir Robert, 184, 185
Rodden [Radene], Somerset, 97
Rode, Church of, 259
Rodeney [or De Rodeney], Walter, 254, 258
Runnymeade, 209
Ryborg, Richard, 106

Sadler, Thomas, 140
St. Swithun's, Winchester, 59, 60, 67, 261, 315
Salisbury, 266
—— Bishop of, 219, 226

Salisbury, Castle of, 214
—— Cathedral, 211, 214, 219
—— Dean and Chapter of, 317
—— Lawrence, Cardinal Bishop of, 299
Sanchare, John, 294
Savoy Palace and Chapel, 185
Selwood, Carthusians in. *See* Witham Charterhouse
—— Forest of, 3, 83, 191, 195
Sheen Anglorum, 189-190
Sheen, Prior of, Rector of Chewton, 317
Sherbourn, Prior of, 136
Sheweston, 315
Shrewsbury, Ralph, Bishop of Bath and Wells, 251-252, 254
Sixtus V., 190
Smythe, John, 178
Sobbury, John, 241
Somerset, Duke of, 196
Soundenham, Agnes, 260
—— John, 260
Spectisbury, manor of, in Dorset, 102, 114, 141, 144, 192
Spencer, Dom Thomas, a Hinton Carthusian, 302-304; his literary works, 303
Spenser, Leonard, of Norwich, 302
Stafford, Lord, 292
Standerwick [Stanrewick], 257
Stantour, Peter, 299
Statute of Labourers, 95, 247
—— of Westminster, 237
Stephen, a Hinton monk, 268, 270-274, 275
Storan or Storer, Dom Edmund, Prior of the London Charterhouse and of Hinton, 268

INDEX

Stourton, John, 99
—— John of, 100
—— Lord, 134, 138, 309; his letter, 135
Stratford, Ralph, Bishop of London, 248
Succession, Act of, 137-138, 309-310
Surrender of Witham Charterhouse, deed of, 170
Surrey, Earl of, 295
Survey of the possessions of Witham and Hinton Charterhouses, 140-145, 313, 314-317
Sutton, Thomas, 142
Swansco [Swymestowe], Brother John, a Witham Carthusian, 187

TALBOT, John, 256, 257
—— William, 207
Tanner, Isabella, 102, 260
—— Thomas, 102
Tannery at Witham and Hinton Charterhouses, 101, 247
Taylor, Brother, a London Carthusian, 184
Temple Street, London, 142
Theodore, a layman, becomes a Carthusian at Witham, 71
Thornbury, Gloucestershire, 287
Thurlby, Father Robert, of Sheen, 188
Thynne, Sir John, 299
Tilshead, Wilts, 85
Toft Monachorum, or Monk's Toft, manor of, and priory there, 102, 103
Trafford, Prior William, of the London Charterhouse, 132

Tregonwell, John, 169, 178, 324-326, 329, 339
Tucker, Thomas, 316
Tynbygh, Prior William, of the London Charterhouse, 300

ULSTROPE, Leicestershire, 192

VILLARBENOIT, Priory of, 45, 49, 51

WALDECOTE, Geoffrey, 99
Walker, Richard, 197, 343
Walter, Prior of Bath, at Witham, 75-77
—— Prior of Witham, 91
Walton, Alan of, 85
Warmington, Leicestershire, 192
—— manor of, Warwickshire, 102, 114, 140, 144, 192
Warwick, Henry Newburgh, Earl of, 102
Watt, Dan Peter, a monk of Witham, 135, 309
Waz, Stephen, 240
Wells, Archdeacon of, 317
—— Cathedral, 252, 260
Wendover, Roger of, 208, 214
Westbarne, a farm or grange of the Witham monks, 143, 159, 162, 195
Westbury, 254
—— William of, parson of Rode, 259
Westwood, Wilts, 257, 261, 316, 342
Whalley, John, 312
Whatley Church, 99, 100, 254, 259
Wherwell, Hants, 77
White Oxmead [Whittokesmede], 258, 315, 342

INDEX

Whitnel [Whytenhull], near Wells, 230, 316, 317, 342
Whoweford [Oldford?], 257, 316
Wilbye, 144
William de Avalon, 45, 47
Williams, Prior, last English Carthusian, 191
Wilscote, Leicestershire, 192
Wilson, Dom John, of Mountgrace, 187
Winchester, 210
Witham Charterhouse, 6–9; the re-establishment under St. Hugh, 12–15; erection of conventual buildings and the church, 18–23; foundation charter, 23–30; the kitchen burnt, 68; effects of the Black Death, 94–95; growth of the property, 80–106; dormitory built, 112; the Prior and convent licensed to erect a font and make a cemetery, 113–114; visited by Dr. Layton, 151; correspondence between the monks and Cromwell and Layton, 159–165; appointment of a steward, the house surrendered, 169; the conventual seal and list of signatures, 174; later history of the monks of Witham and the other Charterhouses, 179–191; site of the Charterhouse granted to Ralph Hopton, 193; later owners, 196; fate of the remains, 196–200; mentioned, 301
Wodeford, John, 256
Woderove, John, 99
Wodewyk, 257; manor of, 255, 261, 262, 315
Wokey [Wokes, &c.], 101, 142, 193, 254
Wolsey, Cardinal, 119, 282
Woodbarrow [Wodebarwe], 258
Worcester, Earl of, 284
Wotton, John of, 97
Wykyng, John, 102, 260
Wyndham, Earl of Egremont, 196
Wynelscombe, Henry, 99

YATWICH, or Zatewick [Shapwick?], in Somerset, 242, 257
Yerdele [Yerdeley, &c.], 101, 142, 193

ZOUCH, or La Zouche, William of, of Totnes, 265

Printed by BALLANTYNE, HANSON & CO.
Edinburgh and London

www.ingramcontent.com/pod-product-compliance
Lightning Source LLC
Chambersburg PA
CBHW020527300426
44111CB00008B/567